A King Betrayed

The Ill-Fated Reign of Farouk of Egypt

A King Betrayed

The Ill-Fated Reign of Farouk of Egypt

Adel M. Sabit

Quartet Books
London New York

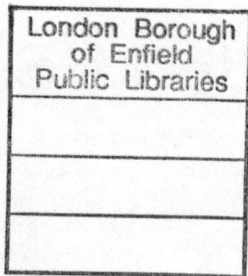

First published by Quartet Books Limited 1989
A member of the Namara Group
27/29 Goodge Street, London WlP lFD

Copyright © by Adel M. Sabit 1989

British Library Cataloguing in Publication Data
Sabit, Adel M.
A King betrayed : the ill-fated reign of Farouk of Egypt.
1. Egypt. Farouk. King of Egypt
1. Title
961'. 052'0924

ISBN O-7043-2711-2

Typeset by AKM Associates (UK) Ltd, Southall
Printed and bound by BPCC Hazell Books Ltd,
Member of BPCC Ltd, Aylesbury

Contents

To the memory of King Farouk's forebear
Mohammed Cherif Pasha
1826–87
whose reforms, had they been applied, would have made this
book unnecessary

Preface

This is not a biography of King Farouk. It is more in the nature of a personal report on the author's experiences in his relationship with the King, starting when he was a remotely situated young cousin and ending after he became a close collaborator and go-between for the King and the secretary-general of the Arab League, Abd el Rahman Azzam Pasha, during the critical years preceding and following the disastrous 1948 war in Palestine.

I have purposely ignored the many horrendous and sensational stories that surround Farouk's memory. These were either false or highly exaggerated. Above all, they were irrelevant to the story of the main events of his reign. In any case, womanizers, gamblers and predators have, in history, also made outstanding leaders.

Readers will notice that the tone of the book is neither harshly critical nor hagiographic. Farouk, I have suggested, was the victim of an endless series of betrayals until, in the end, he betrayed himself. The disservices done him began in early youth when he was the victim of a frustrated and strong-minded mother who bossed and managed his early years, and ran through to the infinitely more serious betrayal of Heydar Pasha, the Commander-in-Chief of his army; which may well be seen as marking the initial phase leading to the abdication. There is nevertheless an even more profound explanation which may be advanced to account for the King's misfortunes.

Farouk was the victim of an experiment. His father, King Fuad, sought to make his son an Egyptian as distinct from an Ottoman or Levantine monarch. The young Prince therefore received a conventional Egyptian education. The Turkish language, which represented the Mohammed Ali's dynasty's residual fealty to the Ottoman Sultan, was denied him. King Fuad, indeed, continued to express a marked hostility towards Istanbul and its rulers long after the disappearance of the Empire of the Bosphorus. Farouk inherited these sentiments and expressed throughout his life a genuine and robust Egyptian nationalism. This, in turn, caused him to clash with the larger-than-life and powerful figure of the British Ambassador, Sir Miles Lampson (Lord Killearn) – with unfortunate consequences.

British tutelage relaxed, however, as the Second World War drew to its close. Farouk took on the formidable task of challenging the British position in the Middle East, seeking in the process to enrol the Americans on Egypt's side. In 1948, within a few years of seizing control of the Arab League on 7 October 1944, Farouk found himself the accepted leader of the Arab world and facing its first major test: the first Palestine war. Though the prime and obvious responsibility for the mismanagement of the war and Egypt's defeat was to be laid at the doors of the military establishment, it was Farouk who faced the blame.

His subsequent attempt to stage a come-back through a reform of the armed forces and the employment of German officers to retrain the army, was undermined by the Commander-in-Chief of the Egyptian Army, Mohammed Heydar Pasha. A further consequence was that Farouk lost the support of the Americans, who seem to have taken a decision to work actively against him and to send to Cairo a CIA 'hit team' to establish contact with anti-monarchist elements. It was Farouk's nationalism and his loyalty to Egypt's Palestine commitments that ultimately cost him his throne. Even so, had he reacted decisively against the Cairo *coup* of 1952, he might still have saved his rule *in extremis*. He preferred to let events catch up with him, and as a result earned for himself an ignominious departure from Egypt.

Farouk, like other Egyptian nationalists, suffered an inability to temper his nationalist ardours with political intuition and reasoned caution. The same inability was shared by such diverse Egyptian leaders as Mohammed Ali, whose victorious adventures provoked an international reaction against him in 1840; Arabi Pasha, whose extreme nationalist postures were the main pretext for the British occupation of Egypt in 1882; and Farouk's uncle, the ex-Khedive Abbas Helmi, whose public rebuke and clash with Lord Kitchener lost him his throne on the eve of the First World War in 1914.

But perhaps the most anomalous aspect of the Farouk abdication was the fact that he was deposed by precisely that element in Egypt which might have been expected to offer him his main political support, drawn mainly from the conservative Egyptian middle class represented by a group of army officers who had already attained the rank of major or colonel and hence who belonged, in Egypt, to a socially prominent sector of the community.

What therefore was it that caused these relatives of the ruling Faroukian establishment to rebel? In the opinion of the present writer, the answer lies in the disunity endemic in the Egyptian body politic, the lack of any institutional machinery capable of curbing the political excesses of its leaders, and the never-ending interference in the affairs of the country by alien hands promoted by the ill-conceived Constitution of 1923.

Yet above and beyond all this, and in conclusion, the determining reason for the abdication was *the absence of any dialogue* between the King and the young and eager officers who were the rising lights of his army. The cause for this may be attributed directly to the palace system, which created a barrier between the King and his subjects. The writer is one of the few people in Egypt who managed to breach that barrier for a while. This book might otherwise never have been written.

ADEL MAHMOUD SABIT

Cairo
February 1989

Prologue

'I'll be King of Bavaria, so he will feel at home here.'

This unexpected remark was made by King Farouk in 1949 in response to an inquiry from General Leutnant Artur Wilhelm Schmitt, late of the Afrika Korps, late of the Royal Bavarian Life Guards regiment. The general had asked me, 'When I am presented to His Majesty, how should I greet him? In Germany it would have been customary for an officer to identify himself when reporting to the sovereign with a special formula and then to place himself under the "orders" of His Majesty.'

The royal office was said to be equipped with a trap-door situated immediately in front of the King's desk. At the pressing of a conveniently placed button, the King could remove an unwanted guest, who would suddenly find himself deposited in the basement. Faithful to royal instructions not to confuse the general, I omitted to advise him of the possible presence of this unusual convenience. The general's presence in Egypt was surrounded with secrecy. He had been smuggled out of Germany under the noses of the Allied occupying powers, only the French, who had quietly and unobtrusively helped with the operation, being in the know.

The transfer itself was masterminded by the Shadow SS, whose main function in that spring of 1949 seemed to be the placing of former German officers and Nazi personages in various parts of the Middle East and South America. Franz, our friendly SS colonel and go-between, was at that very moment building up a German security advisor team to serve General Hosni el Zaim, the Syrian dictator of the day.

General Schmitt turned out to be a diminutive military martinet of a man, clean-shaven and with pale-blue eyes, and

1

the usual German hair-do in the shape of a modified crew-cut. He was the very model of a German officer of the Rommel type, a complete military animal whose opinions on everything were regimented and grounded in the philosophy of his Prussian military academy, which gave to his views on a vast spectrum of subjects the conciseness and clarity of a General Staff bulletin on the operations of the day.

'Dear Mr Sabit,' the general would say, 'we are accustomed always to read everything from left to right. You may therefore be sure that when we list a place on the map it starts from the west and goes to the east. Thus Paris always comes before Berlin. This helps our officers to achieve a visual dimension to their orders.'

There was little doubt that to most questions the general came out with the kind of answers that might be expected from an enlightened computer. Anything with which he had not been programmed by the various military academies and courses he had attended – as, for instance, the eccentric behaviour of a certain rather wild American girl – would evoke in him a puzzled blankness. Indeed, the general was worried for several days after Letha, the girl in question, had kissed him in public and said, 'You make me giggle, you make me laugh, you make me want your autograph.'

'Mr Sabit,' the general explained, 'this is not to be understood by a German officer. We would not allow our ladies to behave in this manner.'

The general was even more shocked when I took him to the Opera, where the Ballet de Jean Babille showed us a dancer committing *hara kiri* to the music of Beethoven's *Requiem* in one of the French dance creations which were so popular at the time.

'Mr Sabit,' protested the general, 'I wish to leave this theatre immediately! I consider the scene we have just witnessed to be outrageous and sacrilegious, an insult to the great Beethoven.'

When we arrived at the Palace together, we were ushered in by a discreet chamberlain. Secrecy was the order of the day and no servants were visible. The prying eyes of British or other agents among the palace staff had been consigned to some temporary limbo in a palace basement or attic. To all intents and purposes we were to be alone with His Majesty.

The order to attend the royal presence had arrived without warning, and all at once the little general had been transformed. He had jumped to attention, his arms stiffly pointing to the floor, though angled slightly outwards, his short, stubby but powerful torso expanded to its maximum, his crew-cut and neckless bullet head held at a supremely precise angle.

We goose-stepped through the open door into the King's presence, with a clatter of ghostly boots, a clinking of innumerable imaginary medals and the clanking of a phantom Bavarian cavalry sword. At precisely one metre from the King's desk, where His Majesty sat, rather startled by the display, the general came to an abrupt stop. There followed a stamping of feet and then a parade-ground bellow, 'General Artur Wilhelm Schmitt, late commander of fortress Bardia, late commander Libya, late *Feldzeuchmeister Armee* von Kluge before Moscow, late military governor of Strasburg, late commander *Kampfgruppe* [Battle Group] Dolman, reporting to His Majesty and standing by for Your Majesty's further orders! *Zum Befehl!*' – all of this accompanied by a splendid salute, followed by a rigid standing to attention.

Nonplussed for a moment by such a display of unfamiliar military pageantry, King Farouk rallied. 'Very pleased to see you, General. Will you please sit down?' he said.

In this and subsequent conversations, Farouk showed a remarkable grasp of the subject of Egypt's military deficiencies mainly the result of the incompetence of the upper hierarchy of Egypt's British-trained officers and recently revealed by Egypt's defeat in the 1948 war against the new state of Israel. 'I want you,' he said to Schmitt, 'to help us to build up the Egyptian Army into an efficient fighting force enjoying all the advantages of the experiences gained by the German Army during the Second World War. We should set up,' said the King, 'a training command officered by joint German and Egyptian staff who will together lay the foundations of a new organization Model Army. We shall call it the *Nizam Gedid.*'

This term, meaning 'New Order', was originally used to describe the army of Farouk's great-grandfather, formed by French officers along the lines of the old Napoleonic pattern in the 1820s. At that time, Egypt's *Nizam Gedid* army defeated the Wahabites, repressed the Greek insurrection and, in a

3

succession of victories culminating in the annihilation of the Ottoman army at Nezib, carried Egyptian forces to the gates of Istanbul. One of King Farouk's own grandfathers was Suleyman Pasha el Franzawi, the Napoleonic officer who, in the 1820s, achieved what Farouk wished Schmitt to do.

A master plan was worked out between Farouk and Schmitt in a series of meetings, Schmitt having proposed Field Marshal Guderian as the German-based anchor-man in the recruitment of suitable officers of the old *Wehrmacht* for the Egyptian Army. (It is interesting here to record that Schmitt suggested the name of General Speidel as Chief of Staff of the Egyptian Training Command, for Speidel subsequently became Chief of Staff of NATO.) The idea proposed as a result of the Schmitt/Farouk discussions was the formation of a highly mobile, integrated modern army in which a merging of armoured artillery and mobile infantry forces would be anticipated. At the time, the Egyptian Army, much to Schmitt's dismay, was still based on separate artillery, infantry and armoured forces and was even contemplating the formation of an artillery division.

'Mr Sabit,' said the general, 'this is military nonsense. I have never heard of an artillery division. Not even in Frederick the Great's army. It is madness. Today all experience points to the conclusion that forces must be integrated and trained into total co-operation with one another. A *Panzergrenadier* division carries men into battle on the backs of tanks and artillery keeps fully mobile by using tank chassis.'

One important aspect of this planning was that the King was in full agreement with Schmitt's suggestion that officers who had shown leadership and capability should be carefully selected on the basis of their performance in actual battle conditions, the recent Arab-Israeli war of 1948 being taken into account. And those who had shown leadership were to be placed in positions of command. Had this ever happened, it is highly likely that Gamal Abd el Nasser, Salah Salem and other officers who had distinguished themselves, and who formed the core of the revolutionary Free Officers movement, would have found fully satisfying and adequate positions in the new army. Unfortunately, intrigue around the King and the ready argument of the political danger present among able officers,

4

and possibly a fear that such officers might indeed be used in a new army, caused the old guard, headed by the then Commander-in-Chief, Heydar Pasha, to banish most of Egypt's best officers to remote garrisons as far from Cairo and King Farouk as possible. The seeds of the Nasser revolution of 1952 were thus already germinating.

Regrettably, though perhaps understandably, the agreement between Farouk and Schmitt was never ratified or even acknowledged by Heydar Pasha and his associates. The whole matter became an internal political issue between those who wished to unseat Heydar Pasha, a redoubtable political figure, and those who, for their various reasons, sought to keep him on. But that is another story. I touch on it here because I feel it gives something of an insight into the personality and problems of King Farouk.

Farouk is quite possibly the most maligned and misunderstood monarch of the mid twentieth century. We live today in a world of instant communication of radio, television, newsreel and newspaper coverage: an audiovisual world in which unprecedented publicity is given to every newsworthy event, in which sensationalism dominates true reporting and sex, sado-masochism and other news and media aberrations are promoted to the utmost limit. Farouk was too vulnerable a figure to escape the attention of the world's sensationalist press, which proceeded to make him into the pastiche, ogre figure of a medieval Muslim potentate. Complicating things further, the pro-Israeli press in the United States, closely influenced by the Eddy Cantor Hollywood version of the Orient and its leaders, made the caricature even more extreme and displeasing. Above all else, enmity against Farouk from within the British community, for example from the former Ambassador, Sir Miles Lampson (later Lord Killearn), inspired a number of particularly vicious quasi-biographies. To such an extent was Farouk vilified that one wonders if a reasonably objective view can even now be arrived at.

The present writer knew Farouk well and personally. He had a rather special relationship with the King, being a cousin and collaborator. Naturally, therefore, a favourable bias can be expected of him, yet biased reports are little use to anyone. And it is only the particularly stupid biographer who engages in the exclusive glossing of his subject. As someone whose association with the King lasted from 1936 to the eve of his abdication – a period during which I had a violent quarrel with His Majesty and was banished from the King's circle for several months – I was possibly in a unique position to observe events from very close to. Indeed, so close was my relationship that it could definitely have had a bearing on my arrest many years later when I was put on trial by the Nasser regime. (Among the accusations then levelled against me were (a) plotting with reactionary elements in the army to restore the old order; (b) intelligence with the enemy; and (c) being an adviser to foreign embassies on the recruitment of Egyptian spies. I was also described as 'a creature of the monarchy, nurtured in the palaces of reaction', and so on and so forth.)

In all systems of government, persons within the immediate ambience of the seats of power are in a position to play roles and apply influence far in excess of any actual position held. For short periods, this was my experience. As a result I believe that I achieved as close an insight into Farouk as anybody. Farouk had charm and – an extremely valuable quality in a King – he had simplicity. This ability to project a disarming friendship and warmth gained him many friends. He was likewise a youthful-minded man, always ready for a joke and possessing the acute Egyptian sense of humour that is one of our countrymen's most valuable and desirable assets.

His youthfulness, however, did lead to his being accused, occasionally with some justification, of excessive frivolity. He would play the most absurd tricks on his ministers and take delight in placing them in ridiculous situations. I well remember the embarrassed obsequiousness of elderly pashas, including an ex-Prime Minister, when, after a large lunch, the King knocked their fezzes off their heads with well-aimed tomatoes and cucumbers. There could perhaps be a certain vindictiveness in His Majesty's behaviour. But I knew him to be often exasperated at the servility of his ministers. 'Look at them,' he would say as they bowed and scraped and behaved with false humility. 'They do not respect themselves. How can I respect them?'

Farouk was a frustrated King. He was surrounded with all the appearances of absolute monarchy; he was given the deference one gave to a god. Yet he knew his power to be a fiction and the devotion of his entourage to be largely a form of theatre. For the greater part of his reign, actual sovereign power was at the disposal of the British Ambassador, an avowed personal enemy who commanded a greater obedience among Farouk's own ministers than Farouk himself could reasonably expect. As we shall see, the Abdin Incident, at the time of the Allied struggle against Rommel's forces in the Western Desert in 1942, was itself precipitated by the compliance of an Egyptian Prime Minister, Hussein Sirry Pasha, to a request from the British Ambassador to expel the Vichy French Minister from Cairo. Sirry had acceded to Lampson's request, even though he was well aware that his King opposed the action and regarded compliance with the British Ambassador's demand as an infringement of Egyptian sovereignty, as indeed it was.

It is my conviction that the high hopes vested in Farouk when he ascended the throne as an extremely popular, young and attractive man, were at the time fully justified, for the young monarch possessed all the necessary qualities to have lived up to them. What Farouk lacked was experience and advice, and the kind of statecraft his father possessed before him. Had King Fuad lived longer and been available personally to educate his son in kingship, history might have been written quite differently and Farouk could still have been alive and ruling today. But let us begin at the beginning.

Part One

King in Waiting

1. Nannies and Governesses

'Queen Nazly, dear,' our nanny would say, 'is rather like the Swan Queen in your *Grey Fairy Book*. She's a lovely person who reads poetry all day.'

To us, of course, she became a lovely, ethereal 'Lady of the Lake', a lady bountiful who sent us magnificent presents. I shall always feel grateful to her for the Pathé Baby movie projector and film camera, for the marvellously detailed all-metal Citroën car-assembly set she sent me, and for a whole sequence of gifts received with pleasure over the years, culminating in a monthly allowance of the then princely sum of £10 to help a teenager on his way.

Queen Nazly's *bête noire* was the British governess to the Royal Court, Mrs Naylor. It seems that King Fuad had sought to put his family on a tight rein, and to this end he employed the disciplinarian skills of Mrs Naylor, who ruled the nursery with a rod of iron and whose authority, supported by the King, overruled that of Queen Nazly. Mrs Naylor is supposed to have imposed a kind of Brixton Prison hold over the young Prince Farouk and his four sisters. Queen Nazly apparently had no say in the early education of her children and was only allowed to see them for about an hour a day so that she should not disturb their studies.

As far as Naylor is concerned, so many contradictory things have been said or written about her that it is hard to define her. To some she was a dreadful middle-aged harridan who hated the Queen and had been encouraged by the ageing, jealous King Fuad to maintain a tight control over the children and remove them as far from their mother's influence as possible. (I learned later that Queen Nazly, as a girl, tried to elope with my handsome Uncle Chahine, hence perhaps King Fuad's unease.) Others saw Mrs Naylor as the instrument of that sinister abode of power, intrigue and influence, the British Residency in Kasr el Doubara, to which, it was assumed, Mrs Naylor dutifully sent secret reports on the doings and misdeeds of the royal children.

It is necessary to try to visualize all this against life in Cairo in the years following the First World War, when there was frequent rioting accompanied by sudden changes of government, for the Egyptian internal political scene was particularly volatile. Bitter recrimination had originally followed the clumsy handling by Britain of the Egyptian Nationalists after the heavy-handedness of Whitehall managed to provoke what some 5,000 years of absolutist government was never able to achieve: namely, a mass popular uprising. This event, in 1919, had epitomized, as we shall see, the peculiar inability of the British to decide upon the exact status of the relationship between the Egyptians and themselves. For Egypt was neither a colony nor independent. Rather was it a hybrid, an unidentifiable bedfellowship termed at the time a 'veiled protectorate', a situation exacerbated by the dethronement of the Egyptian Khedive during the panic of 1914 when war broke out and a British protectorate, to be administered by the admired but disliked military martinet, Lord Kitchener, was proclaimed.

We children grew under the firm conviction, notwithstanding our nannies and people like the delightful Miss Staunton (a retired visiting governess, a gentle and genteel Edwardian, who would interject an exotic French *sac à papier* into the conversation and give us gifts she could ill-afford), that these seemingly friendly English people were somehow demons in disguise. To some of us they were secret members of the 'Intelligence Service', this latter expression being pronounced in the French manner with an accentuation of penultimate syllables.

Here was a contradiction and an ambiguity which was to last many long years: how to reconcile British political posturings and pretensions with the loved and liked English persons whom we knew and grew up with. For me there would be no answer until much later in life. Obviously, Farouk was to encounter the same problems, and I believe that this does give us a key to understanding him and his later development.

His father had suffered at the hands of the succession of British proconsuls who followed the great and liked Lord Allenby. Apart from the vaguely humiliating circumstance of Fuad having risen to the throne under alien patronage, the camouflaged British Raj in Kasr el Doubara would actively, and sometimes with malicious relish, play the game of balance of power, pitting kings against pashas and vice versa. The game was illustrated by comings and goings, by secret rendezvous of Egyptian politicians with the Residency.

During the whole of Fuad's reign, the shadowy socializing of British salon diplomats with enemies of the King, the prevailing atmosphere of *complot d'alcove*, could hardly have been reassuring. Every other princely member of his large and charismatic family had some pretension or other which might be used as a counter for the acquisition of loyalty and confidences by the omnipresent Savile Row-clothed, Lobb- or Maxwell-shod Residency representatives. (The bourgeois takeover of the Foreign Office had only just begun and diplomats were still required to dress 'properly'.) If Fuad had felt himself to be target number one, this was understandable, for suspicion was only natural. Political discussion was rife at our own luncheon table.

We knew, as everyone else did, that an efficient intelligence service was masterminded by the King's own Sudanese butler, who had enrolled the ubiquitous army of Nubian and Sudanese *suffragis* (house servants) to be found in every home, to eavesdrop and report on the thousands of conversations that took place in Cairo about the doings of the times.

At table, King Fuad was always 'Bosambo', and, of course, the British High Commissioner, Sir Miles Lampson, was 'Sanders of the River', Edgar Wallace being very popular at the time. Sheikh el Maraghi, the clerical *éminence grise* of the Palace, was naturally 'Rasputin', for he was supposed by some to have presided over the British-inspired alliance between the religious University of el Azhar and the Palace, an Anglican 'church and state' situation. Egyptians at the time suspected the British occupation authority of using el Azhar, which plays an important political role in Egypt, to prop up an unpopular monarchy (el Azhar being, in effect, a part of the royal team in the internal political line-up).

To be anti-British was therefore fashionable, indeed normal. These sentiments were shared in the nursery, and I vividly remember an incident when, being pushed in my pram by a housemaid past the British Residency, I shouted, 'Fucking Ingleezy,' at the imperturbable and gigantic British sentry at the gates. The maid fled in terror, expecting violent punitive action. This confirmed to my small mind that the word 'fucking' was somehow an aggressive expression. No amount of questioning, however, was successful in securing a precise definition of its meaning. All we knew, I and the Egyptian nursemaids, was that the British used it on every possible occasion and that it was presumably an important ingredient in their conversation. Nanny, who did know, was not telling.

One area in which English came into its own was that of the 'books'. Whenever anyone inquired as to what sort of present would be acceptable to little Prince Farouk, the answer had always been books. In those days, British publishers brought out superbly printed and bound annuals, it being a tradition in England that an annual made a splendid gift for Christmas. These books were lavishly produced. Distinguished artists were mobilized to paint or draw the wonderful illustrations. The volumes were given glossy indestructible covers printed in lovely colours. The *Oxford Annual* for boys and girls and various other monuments of the Edwardian nursery library were still being published.

Wholesome adventure stories, books about courage and loyalty and, in fact, all the great Victorian virtues which had helped to build the British Empire were available: a veritable cavalcade of reading material calculated to further and complete the noble exhortations of Kipling's 'If'. We were familiar with Captain Marryat, R. L. Stevenson, James Fenimore Cooper, G. A. Henty, Charles Kingsley and various others. We in a sense graduated imperceptibly from Beatrix Potter via J. M. Barrie's Peter Pan and A. A. Milne's Christopher Robin and Pooh, to Herbert Strang and Captain W. E. Johns's creation Biggles.

Farouk, of course, had read everything available in this cornucopia of British *Kultur*, and by the time he reached his teens was thoroughly briefed in the ways of the British. This produced a kind of ambivalence, no doubt similar to that

14

experienced by the sons of Indian maharajahs or Austrian dukes who rated English nannies and were subjected to the nursery drill of Edwardian England. Much has been written about that most distinguished breed, the English nanny. When one had grown a bit older, an even more superior English-woman would arrive on the scene: the governess. Her job was to bring cultural enlightenment to her charges' little minds, a large part of her effort being directed at the eradication of the Cockney accents that some of the less 'noble' nannies had spread among them. We came to feel something of that 'élitism' so dramatically presented to the modern world by TV's *Upstairs, Downstairs*.

Our governess, or teacher as Miss Broadbent preferred to be called, was chiefly there for the sake of my sister, who was to be educated entirely at home. My mother, fearing the corrupting influences and wandering infections of schools, wanted her daughter to be given the kind of upbringing that she experienced in her own youth. Indeed, it was my mother's gaunt Kitchener-like former governess, Miss Weightman, who had been charged with recruiting a suitable lady for our household. She found her in what might have been a Suffolk vicarage, except that Miss Broadbent's family were devotees of a rather mysterious branch of Protestantism that held strong views concerning anything that smacked of popery. Their reservations extended to the Pope himself, the Anglican Church and any man dressed in skirts, be he Catholic or otherwise.

Miss Broadbent's father, E. Hamer Broadbent, was a writer on religious subjects, and his publishers, Messrs Pickering & Inglis, would send his daughter in Cairo review copies of his latest books, such as *The Pilgrim Church* and *Jeremiah*. Mr Broadbent earned our admiration by demonstrating, with complete success, the Malayan technique of shinnying up a palm tree with bare feet, his toes clamping themselves to the knobbly parts. He was a small, bearded man with a twinkle in his eye, and he had, we were told, extracted his own appendix while engaged in a camel trek across the Gobi Desert. A most unusual man!

Miss Broadbent, whose first names were Dorothy Ethelwyn, came to us when in her thirties. She had never married, but she always placed beside her bed a Union Jack-decorated picture of Geoffrey, her fiancé, killed at Mons during the First World War. She was far from maudlin about her loss, but nevertheless was fiercely loyal to his memory and, though attractive enough to inspire male interest, was hopelessly unapproachable. Instead, she dedicated herself to Christianity. My sister and I, and later Farouk and his sisters, provided targets for her proselytizing activities.

She did not hide her intentions and quite clearly informed my mother that she would teach us her religion, her conscience forbidding her to do otherwise. Since I was at that time exposed to the ministrations of the good Jesuit Fathers at school, my poor parents were convinced that their children were in danger of being converted to Christianity; a fate worse than death in their eyes. And since my mother was unaware of the intricacies and doctrinal rivalries of confronting churches and creeds, she did not realize that the militantism of Miss Broadbent's Cromwellian Puritanism would most likely cancel out any progress that Jesuit Popery could hope to make. She therefore rushed Sheikh Shindi, an ancient el Azhar teacher, to the rescue.

Sheikh Shindi came to give us a onehour Koran lesson every Thursday afternoon. He would start by distributing sweets and then, in a melodious voice, begin to recite the splendid words. We had to repeat these after him, but the exercise was usually too much for him. It was, after all, just after lunch, and very soon Sheikh Shindi's head would nod as he slipped drowsily into his afternoon nap. With relief my sister and I would turn to more attractive pursuits. Needless to say the experience made us into confirmed Muslims.

Dorothy Ethelwyn Broadbent was petite but very muscular. She had blue eyes and long golden hair. The Bible, she told us, referred to a woman's hair as 'her crowning glory'. It was possibly for this reason that Miss Broadbent gave her hair much attention. 'You must not wash it in water,' she would say. As a substitute, she used a bottle of pale-yellow liquid that had a pungent odour. It was, however, all right for her to rinse her hair in water afterwards. She would then sit and comb the splendid golden locks in the sun. She had pleasant regular features of the kind that would have made her very pretty had she had the desire or the inclination to do something about it. Alas, after the demise of Geoffrey, 'DEB', as she called herself, lost all interest in the opposite sex; except as rivals to be out-stripped by a greater proficiency in Empire-building virtues.

Miss Broadbent was an unsung pioneer of Woman's Lib, for she claimed she could throw a cricket ball as far as any man, and was ready to take on any mere male at Graeco-Roman wrestling or that most English of sports, single-stick! She had also been captain of the Leinster House School first-eleven hockey team, and would proudly wear her first-eleven blazer on special occasions. It was a splendid white blazer with gold trimming. On the pocket, the initials 'LHS' in gold filigree gleamed at us. We were very impressed.

On lesser occasions, Miss Broadbent wore the dark-blue second-eleven LHS blazer, but on Empire Day or Armistice Day she would put on the regalia of a full-blown Ranger Girl Guide Scout. This consisted of a uniform topped by a 'digger'-style hat, the type worn by the 'Guides', a crack regiment of the old Indian Army. Hat and uniform were augmented with whistle, lanyards and other smart pieces of Girl Guide gear. Out for a walk, 'DEB' invariably took along a compass, a whistle, a rope if in the country but string if in town, and, of course, a multi-purpose Boy Scout knife. Thus even our peaceful strolls in the highly urban shop-filled streets of the Egyptian capital took on the brave aspect of expeditions into the wilds.

The ethos currently associated with the Outward Bound schools, where the Duke of Edinburgh and the Prince of Wales were sent in their time, was ever-present about Miss Broadbent, and clearly we, too, were destined to be trained in the tradition of young British Empire-builders. If Miss Broadbent receives a special amount of attention here, it is because she was destined to take over from Mrs Naylor the upbringing of the royal family. The energetic diffusion of Britishness to which she subjected us was similarly directed afterwards towards King Farouk and his sisters. To say that 'DEB', given the chance, would have outdone the Pilgrim Fathers is not to exaggerate.

From the very beginning she began to work with gusto on what she called our souls. Life with Miss Broadbent was interesting, enlightening and challenging. After a morning of lessons, we lunched at the request of Miss Broadbent with our parents.

'The children, Madame, should be taught to sit at table, to make conversation, be polite and observe the disciplines of eating in company.'

Thus from the age of ten onwards, thanks to her, we ate with the grown-ups, at least at lunchtime. Even when guests were present we were expected to participate and share in the conversation so long as we managed to avoid being 'silly'.

In the evening, life passed to the schoolroom, which doubled as a kind of playroom. After bath and dinner, Miss Broadbent would read to us for an hour or so, not only from the Victorian authors but, on more festive occasions, from the William books by Richmal Crompton. The latter was small beer compared to *It is Never Too Late to Mend* by Charles Read, a heavy and lengthy adventure book which, according to Miss Broadbent, had constituted a major factor in reforming the British penal system. Other books were more conventional: *Westward Ho!, Salute to Adventurers, Ivanhoe, The Last of the Mohicans*, the usual Victorian nursery fare. Having disposed of the reading for the night, Miss Broadbent would tuck us into bed and then kneel in prayer silently beside us.

'When people to whom I am close are destined to go to the other place, I pray for them,' she would explain ominously.

Prayers completed, she would pass to the living room and play a rather muffled series of hymns on the piano. I remember 'Roses of Galilee', 'Abide with Me' and many others. Occasionally she would pull out her extremely valuable violin.

'It's an Amati,' she would tell us.

On this, she fiddled Kreisler's rendering of the *Humoresque* by Dvořák and usually ended with a Schumann lullaby.

Miss Broadbent was passionately interested in flying, and at that time learning this new sport was easy in Egypt. It cost some fifty piastres an hour to get flying tuition on Bucker 'Student' biplanes, and she indulged in the activity with characteristic energy. She passed all the tests necessary for her various licences, and over the years achieved her ambition to qualify as a multi-engined pilot. Since she had more or less grown up with the first generation of Egypt air captains, they

18

were always ready to invite her into the cockpits of their Viscounts and Comets when, in later years, the elderly Miss Broadbent would travel back to England to spend her summers there. At one point the *Sunday Times* wrote her up as one of the figures of the British community to have survived in Egypt into the late 1960s.

Such was the lady who took over from the redoubtable Naylor when Queen Nazly, after the death of King Fuad in 1936, dismissed her inconvenient nanny. Miss Broadbent took to palace life with her usual energy. She brought in a supply of evangelistic tracts, of Bibles and Gospels, for distribution to His Majesty and to the palace personnel. The task she undertook would have daunted the most determined Pilgrim Father, namely the evangelizing of the staunch Muslim stronghold of Farouk's palace. But then Miss Broadbent had faith in miracles.

With Farouk, she enjoyed a friendly relationship. After all, her main charges were his sisters. But no doubt the *Boy's Own Paper* background of the young King, for he had become King by the time Miss Broadbent reached the Palace, created bonds between the two, and if it was not up to the 'Anna and the King of Siam' level, there was even so something familiar about the confrontation between an English governess (or teacher) and a young and at the time still hopefully idealistic monarch.

2. The Cadet Prince

My own first meeting with Farouk took place in the summer of 1936 after his return from military academy in England following the death of his father King Fuad that April. Queen Nazly, on the death of her husband, had promptly fired Naylor and asked my mother if she could provide her with a replacement. Miss Broadbent was proposed, and also Miss Lindsay Ellis, until then Matron of the Kasr el Ainy Hospital. The last days of King Fuad's life had been eventful. When the old King was clearly passing away, Queen Nazly called my mother on the phone.

'Fuad is dying,' she said, 'and there's a rumour the British will try to put Prince Mohammed Ali on the throne rather than Farouk. We must do something quickly.'

A hasty conference was called with Cherif Sabry Pasha, Queen Nazly's brother, at the time Under-Secretary of State for Foreign Affairs, in our house in Kasr el Doubara. It was decided that a cable be sent to Farouk to return home from England as quickly as possible and that the Egyptian government officially request the British authorities to fly the young heir to the throne back from the Woolwich Military Academy. Appropriate publicity was organized in the press.

It is likely that the British were taken by surprise before really having time to organize any alternative king-making arrangements. These might well have taken the form of a suitably worded communiqué suggesting that Farouk was too young, that he should be given a chance to finish his education, and that, in any case, since the automatic right to inherit a monarchy did not really exist in a Muslim country, it would be better for all concerned if an older man were placed on the throne, and that there was no better candidate than the septuagenarian heir-apparent, Prince Mohammed Ali Tewfik.

Here we may pause to digress a little. King Fuad had been anxious from the start to make his son into an Egyptian as distinct from an Ottoman or Turkish monarch. He, himself, had married an Egyptian commoner in Nazly, who was the daughter of Abdel Rahim Sabry Pasha. Farouk's schooling, apart from a finishing at a British military academy, was entrusted to Egyptian generals and ministers of proven nationalist Egyptian sentiments. General Aziz el Masry Pasha, a leading military firebrand, was then the young Prince's military tutor at Woolwich, much to the probable disapproval of the British Residency in Cairo. By contrast, Prince Mohammed Ali Tewfik, the ageing son of Khedive Tewfik, lived with his French mistress in the Manial Palace, was partial to the elegant and gentlemanly pursuits of the Edwardian era, such as cock-fighting and billiards, and was a far cry from the kind of charismatic national political figure whom the British might regard as inconvenient.

The Residency might justifiably suspect that King Fuad was nurturing in Farouk a nationalist Egyptian prince of the type who would inevitably clash with them, especially if General Aziz el Masry Pasha had anything to do with it. Hence the 'Prisoner of Zenda' atmosphere prevailing at the time in Egyptian court circles. The somewhat inexplicable grudge that at once developed between the British High Commissioner, Sir Miles Lampson, and the young King might well have been prompted by the circumstances being described, for there was no obvious reason for Lampson's endemic dislike of the 'Boy', as he called Farouk, who was at the time a sixteen-year-old schoolboy who could well be seen as deserving a degree of paternalistic and friendly handling. It is possible that Sir Miles felt strongly about the suitability, in terms of British interests, of Prince Mohammed Ali Tewfik, and that Farouk unwittingly became the symbol of the Ambassador-to-be's diplomatic failure to get away with some judicious king-making. One factor that was soon apparent was the delirious support the young Farouk managed to generate among the Egyptian masses. Here, for the first time, was an entirely Arabic-speaking member of the Mohammed Ali family. He was likewise to become an unapologetic Egyptian nationalist, a fact that would in the long run cost him his throne.

Looked at with hindsight, it might well have been better for Farouk not to have ascended the throne when still a teenager. Instead, Prince Mohammed Ali could well have reigned for a while, a colourless, harmless and uncontroversial monarch whose main interest was that correct protocol be observed at official ceremonies at all times.

The Prince's main passion, however, was looking after his Moorish-style Manial Palace (today a French-managed hotel) on the island of Rhoda, and sitting in the shade of his impressive banyan-tree gardens. Prince Mohammed Ali Tewfik was a harmless elegant snob, chiefly remembered for two booklets he had printed which consisted entirely of long lists of the celebrities His Highness met during his lifetime. It was a list that included King George V and Douglas Fairbanks and Mary Pickford as well as Charlie Chaplin. A short fragile man, he sported an elegant Van Dyke beard and could have passed any day for a repertory version of Charles I. He wore a fez, a wide 'Augustus John' tie, a black morning coat, striped black trousers (*pantalons bonjour*), polished black pointed shoes and pearl-grey spats. There was something dignified, endearing and a little pathetic about him. He eventually died in exile, in Nasser's day, in Lausanne.

At the time, though an ailing man, epileptic and fragile, the Prince belonged to the breed of aristocrat who could be relied on to live long despite illness. An uncomplaining rubber-stamper, he would have been supremely convenient for a myth of national home-rule promoted by concealed alien hands; a finely tooled, delicately balanced implement of colonial rule. This the young Farouk was not! But we shall return to these matters.

It had been at the ripe age of fifteen, with many tears from his adoring mother and sisters, that young Prince Farouk left Egypt for England and the Royal Military Academy of Woolwich. But why Woolwich and not the Royal Military College of Sandhurst? There is a possible hidden reason, though it is impossible to say whether the choice was King Fuad's or if the suggestion came from the British. Sandhurst, with its more aristocratic background, would have seemed to be the appropriate destination, but possibly Woolwich's reputation in the scientific fields of gunnery and range-finding was considered to make a safer school for someone who could become a young and active nationalist king of anti-British persuasion. Sandhurst, after all, was the road to Staff College and an eventual appointment on the General Staff where skills could be obtained that might be used against the British.

Such were the preoccupations of Empire. We should also remember that too close an acquaintanceship between Farouk and young British anti-establishment aristocrats was likewise undesirable. This was a time when an anti-establishment king was about to ascend the British throne and Kim Philby, Donald Maclean and others were being recruited with remarkable success by Communist agents. And when, at the notorious debate at the Oxford Union, young well-born Englishmen voted against dying for 'King and Country'.

Life at the military academy was, we are told, pleasant. As a special dispensation, Farouk was allowed to sleep out of school. A convenient home was rented in the shape of Kenry House, Richmond, and here the young Prince established a household dominated by the suave and worldly Mohammed Hassanein Pasha and his military tutor, the highly intelligent, inconvenient and dangerous Aziz el Masry Pasha. As el Masry Pasha's diplomatic counterpart in the Prince's entourage, Hassanein Pasha had the reputation of being an agent of British policy. This was unfair. He was, to a large extent, an English-minded man, firmly convinced that the Battle of Waterloo had been won on the playing fields of Eton and that the British addiction to sport and the healthy life was the essence of effective rule. As a product of the Rudyard Kipling 'If' era, it was really not very difficult for Sir Ahmed Hassanein Pasha to fall in completely with the *Boys' Own Paper* syndromes of the Residency in Kasr el Doubara.

He was also an exceedingly attractive man who carried with him an irresistible appeal for the ladies. British-educated, public school and an old Oxonian, he had been secretary to General Maxwell, the notorious hangman of the ring-leaders of the Easter Rising in Dublin in 1916. He accompanied the beautiful Rosita Forbes on her trip to the secret oasis of Kuffra in southern Libya, and was an *héros d'alcove* in many a Cairo drawing room. Hassanein was slim, long-nosed and intelligent. I do not wish to pass any judgements here on his motivations. Whether his main loyalty was to his British friends or whether his loyalty to Farouk was greater is a matter for future study and discussion.

Hassanein belonged to that group of Egyptian politicians, and there are many still, who believed that Egypt was too small and too weak a country to practise an independent national foreign policy and that the royal interest therefore demanded a more than normal co-operation with the occupying super-power. For Hassanein, Farouk's future, like his country's, depended on the continued existence and well-being of Britain. He also became the hero of a well-publicized liaison with the King's mother, Queen Nazly, and was supposed to have contracted a marriage with her, much to Farouk's dismay. He died in a traffic accident on Cairo's Kasr el Nil Bridge on a rare rainy day in 1946.

Aziz el Masry Pasha was quite a different kind of man. He was, to look at, short, slim and lightly built. But like many of his type, what he lacked in substance was amply compensated by intelligence and energy. He could be deceptively calm and benign when he wished, but behind this reassuring façade there lurked a revolutionary's mind and a ruthless energy and resource. He had grown up, a companion of my nine uncles, under the patronage of my grandfather, Mohammed Sabit Pasha. From the Nasrya School in Cairo, a hot-bed of Egyptian nationalism, he went straight to the Military Academy in Istanbul. Among his companions there were Enver Pasha and Mustafa Kemal, known to posterity as Atatürk. He passed out of the staff college in 1904 and was posted to the staff of the Third Army in Macedonia.

El Masry had barely left the academy before becoming an influential member of the Revolutionary Committee of Union and Progress that master-minded the successful revolution against Sultan Abd el Hamid in 1908. He commanded the company which captured the Galata Bridge, assaulted the Sultan's palace and talked the Sultan's bodyguard into surrendering.

He went on to take an active part in Turkey's war with the Italians in Libya in 1912. Soon he clashed with Enver Pasha over his Pan-Arab convictions. Ever the revolutionary, he was the instigator of a number of political initiatives distasteful to the Turks and was correctly accused of plotting an Arab military revolt within the ranks of the Turkish Fourth Army. In 1914, this body contained no less than 490 Arab serving officers, of whom 315 were members of Aziz el Masry's secret society, 'El Ahd'. The constitution of that body makes interesting reading. It provides an indication of what could be expected from any great influence he might have exerted over the mind and activities of the young Prince Farouk – a prospect that undoubtedly disturbed the British. The text of the constitution and the definition of its aims ran as follows:

1. El Ahd is a secret association founded in Constantinople. Its purpose is internal independence for the Arab countries, provided they remain united with the government of Constantinople as Hungary is united with Austria.
2. The association, El Ahd, sees the necessity of maintaining the *Khilafa* [Caliphate] as a sacred trust in the hands of the Ottoman family.
3. The association believes that Constantinople is the head of the East. The East cannot survive if it is stripped away from it by a foreign state. Therefore the association is especially concerned with defending it and preserving its security.
4. The Turks have established for six centuries the first lines of defence of the East in the face of the West. The Arabs must be prepared to provide the reserve forces for these lines.
5. The members of El Ahd must do their utmost to cultivate their virtues, and to exhort the people to good morality. No nation can preserve its political national entity if it lacks good morality.

It is not difficult to imagine the reaction of the bullish Lampson to the news that Aziz el Masry Pasha was the general selected to accompany young Farouk to his English academy. El Masry could certainly be trusted to set out to undo the effects of any British brainwashing on the young and royal mind. He might, in Lampson's view, fill the boy's head with silly and dangerous notions. In fact in the contest that followed the wiles of the diplomat outwitted the tactical skills of the soldier. Hassanein appears to have encouraged Farouk, who was enjoying his release from the oppression of Naylor and tasting some of the pleasures of freedom. This was made possible by the special dispensation of allowing the Egyptian Prince not to have to sleep in barracks with the rest of his fellow cadets but to live in style at Kenry House.

One may fairly conclude that the references to the maintenance of *Khilafa* or Caliphate in Article 2 of the Ahd Manifesto revealed a conviction in Aziz el Masry's outlook that such an institution, though extinguished in Istanbul, could well be revived in Cairo at a later stage with the promising young Arabic-speaking Farouk as its principal actor. Such an eventuality was hardly likely to impress or please the British or, in the process, Hassanein Pasha. Predictably, therefore, Aziz Pasha's presence in Farouk's entourage at Kenry House did not last long. There is strong evidence to indicate that an intrigue to unseat the general was in train at Kenry House. Hassanein appears to have encouraged the young Prince to lead in England a freer existence than was compatible with the abstentions and rigours of the life of a cadet.

In the end, General Aziz's resignation was precipitated by Farouk's behaviour. The general, taking a dim view of nocturnal pleasure-seeking, tried to impose military discipline.

'The fact that Your Highness does not sleep in the dormitory like the others does not mean that you can behave with total freedom. On the contrary, as a future king you must set a good example and go to bed at least as early as the others, if not earlier.'

Farouk's reaction to this was defiance, covertly condoned by Hassanein.

'I did not escape from one Naylor to fall into the clutches of another governess,' he said.

Aziz Pasha el Masry wrote an angry report back to King Fuad and submitted his resignation, which was accepted. El Masry went on to become in later years Farouk's implacable enemy, and he it was who groomed Gamal Abdel Nasser and his fellow officers into becoming effective revolutionaries. There could have been no better person or more suitable man for such a task.

During his stay in England, Farouk engaged in his first official international role when he represented his father King Fuad at the funeral of George V, at which he seems to have struck up a friendly personal relationship with the new King of England, Edward VIII. Within six months, however, his own father, King Fuad, was also dead and he returned to Egypt. Back home he was an instant success. A handsome fresh-faced Arabic-speaking boy, he was everybody's Prince Charming. Since he was still too young to be officially invested in the kingship, a Council of Regents was formed to rule on his behalf.

The council consisted of Prince Mohammed Ali, Aziz Pasha Izzet, Ali Pasha Maher and Cherif Pasha Sabry, the King's uncle. Aziz Izzet was a splendid-looking gentleman of the old school. Trained as an army officer, he had been Egypt's first diplomatic representative in London and was married to a royal princess. Cherif Sabry was tall and elegant and was quite close in looks to his sister the Queen. He was an efficient Secretary of State for Foreign Affairs and something of an art connoisseur since he owned one of the world's most complete collections of Persian miniatures.

Ali Maher was a favourite figure for the many able caricaturists of the Egyptian press. He wore his fez at an angle and personified the little-man caricature 'el Misry Effendi' that the popular press used to symbolize the middle-class Egyptian. Since such symbols have their importance, being a part of folklore, it may be useful to look at 'el Misry Effendi' rather more closely. Two pieces of equipment were essential: a fez at a rakish angle and the inevitable prayer beads. 'El Misry Effendi' was a mild little man, good-humoured and good for a joke, but ready to bristle with anger when provoked. In the eyes of the caricaturists, among them the sharp, witty Armenian, Saroukhan, 'el Misry Effendi' personified the modern middle-class Egyptian. Peaceful, generous, clever, critical and apparently of a mild disposition, he was nevertheless subject to strong feelings and nationalist ardours.

Ali Maher, though he lacked the massive public support his Wafdist competitors enjoyed, could suggest with some justification that he was fairly representative of an important segment of the Egyptian voting public. Had there been better electoral turn-outs in the urban areas of Egypt at the time, Ali Maher might have achieved a certain eminence as a popular leader. He was doubtless disliked by the Residency Establishment in Kasr el Doubara.

3. The Queen Mother

By the time Farouk returned from Woolwich to the arms of his adoring mother and sisters, Queen Nazly, still a young woman, was firmly at the helm. A strong-minded lady, and a beautiful one, her married life in King Fuad's time had been severely restricted. She lived a virtual prisoner behind the walls of the three great royal residencies, the palaces of Abdin, Koubbeh and Montazah.

Abdin Palace was the central official residence, a large structure reminiscent of Buckingham Palace or one of the more splendid South American presidential residences. Its style was that of nineteenth-century baroque. The presiding genius behind its splendid façades and columned marble halls was Verucci Bey, a somewhat sinister elderly Italian architect, and confidant of King Fuad, for whom he acted as a kind of private go-between. Koubbeh Palace was something different again. Set in vast gardens in the Cairo suburb of Koubbeh Gardens, the palace was a splendid location in which to site King Fuad's harem. It was here that Queen Nazly spent the better part of her life.

The Queen was a keen amateur photographer who did her own developing and printing. She was also a good artist, specializing in graceful paintings of flowers. Since Nazly had been a romantic and strong-willed girl, King Fuad clearly felt the need to ensure that she would be sealed off from the rest of the world. Even her brothers and family were excluded from the Palace, and only my mother, presumably regarded (with some solid justification, I might add) as a very respectable person, was allowed access to her, apart, of course, from the various ladies-in-waiting recruited from some of the most prominent families of the pasha class.

Her chief lady-in-waiting was a Jewess, the stately and delightful Madame Cattaoui Pasha, who had been in earlier times a great friend of King Fuad and one of the brilliant Kasr el Doubara hostesses. Madame Cattaoui was a graceful, angular, aquiline-nosed brunette of the Boldoni school, always elegantly dressed and a splendidly patrician example of the Cairo Jewish aristocracy of the time. The Cattaouis were Sephardic Jews, probably of rather remote Spanish origin, who belonged to that glittering community of Jewish families which had built the smart residential quarter of Kasr el Doubara. They included the Adeses, the Rolos, the Toledanos, the Hararis and many others who developed Kasr el Doubara into a never-never-land of stately *hôtels des villes* and mini-palaces. They were, in essence, an Edwardian crowd whose activities ranged between high government posts and big-business prominence. Cattaoui Pasha had been a minister, and his son Aslan a distinguished member of King Fuad's Parliament. The Adeses came from Manchester, where they were a family important in the cotton trade, while the Hararis, besides being leading Jewish citizens of Cairo, also played a part in the British administrative machine. Ralph Harari, from an Egyptian childhood, became finance officer on the staff of Sir Ronald Storrs and ended his career as manager of a prestigious bank in London. His wife, Manya Harari, was the co-translator with Max Hayward of Pasternak's *Dr Zhivago* into English.

Life was for Queen Nazly quiet and restful. She attended the opera during the winter season, when every major première started with something akin to a command performance with the diplomatic corps and members of the government present. The opera house was a small, rapidly built but accurate replica of a baroque theatre of the style favoured by people like the King of Bavaria or the Elector of Hanover. Indeed, similarities between the Egyptian court and the court of some small German king or princeling were striking. Opera nights were exciting affairs, crowned, of course, by the annual set of performances of *Aïda* by the Scala di Milano.

It should not be forgotten that King Fuad was educated in Italy and had been attached to the Italian Army as well as having been, in his princely days, an ADC to King Victor

Emmanuel. He was at school with the latter when the Khedive Ismail was sent into exile by the Ottoman Sultan in 1879. A certain Italian operatic influence was therefore understandable.

Grand opera openings had all the charisma of the times. Audiences wore high evening clothes, miniature decorations, monocles and all the trappings of smart Edwardianism. One carried binoculars to the performance, not only to observe the stage but also to scan the other boxes, to see and be seen, to record the gossip and scandal that these events inevitably brought out when royal presences attended. The arrival of the Queen and her ladies was an exotic and most discreet affair. The Queen's box being screened with an ornate *musharrabiyya* screen, one could just sense the royal arrival as the silent box began to stir with the murmur of ladies' voices and the movements of muted colours briefly glimpsed through the screen's wooden diagonals. From the ceiling, framed in ornate rococo stucco, the great composers of the nineteenth century looked down on the audience. In the intervals, the foyer would glitter with dresses, diamonds and jewel-studded plastrons.

Other grand occasions were the yearly levees held on the great Islamic feast days of Bayram or Eid. Then the King would receive the diplomatic corps, the ministers and the ruling members of the establishment, and especially his own family of princes and nabils. The Queen likewise presided over audiences with the ladies of the foreign diplomatic corps, the wives of ministers and distinguished members of the establishment. These were occasions of pomp, circumstance and gossip.

There can be few palaces anywhere to combine the attractions of the third royal palace, that of Montazah in Alexandria. Set on a series of low-lying cove-framing cliffs, shaded by pine trees in a luxurious garden setting, Montazah was the sort of dream palace that King Ludwig of Bavaria or Walt Disney might have thought up. In style it was broadly Italianate, with a strong Mediterranean inspiration. It was a bewildering conglomeration of forms and architectural frills, where arches, balconies and towers exuberantly jostled each other and presented a sometimes clashing contrast of widely divergent styles. To some the palace was an architectural

31

monstrosity, but to those who had the pleasure of living there, it made a delightful home, a place of sunlight and blue seas where wide heroic balconies overlooked gardens of multi-coloured flowers, of ancient exotic trees, of lawns and pathways that led to sheltered bays and the ever-present sea and its sounds. This was the pleasure palace in which Farouk and his sisters spent their summers, that in those days lasted some five months, and during which time Alexandria became the capital of Egypt as King, court and government lived and worked in the city.

'You'll have to tidy up, wear a fez, morning coat, striped trousers and clean shoes,' said my father one day, always on the ball so far as dress was concerned. He was at the time Chef du Protocole at the Ministry of Foreign Affairs, and as such was an authority on the forms and precedences of diplomats. Since I had hardly any of these garments, and no facilities existed to hire them, I approached friends and relations to help me complete my wardrobe.

The emergency had hit us with unexpected suddenness. 'Adel and Dodie must come and have tea with the King and his sisters tomorrow afternoon at 4.40,' was the telephoned command from Montazah.

'Queen Nazly wants Farouk and his sisters to meet children of their own age,' my mother said. 'You must behave perfectly.'

My sister Dodie was something of a tomboy, gay, mischievous and, according to most people, very beautiful. I, as a brother, was unaware of these attractions. To me she was a good friend and a companion, if sometimes an aggravating tease. From Miss Broadbent she had picked up a somewhat puritanical outlook and seemed to have inherited some of 'DEB''s scorn for males. A good rider, she was quite fearless and showed the beginnings of that rare combination, moral and physical courage.

'There'll be other children with you,' said Mother. ' "Fafette" Zulficar and her sweet young brother Said and also, Adel will be happy to know, "Toats", the son of Princess Abbas Halim.'

Toats and I were great friends and had shared many thrilling experiences, such as being caught in the middle of Alexandria Harbour one afternoon in a rudderless and unmanageable sailing craft just as the British Mediterranean

Fleet was sailing majestically in. We had had to run the gauntlet of huge dreadnaughts and cursing sailors and only managed to get out of the way of HMS *Queen Elizabeth* by jumping overboard and towing our small light craft to safety. We also once sank spectacularly in the Nile on a boat of my own construction that turned out to be a good deal less watertight than I fondly imagined.

Toats had been brought back to Egypt by his mother after a stint in a British prep school where he had picked up all the brash cockiness of the English schoolboy. His mother had remarried, his stepfather being Prince Abbas Halim, an exotic and romantic figure. While in England Toats had also developed a taste for Gilbert and Sullivan operettas, and we would spend hours memorizing *Trial by Jury* and *The Pirates of Penzance* in between swimming, sailing and indulging in the good life of the Alexandrian summers of the 1930s.

And so, brushed and dressed up, balancing our fezzes at rakish angles under the disapproving gaze of the grown-ups, we accompany the girls to Montazah. Safinaz, nicknamed Fafette, is an unknown quantity, a pretty dark-haried girl who is clearly well in front of our own country-bumpkin levels.

'She's supposed to be a real fast one,' says Toats, 'only interested in older men.'

Her brother is a handsome bouncy boy whom we know vaguely from having been, over the years, guests at various summer birthday parties in Alexandria. Her parents live in Alexandria, where her father, a delightful pink-faced and hearty gentleman, Yussef Bey Zulficar, is a Supreme Court judge who will later become Ambassador to Iran. Zeynab Hanem, her mother, is a lady-in-waiting to Queen Nazly. She is a plump, pleasant, motherly person, the daughter of a former khedivial prime minister.

We check in through the enormous portals of Montazah and enter a fairy-tale world of lovely garden alleys, of rows of smartly dressed sentries of the royal bodyguard, of heavy ancient trees and multi-coloured flower beds. We drive along winding paths through a small pine forest till the car stops at

33

the foot of a palatial marble stairway that leads upwards towards the entry of the fairy palace itself. We are taken to a large room overlooking the sea. The furniture is heavy – solid tables and a minimum of breakable bric-à-brac – a fact that is noted with approval. Outside, the gardens look inviting, the sea glints further off and the sound of bugles wafts in on the afternoon breeze. I look at Toats.

'This is the life. Beats Sidi Bishr any day,' he says, Sidi Bishr being the beach where we usually bathe.

There is a sound of movement, a rustle of skirts, and led by Miss Broadbent four pretty doll-like girls come tripping into the room. They are all pretty, but the eldest two are beautiful, Fawzia with the blue eyes being quiet and shy, and Faiza dark-eyed and slimly graceful. They are dressed alike in smart white dresses, long white socks, white shoes and pig-tails, except for the youngest, Fathia or 'Atty', who has bobbed hair and has a vaguely Shirley Templeish look about her.

Had we suddenly been dumped by magic on a Cytherean desert island and approached by its attractive natives, the effect would probably have been comparable. We discover that the princesses are models of innocence, that they call each other 'dear' and 'darling', and that apparently no cross words are ever uttered. Quarrelling is something unheard-of in this Garden of Eden. Clearly Mrs Naylor's influence still lives on. She has obviously, by dint of sheer single-minded discipline, brought about a complete isolation of her charges from the outside world. We are, in fact, the first children the young princesses have ever been able to see or talk to, within reaching and touching distance. Lacking nothing, living in bucolic surroundings, mobbed by adoring servants, aunts, ladies-in-waiting and a romantically beautiful mother, the little princesses belong to another world. They are supremely naïve, over-protected, cellophane-wrapped, gift-packaged little girls of a type rarely to be found anywhere off the covers of a chocolate box. We are all led outside into the gardens to play.

'Do you like running, dear?' says little Atty, coming up to me.

'Yes, Your Highness!'

We, too, have undergone some hurried training, and calling them Highness is a part of it.

34

'Then catch me!' says Atty, disappearing into one of the many bushes.

Utter confusion . . . What do I do now? How appallingly undignified for a sixteen-year-old man to go chasing a tiny doll-like girl through the underbrush. Nevertheless, discipline and instructions have to be obeyed, so I lurch off after the bobbing bundle . . . and get myself hopelessly entangled in shrubbery. Atty, not much larger than a good-sized rabbit, knows the terrain pretty well and disappears through impenetrable gaps in the bushes, suddenly to reappear somewhere unexpected to crow triumph and derision until finally she rejoins the main party, having outflanked and outmanoeuvred me six or seven times. I return, dusty, dishevelled and vaguely humiliated. The princesses help to dust me down. Atty looks on with interest.

'Not much of a runner are you, dear!' she says.

Queen Nazly now suddenly arrives on the scene, accompanied by her ladies. She is dressed in white, something frilly and rustling, and brings with her an aura of fragrant perfume. I can visualize her strewing roses as she walks, white roses. All around us is serenity, transparent blue skies, the sea glinting gold in the distance, puffy white summer clouds in the sky, languorous groups of lovely ladies and delightful young girls, basking in the tree-rich glades amid the banks of flowers.

'And this is Adel,' says Queen Nazly. 'My, you look just like Adolphe Menjou, *en plus jeune, chéri!*'

I am not quite sure how to take this. Adolphe Menjou is definitely before my time. I vaguely remember him from films as an elderly and somewhat disreputable roué.

The Queen has now turned her attention on Dodie and Fafette. There is a general cooing going on as the ladies flutter about Her Majesty. The girls smile back as royalty examines the little group of children from the 'great outside'. Toats, who is plumpish and homely, is mercifully neglected.

'*C'est le fils de Tawhida, n'est ce pas?*' says the Queen sweeping past and not waiting to hear his mumbled reply.

We move on towards the tea party. A military band in a near-by pavilion observes the arrival of the royal group and the bandmaster, in red fez and dazzling blue and white uniform, swings into action.

35

'*Nimra sitta,*' he roars at his men, meaning No. 6.

No. 6 turns out to be the stirring Overture to Rossini's *William Tell.* His bandsmen look like elaborate and expensive mechanical toys. They have clockwork arm movements and have clearly been drilled to a high standard of military precision.

An enormous table has been laid out, with cakes of every conceivable size and type spread on it. A voluptuously inviting *sacher torte* rubs shoulders with lemon chiffon pie, strawberry shortcake, Black Forest *gâteau, mille feuilles en masse* and an absolutely enormous *crème Chantilly* filled with meringues. There is, of course, the usual collection of *batons sales,* canapes, savoury pies and sandwiches *à la Bourbon.* There is tea, lemonade, orangeade, mango juice, sugar-cane juice and strawberry sundaes. Small tables are spread around the glade.

'Sit with the children,' I am ordered by a lady-in-waiting.

I try to avoid Atty, who has a mischievous glint in her eye. When we bring our cake-laden plates to the table I sit next to Fawzia, who seems rather comfortingly shy and talks in monosyllables. We are both tongue-tied and seek comfort and consolation in eating cake. Splendidly liveried Sudanese *suffragis* serve us drinks. They are clothed in blue and gold, and some wear war medals. One cannot help feeling important here. The service, the implied flattery, is heady medicine. Luckily and opportunely, having recently read *Great Expectations,* I was much impressed with Pip's illusions concerning Estelle. Queen Nazly seems to be a kind of Miss Haversham, and possibly these girls are so many royal Estelles. I had better watch my step.

With tea coming to a close the band is playing *nimra ashra* (No. 10), an arrangement of the 'Last Post' with mournful bugles sounding lights out and merging with other muted martial sounds. Tea is clearly over.

'Time for the cinema,' cries little Atty. 'It's Shirley Temple tonight.'

As the ladies-in-waiting officiously marshal us into our seats, a certain protocol is being observed. We two older boys find ourselves placed on the periphery. No funny business, such as holding hands or other approaches, is to be tolerated. Toats and I are obviously too old to be trusted; the little princesses must be protected. Judging by the highly subtle surreptitious glances that emanate from the latter, precautions are possibly wise. But if they only knew what little experience we two boys possess, they would hardly bother. We are certainly not the ones who need watching. Unlike her ladies, the wise Queen Nazly is fully aware of the situation. She knows her girls, having been one herself not so long since.

The Shirley Temple movie comes on. The heroine is all that is most off-putting to boys of our age. She sings 'The Good Ship Lollypop' quite horribly. We are frozen into suffering politeness but we deceitfully smile approval as a gushing lady cries hysterically, 'Isn't she sweet!' Atty is bobbing up and down on her seat, clapping her hands and singing. Obviously she identifies with Little Miss Hollywood.

'The children are having a wonderful time, darling!' my mother says to the Queen as she looks disapprovingly at our glum faces.

I hastily restore a hypocritical smile. It can't be long now. The King, I suddenly realize, has not been seen at all. Where is he? His presence, observing us from the palace windows, might be felt. I suddenly realize that, poor King, he's shy, and who wouldn't be with this mob of women? As we are all getting ready to leave, suddenly Farouk arrives. He is about our age, nice-looking, a real boy. He has in his hand a .22 rifle which he shows to me.

'I use it to shoot rats,' he says, 'but I have an elephant gun upstairs.'

He promises to show me his collection of guns and disappears again. We are ushered out by the ladies, Queen Nazly having retired to some palace limbo. The children, too, depart. So ends a memorable occasion. That summer of 1936 we see some dozen Shirley Temple movies.

My sister and I in fact get to know the little princesses well. I am happy to go to tea and cinema events. At least the tea and cakes are very good. I am likewise happy to find myself banished from morning operations when the girls go swimming in the little natural harbour on Montazah. My banishment provides an interesting example of the way Queen Nazly's mind works. Arriving one morning at Montazah with my bathing suit, I am intercepted by a lady-in-waiting.

'Adel comes with me,' she says. 'The Queen wishes to see him.'

I am taken upstairs into a large room and told to wait. Five minutes later a trolley stacked with goodies is trundled in. 'Eat,' I am ordered. After I have tucked into a hearty second breakfast, the lady returns and says, 'Come with me.'

I am taken to a large room where Queen Nazly is trying on new shoes. A prominent shoe-maker is in attendance; dozens of pairs are lying about. The Queen is trying on everything. She sees me.

'Ah, Adel,' she says, 'did you have something to eat?'

'Yes, Your Majesty.'

'Well, Adel, you are a big boy, nearly a man, and you look like Adolphe Menjou! Do you really think it's suitable for you to go swimming with Fawzia and Faiza, who are also grown up? You would see them in their swimsuits, undressed . . . Anything could happen! So I think it is better that you do not go swimming with them!'

What a welcome release. It means I can go to Sidi Bishr again, see my friends and return to the normal world. Still the princesses are rather pretty. But never mind, there is always Shirley Temple.

4. Queen Nazly's Family Background

The most important among Queen Nazly's forebears was Mohammed Cherif Pasha, who was one of the most distinguished figures in the history of modern Egypt. Cherif Pasha was the son of Mohammed Cherif Effendi, the Ottoman *Kadi el As'kar* of Egypt in the early stages of Mohammed Ali's rise to power at the start of the nineteenth century. The function of *Kadi As'kar*, or Military Judge Advocate to give an approximate modern rendition, was that of the supreme representative of the Ottoman judiciary in what was then the tributary territory of Egypt – the *vilayet* of Egypt. In this function he shared power with Mohammed Ali himself, who was at the time the Ottoman governor of the country. The two men had been close friends, and during Mohammed Ali's quarrels with the Turkish Prime Minister, or *Sadr Az'am*, Mohammed Cherif Effendi sided with Mohammed Ali and used his own substantial influence in the Ottoman capital on the latter's behalf. Upon his return to Istanbul, he was to become the *Sheikh ul Islam* of the empire, which was, in effect, the supreme religious legal authority in the Muslim world of the time.

On going back to Turkey, he left his son Cherif behind in Egypt, to continue his later education. Cherif was a contemporary and school-mate of Ismail Pasha, later Khedive (Viceroy) of Egypt, who was the son of Mohammed Ali's Viceroy Ibrahim Pasha, formerly the great commander of the Egyptian armies in Syria and Anatolia. At eighteen years old, Cherif was sent to Europe as a member of the fifth mission of students to France in 1844. This mission, called the 'Princes' Mission', was one of the most important to be sent to Europe. Selected from the most brilliant students of the Mohandess Khana, which in English could be translated as School of

39

Engineers, the mission also numbered several princes of the Mohammed Ali family, including the Emirs Ahmed and Abd el Halim Hussein, as well as Ismail Pasha, with whom Cherif enjoyed a close relationship.

The period of Cherif's student years in Europe was one of the most significant in that continent's history of social progress. In Britain, the age of Peel, with its great parliamentary reforms and its worker-orientated legislation, was in its prime. In France, the moribund monarchy of Louis-Phillipe was in its last years before the 1848 revolution. The French public had grown restless at the unimaginative compromises of such personages as the doctrinaire and cautious François Guizot, Foreign Minister and leader of the monarchist party. Bonapartism was slowly emerging as a vocal opposition in the French Parliament. Certainly the Second French Empire was in the making from 1840, the year of the transfer of the late Emperor Napoleon Bonaparte's remains to his last resting place in Les Invalides in Paris, where they remain to the present day.

The year 1844 lay a bare four years before 1848, and the spirit of revolution was already smouldering in Switzerland, Italy and Poland. The liberals, socialists and disciples of Karl Marx were actively and industriously preparing the great social upheaval that would, less than a century later, sweep most of the European monarchies off their feet. It would have been impossible for young Egyptian students living and learning in France to have remained indifferent spectators of the turbulence and turmoil. Cherif's tutor in the early stages of his education had been none other than Rifa'a el Tahtawy, a distinguished Azhar scholar of an earlier generation who had accompanied the first mission to France in 1826. Rifa'a el Tahtawy had taught himself French and translated Montesquieu's *Esprit des lois* into Arabic. He was subsequently to father the great legal reforms in Egypt under Ismail Pasha and to be one of the major influences on Cherif's constitutionalist and socio-political reformist ideas.

In Paris, Charif attended the prestigious military academy of St-Cyr. Passing out of this institution with distinction, he spent another two years in the French Higher Institute of Military Sciences, from where he was seconded to the French

General Staff, there attaining the rank of captain. On his return to Egypt, these talents earned him a position on the staff of the Commander-in-Chief of the Egyptian Army, Suleyman Pasha, the former French Colonel Joseph Anthelme Sève, whose daughter Nazly Cherif wooed and married. Under Said Pasha, the next Khedive, Cherif achieved the rank of *amiralay*, commander of the Viceroy's Bodyguard.

In 1856 he was promoted to general and assumed the title of *pasha* in accordance with this rank. The next year he was transferred from military duties to become Minister of Foreign Affairs. Following the death of Said in 1863, and the advent of Khedive Ismail, his former schoolmate, he was given a further ministry, that of the Interior. Then, in 1865, Ismail, in a unique gesture of confidence and trust, nominated him *Kaim'makam*, or, literally, place-holder, to rule the country during the Khedive's long absence in Istanbul. It was an appointment that would normally have been given only to a member of the royal family, for it meant a virtual assumption of sovereignty over the whole country. Under Ismail, Cherif assumed high honours. He held the prime ministership on several occasions and began to take an active role in Egypt's budding parliamentary institutions. In 1868, he was elected to the leadership of the Privy Council, whose function was supra-ministerial at the time.

During these years, Cherif's mind turned increasingly to social and political reform, and, as we have seen, his formative influences came from a Europe in the full ferment of the nineteenth century's social tensions. He had absorbed at first hand the teaching and views of Montesquieu, Rousseau and others among the French Revolutionary intellectuals. He was closely in tune with the views and outlook of Rifa'a Bey el Tahtawy, tutor and chaplain to an earlier generation of Egyptians in Paris. These views were both Islamic and nationalist. Since he found no conflict between reformist European ideas and the ethics and principles of Islam, an adaptation of the latter principles to the Egyptian legal codes was regarded as desirable. The decision by the Cherif ministry to engage in judicial reform was therefore part of a continuing progression.

It is a measure of the discipline and restraint applied in the process that it was Rifa'a el Tahtawy himself, heading a working group composed of Abdullah Bey el Sayed, Abd el Salam Ahmed and Ahmed Helmi, who elaborated the adaptation of the French Civil Code, the *Code Napoléon*, to the prevailing laws in Egypt. In the context of a Muslim community of the nineteenth century, these were indeed revolutionary measures, so advanced that they excite controversy to this day. It is unlikely whether such measures could have been instituted had they lacked the firm and convinced patronage of Cherif backed by the far-sighted support of Khedive Ismail. Writing on this subject, Professor E. I. J. Rosenthal has this to say in his book, *Islam in the Modern State*:

But before we can discuss their important contributions, we must touch briefly on an earlier Egyptian thinker Rifa'a Badawy Rafih El Tahtawy whose five years stay in Paris made a deep impression on this Egyptian. He translated Montesquieu whose praise of patriotism strongly appealed to him, just as Silvestre de Sacy awakened in him an interest in ancient Egypt. Both interests prompted El Tahtawy to encourage the publication of Arabic classics, amongst them the works of Ibn Khaldun. His political thoughts are in accord with the classical Islamic theory of the authority of the Shari'a which the absolute ruler must respect. He divided society into four estates: the Ruler, the men of religion and law, soldiers and those engaged in economic production. Incidentally we find the same four classes already in El Diwani. The influence of the French enlightenment is evident in all Tahtawy's views, that the principles of Islamic law are not very different from natural law which forms the basis of modern Europe.*

It seems that what Plato was to el Diwani, so Montesquieu and Rousseau were to el Tahtawy. His equation enabled him to *legitimize recourse to modern law codes, gaining an interpretation to bring about a modernization of Islamic law to meet the exigencies of the time.* According to A. Hourani, this

*E. I. J. Rosenthal, *Islam in the Modern National State*, Cambridge University Press, 1965, pp. 65–6.

42

Egyptian reformer held education to be the key to *Hubb Al-watan* (the love of the fatherland), which has the same significance as Ibn Khaldun's *Asabiya* (group loyalty). One interesting development occurred through el Tahtawy's widening the circle of important builders of state and society by including doctors, engineers and other scientists, with the *Ulama* (men of intellect) coming next in importance after the ruler, the fatherland being Muslim Egypt.

Cherif's greatest achievement, however, was the elaboration and voting into law of the Cherif Constitution of 1879. This document represented a startling change in the Muslim world, long accustomed to autocratic and totalitarian regimes. The Khedive became, from an absolute monarch, a constitutional sovereign who reigned but did not rule, something after the style of Queen Victoria. State authority was vested in the National Assembly. The Cherif Constitution was presented to the National Assembly on 17 May 1879, and a few days later Cherif submitted an electoral law to take effect after the deposition of Khedive Ismail on 10 November 1881, when Egypt witnessed the first free election for the new assembly of delegates. He personally supervised the elections and issued a stern warning to officials against attempting to influence them.

The passage of Cherif's reforms did not enjoy plain-sailing, either within Egypt or abroad. Such personages as the two former prime ministers, the Armenian, Nubar Pasha, and Riaz Pasha, were convinced Europhiles and alarmed at developments. They opposed Cherif strongly, believing in the virtues of greater foreign intervention and interference in Egyptian affairs. The great powers themselves, of course, also objected to reformist trends, led by France and Britain, whose motives ranged from concern over the repayment of various debts contracted by Ismail through extortionate bank loans to, in the case of Britain, designs over the control of the newly inaugurated Suez Canal waterway.

All these elements were openly hostile to the national cause, but it was left to Bismarck to engineer the abdication of Ismail in favour of his son Tewfik, a person of considerably less talent than his father. The German Chancellor, taking up the cause of various creditors and usurers, delivered an ultimatum to the Khedive Ismail in May 1878 that he must pay his debts. Since the latter was in no position to do so, Bismarck made representations to the Sultan in Istanbul, and on 24 June 1879 Ismail was forced to abdicate.

There is no doubting that the various creditors who had serviced Ismail's debts were appalled by the prospect of authority passing out of the Khedive's hands and into those of a democratically elected National Assembly who might renege on repayments and call for a moratorium. Some idea of the vulpine nature of these creditors may be gathered from the information given in *Spoiling the Egyptians: A Tale of Shame* by J. Seymour Kray. Kray states in his Preface that a debt of about £90 million had been imposed on Egypt by European speculators, in consideration of which only about £45,500,000 was even nominally received.* This means, in modern parlance, an emission or discount rate of nearly 50 per cent!

An appreciation of Cherif's work can be deduced from an analysis of his outlook. Cherif's main preoccupations were two-fold: to end foreign interference in Egypt's affairs and to bring about the necessary constitutional reforms permitting the government of the country to develop normally within a democratic mode. And although such processes would inevitably transform the khedivial status to that of a constitutional ruler, his personal relationship with Ismail was such that he gained the latter's agreement to co-operate in the process.

Matters came to a head when Riaz Pasha, then Premier of a Cabinet containing a British and a French minister, addressed the Consultative Assembly on 27 March 1879. The purpose of this meeting was the dissolution of the assembly, which Riaz Pasha proceeded to proclaim. The assembly, however, declined to react positively and refused to dissolve, and a crisis developed which was at the time regarded as a revolution. The Khedive's hand was now forced (needless to say, not unwillingly on his part) and Cherif Pasha came to power and immediately proceeded with the issuing of his Constitution.

The Constitution of 1879 was revised and reissued in 1882. As the highlight of these documents, the Second Constitution

*J. Seymour Kray, *Spoiling the Egyptians: A Tale of Shame, Told from the Blue Books*, Kegan Paul, Trench & Co., London, 1882.

of 1882 was a continuation and an elaboration of the first. Since both were promoted under the direct leadership of Cherif, they reflected his personal touch. Articles 23 and 24 of the 1882 Constitution defined a procedure whereby the National Assembly might overrule the khedivial authority. This meant, in effect, that the sovereign had neither the power to impose his policies on the government nor the right to veto decisions of the assembly. Articles 30 and 31 gave the assembly a complete right of supervision and control over the national finances. Article 30, in particular, gave the assembly the right to defend the sanctity of property and to control the levying and administration of taxes.

The tone of inspiration behind these instruments of political reform was clearly strongly nationalist. Cherif deplored the inroads that had been made into Egypt by assorted groups of foreign 'get-rich-quickers', alien debt controllers, foreign advisors and so on. The Khedive, in his enthusiasm for the task of modernizing Egypt, had regrettably become a vulnerable target for the foreign exploiter. These were the bad old days of unashamed imperialism, a time when both France and Britain were in a full flush of imperial acquisitiveness, when the carpet-bagger and empire-builder plied their trade in Africa, Asia and South America, and even indeed in the defeated Southern states of the United States.

There is little doubt that one of the intentions behind the Cherif Constitution was to remove from khedivial hands the operation of loans and the right of the sovereign to commit the country's responsibility for guaranteeing collateral. This is made very clear in the articles of the new Constitution. It was, of course, no easy task to persuade Ismail that these reforms were necessary, and it is unlikely that anyone in Egypt other than Cherif possessed the stature, or the personal regard of the Khedive, to achieve these ends. It is in the personal relationship between the Cherif and the Khedive Ismail that an insight into the source of Cherif's influence may be discerned. Both had been sent as students to France, although Cherif was older by some four years. They were close friends in spite of this, but their characters differed.

Ismail had, as a student, been attracted to the flesh-pots of Paris and been somewhat negligent in his studies. Cherif, on the other hand, was an assiduous and industrious scholar who passed with honours through the prestigious military academy of St-Cyr and the Institut des Hautes Etudes Militaire to become a member, for a while, of the French General Staff with the rank of captain. Cherif, thanks to his background and the special position his father occupied in the Mohammed Ali hierarchy, was, of course, treated more or less as a member of the viceregal family and enjoyed with young Ismail an intimacy that allowed him to adopt critical attitudes and sometimes to proffer unpalatable advice. He was thus able to play a valuable role at a time when the Egyptian crisis, brought about by a growing indebtedness to the Europeans and an increasing European penetration, was coming to a head.

Cherif's solution was, in a sense, to constitutionalize the issue, to create a representative National Assembly that would acknowledge Egypt's liabilities, but do it by applying a repayment procedure in keeping with Egypt's resources. His main aim was to forestall any attempt by Britain and France to exploit the situation for political ends, and this could only be done by replacing the autocratic rule of the Khedive by a duly elected democratic system that would ensure that the repayment of debts was governed by acceptable procedures and legal guarantees. Cherif was successful in securing the support of the Khedive for his constitutional reform, and under his ministry a whole series of reformist measures were undertaken, making him, in the opinion of the eminent Egyptian historian, Abd el Rahman el Raf'ai, the founder and undoubted leader of the Egyptian nationalist movement in the nineteenth century.

Cherif's solution was, if anything, strengthened by the deposition of Ismail. The new Khedive, Tewfik, inherited an awkward situation. After the departure of his father from the scene, he was caught in a cross-current of political intrigue between the predatory foreigner and the discontented stirrings of the Egyptian public body who now had the support of the army. The country, represented by the members of the National Assembly, called on Cherif to form a government of national union in September 1881. He did so, on condition that the army officers, headed by Arabi Pasha, refrain from interfering in politics since any such interference could provide an excuse to the foreigner to intervene militarily in Egypt. The officers accepted these conditions, their agreement taking tangible form in the withdrawal from Cairo in October 1881 of the two main forces commanded by Arabi and Abd el Aal Helmi. It was not long, however, before the assurance was breached, and Cherif, unable to restrain the excessive nationalist zeal of the military, resigned. The subsequent ministry, headed by Arabi and Baroudi, threw caution to the winds and proceeded to make a foreign occupation inevitable by adopting the kind of nationalistic postures that can only have delighted the warlords of the West. The latter were then able to launch a satisfyingly easy conquest of Egypt and thus begin an occupation that would, in effect, last until 1954.

The plain and brutal truth of it was that, behind the screen of occupation, British policy was intent on securing the Suez Canal and dismantling the Ottoman Empire. These intentions were of paramount importance and of course had to be served. Cherif reassumed the office of Prime Minister immediately after the occupation, and although he was able to supervise the continuation of the legal and administrative reforms he had initiated before that event, he inevitably clashed with the British representatives, and in particular the British Agent and Consul General Sir Evelyn Baring, the future Lord Cromer.

Matters came to a head over Baring's obstructions with regard to the Sudan and the British Agent's advice for its abandonment. Cherif resigned on 7 January 1884 following a clash with Baring over what he saw as the necessity of relieving Khartoum and his refusal to accept Baring's suggestion that the Sudan be abandoned. The months subsequent to his resignation saw British public opinion, headed by no less a person than Queen Victoria herself, overrule Baring and decide on the relief of Khartoum and the retention of the Sudan. But by then Cherif was a sick man, a victim of the strains of office to which he had been subjected. He died in April 1887 under treatment at Graz in Austria. He was buried in Cairo. His funeral cortège, some 10,000 strong, passed through streets thronged with a mourning population.

We may therefore see how, on the distaff side, Farouk could claim descent from an authentic Egyptian nationalist with a hereditary connection to the Muslim Prophet himself through his forebear, el Hussein. To this day, Cherif remains in the memory of the Egyptians as one of the greatest of modern Egypt's founding fathers – a decidedly honourable forebear.

The causes and circumstances that led to the occupation of Egypt in 1882 continue to generate an enormous controversy. The action was a classic example of the gun-boat diplomacy so fashionable at the time. Yet, for it to succeed, a certain innocent complicity was required on the part of the potential victims. They had to be made to appear as baiters and bulliers of Christian minorities, as ravenous supporters of mob violence, as terrorists threatening human values and Christian principles. The vocabulary of aggrieved colonialism was a rich one, and the task of presenting the dog with a bad name was easy. Back in England, where a generally naïve public still lacked the awareness to distinguish between propaganda and reality, publicists and polemicists alike had a simple task convincing people as to the virtuousness and righteousness of the imperial cause.

Securing public support was a tactic the colonialists had to succeed in in Britain, where public approval for overseas adventures was necessary, even though some of the more prestigious empire-builders were successful in bypassing it. British public opinion still exerted at least certain decisive influences. This could have led to the conclusion, had Cherif remained Prime Minister, that no justification for an occupation emerged strongly enough to allow the expedition. As it transpired, the excessive and unwise attitudes of Arabi Pasha, his officers and of the more sanguinary members of the National Assembly, who had rejected the cautionary discipline requested of them by Cherif, eminently created the precondition without which no occupation could have been triggered by the British.

5. The Legacy of King Fuad

An examination of Anglo-Egyptian relations is essential for any understanding of the complex problems that faced young Farouk after the death of his father. Looking first at that initial event of the British occupation of 1882, it is sad to note how very little light has been thrown on it and the circumstances leading up to it which could be said to plead a case on Egypt's behalf. Learned books, dissertations and after-the-event conclusions are all weighted heavily on the side of the European viewpoint. In the process, the Egyptian perception of events has been obscured as well as seriously distorted by the well-meaning but often impassioned nationalist Egyptian accounts of the time.

We may by the 1980s allow ourselves a certain clinical detachment in our assessments and evaluations. In 1882, the prime British object was to re-establish Khedive Tewfik on the Egyptian throne within a British-controlled political environment, and in the process to suppress Egyptian nationalist reactions, whether or not these were justified. As a result, the spectacle followed of the British government supporting an unpopular and devious khedivial absolutism against democratic and educated liberals who had already won their point against monarchist absolutism. It is possible to explain the mystery of what may seem to some to be an illogical and uncharacteristic British policy, though it is difficult to reconcile the contradiction. The parodox consisted, in effect, of a support for royal absolutism on the part of a country dedicated to a democratic constitutional monarchy. The purely cynical observer might have added that, quite apart from the problems of politically and militarily occupying Egypt, there was also the important question of securing a guarantee from the Egyptians

49

for the debts of the preceding administrations. These, of about £90 million, had, as we saw, been lent under the most usurious terms to Khedive Ismail.

There is no doubting that Khedive Ismail, in his laudable attempts to develop Egypt into a modern state, did allow himself to become the victim of some of Europe's most rapacious nineteenth-century speculators. There is also no doubting that the loans had been negotiated and given out in terms and under conditions that could in no case be reasonably fulfilled. The cynical cut-rate selling of Egypt's own Suez Canal shares to Britain via the Rothschild Bank and Mr Disraeli provides a case in point and needs little Egyptian explanation or comment.

There are some, both then and now, who see in the occupation of 1882 the culmination of a grand international scheme to exploit Egypt's considerable economic and strategic advantages. For Egypt to become, as she did, the great base from which Britain's African empire was built and the Indian and Asian empires retained and controlled, it was necessary to keep a strong British hand on Cairo. There would be no democratic or parliamentary nonsense to get in the way of imperial designs. What Britain in effect needed was a khedivial puppet supported by a puppet government and people, the whole set-up to serve British interests.

To achieve such a situation was not as easy as might be imagined. The nationalists in Egypt were no African bushmen. They were educated, determined and, for the most part, French-speaking Muslims who had been engaged in creating a new concept within Islamic statecraft. They were far ahead of the rest of the Muslim world, including Ottoman Turkey. Many of the leaders who opposed the British were better educated, and of higher intellectual calibre, than the middle-class English bureaucrats so soon to be off-loaded on to the Egyptian administration.

Another factor that is not to be discounted was the fact that the Egyptian establishment was free from the social pre-occupations of the hierarchy-sensitive English middle class. Too many of the latter, snubbed by their British social 'betters', looked forward to working off their complexes on the

Egyptians. The British diplomat, Sir Ronald Storrs, makes the following comment in his *Memoirs*:

> Nor was there the faintest effort on the part of the official's wife to make acquaintance and still less to cultivate the friendship of the wives and daughters of her husband's colleagues or subordinates and it was with an air of virtuous resignation that she steeled herself to sacrifice an afternoon for a call on an Egyptian or Turkish lady as likely as not better born, better bred, better read, better looking and better dressed than herself.*

Such reflexes provide the breeding-ground for racism. The nationalists, however, were not to be suppressed, and were indeed able to carry a strong popular support partly because the Mohammed Ali administration had not, as some people thought, been an attempt by a Turkish oligarchy to maintain itself at the expense of the *fellahin* (native Egyptians). Quite the contrary, it had been Mohammed Ali and Ismail's intention to bring as many indigenous Egyptians as possible into the administration and development of their country.

The democratic Constitution, suppressed at the British occupation, had been drafted by Sheikh el Tahtawy who, as we saw, accompanied the first of the missions to France and later translated the revolutionary jurist Montesquieu's *L'Esprit des lois* into Arabic. Education lay in the hands of Ali Pasha Mubarak, who had created and led the educational reforms of the period. Both these intellectuals, and many others, were of poor *fellah* origin, selected by a system that relied on merit, not on patronage. It is significant to point out that King Farouk was himself, on his mother's side, the descendant of the French officer Sève, later Suleyman Pasha, who laid the foundations for the army Mohammed Ali used to defeat the Turks in the 1830s. Suleyman Pasha was head of the selection committees for the missions to Europe, and was a prime factor in the application to candidate selection of merit and adequate testing. This is hardly surprising, since Suleyman was himself of poor peasant stock.

*Sir Ronald Storrs, *The Memoirs of Ronald Storrs*, G. P. Putnam's Sons, New York, 1937, p. 89.

Thus, quite possibly to the surprise of the British, the Egyptian national movement was widely supported and able to rely on a grass-roots suffrage. As Landau records in his *Parliaments and Parties in Egypt*, the Assembly of Delegates of 1866 contained 58 *umdas* (head village dignatories) out of 75 delegates, which is to say about 82.86 per cent *fellahin.**

Not least among the British problems were the British liberals themselves, of whom the explorer and poet Wilfrid Scawen Blunt was an example. Led by Lord Randolph Churchill and representing a strong factor in the Parliament at Westminster, they called for the evacuation of British forces from Egypt. The consequence of this was that activities in Cairo fell directly under the eye of London and had the effect of generating often polemical debates in Parliament and in the press.

All of these were basic factors in the play on the British political and military chessboard. Egypt, falling under the suzerainty of the Ottoman Sultan, could not easily be annexed by Britain as a colonial territory, and lip-service needed to be paid to Istanbul. At the same time, other European countries pursued their own aims and ambitions in Cairo. Most important among them was France, who until her humiliation over the Fashoda Incident in 1898 and the birth of the *Entente cordiale* in 1904 could be expected actively to encourage opposition to the British occupation.

By force of circumstance, the policy of maintaining a balance of power became central to the activities of the British Residency and High Commissariat of Kasr el Doubara. One particular British problem was an endemic one, namely, the 'anti-establishment' Englishman who, rather than confining himself to the usual ghetto of local British diplomatic or administrative expatriates, preferred to taste the pleasures of socializing with the Egyptians. This sort of thing gave rise to much confusion, for it was not always easy for the Egyptian side to define the exact standing a 'friendly' Englishman enjoyed with the British authorities. All too often these private contacts were regarded as, indeed sometimes were, relation-

*Jacob M. Landau, *Parliaments and Parties in Egypt*, Praeger, New York, 1954.

ships inspired and clandestinely approved by the British 'Raj', thereby promoting an often undeserved picture of how devilish the British were in their political subtlety and Machiavellianism.

There is little doubt that the Egyptian ruling establishments of the post-occupation period were generally ignorant of the cross-currents affecting the Egyptian situation in Westminster. Wilfrid Scawen Blunt's flirtations with Arabi Pasha and the nationalists, well-meaning as they may have been, ended with the complete disaffection of the latter. They were moreover often interpreted as a vast and sinister charade whose purpose was to encourage Arabi's revolt so as to give the British a pretext for military intervention. It is probable that the strong Francophilia of the Egyptian ruling classes also strengthened Egyptian suspicions of the always *perfide Albion*.

It may be suggested with hindsight that, had the Khedives understood the internal situation in London better, they could well have enrolled strong factional support in the Parliament at Westminster, where the Egyptian Question would have been regarded as important enough to lead to clash and debate in the House. Similarly, it would have been 'natural' for Abbas Helmi, the last Khedive from 1892 to 1914, to have allied himself with such a scheme as the Cape to Cairo Railway. No mutualities of material interest seem, however, to have contributed to close relationships between the Khedive and the British proconsul. But then, what had the Khedive to offer?

Possibly the veiled secrecy attending the setting up of the National Bank of Egypt by a group of Edwardian financiers, headed by Sir Ernest Cassel, would belie this question. Reports have it that a 'deal' was agreed with the Khedive whereby the royal properties, communally owned by the Mohammed Ali family and at the time held by the Caisse de la Dette in the Crédit Lyonnais as collateral for the Egyptian Debt, were to be purchased by a British consortium represented by the National Bank of Egypt, which was to be set up as an issue bank. The lands would then be sold at a substantial price, financed through the National Bank, to selected Anglophile rural landowners. The latter would be required to pay for the land by committing their cotton crop year by year through a transaction masterminded by the bank and uniting the Lancashire millowner with the Egyptian cotton producer.

The Khedive is said to have received a considerable commission from the sale of these lands. Whether or not this be true, it is a matter worthy of future study and investigation. Plot or no, the political interests of Britain were served splendidly. Not only did they establish the National Bank of Egypt, Egypt's central note-issuing bank, but they simultaneously created a politically strong voting body in the National Parliament represented by a new indigenous land-owning class, the *fellah* pashas.

The *fellah* pasha was the new political element to come into its own in the Parliaments of King Fuad's time. These were farmer pashas of doubtful loyalty to the sovereign who owned vast landed properties and were in alliance with the Lancashire mills who were their prime financial partners. As such, they were a ready-made political factor of quite formidable implications which the British High Commissioner had at his disposal. The farmer pashas all too often achieved prominence in the Wafdist Party, where their patronage and financial support could be counted on to rally votes for the nationalist politicians in Cairo and indeed to fuel the latent republicanism in that quarter. So, from the outset, strong elements of political corruption were discernable in the fabric.

In 1923, the year after he became the first King of Egypt, King Fuad inherited a Constitution of a new kind. In this a latent confrontation between the Palace and the Cabinet was endemic. The document had been put together under the influence of strong interference from forces alien to the purely Egyptian scene. The British Resident, being the third party in all the local confabulations, was naturally directly on the line to London whenever the occasion required, and here, whether they were of Machiavellian origin or not, we may pause to admire the way in which circumstances seem to have led to the serving of British interests.

As we have seen, direct colonial rule was ruled out for international reasons. Since the nationalists in Egypt were non-eliminatable and indigestible, the game had perforce to be the one of balance of power. The elements in the game required two internal teams, representing the Palace, khedivial or royal, and a national Popular Front represented by those political parties who could rally a strong popular nationalist support. These two needed to be confronting forces, neither side disposing of sufficient authority to unseat the other totally. The British Residency's role was then that of arbiter and weight-maker, able to cause the scales to tip towards either the Palace or the parties.

The 1923 Constitution, drafted under British supervision and intervention by an unofficial group of jurists, provided the machinery to permit this kind of operation. Its chief feature was an ambiguity in defining the royal prerogative and the government's rights to veto. It was not a constitutional system whereby the royal rights might be strictly limited and defined, as in Britain, neither was it an absolutist document in which the King could overrule the executive authority. It was a constitution that could not but invite a continuous bickering between the King and the people, represented by the parties; a bickering which led eventually to intervention of the British referee, who would apply the decisive touch, usually in line with the British interest. Such, in essence, was the 'divide and rule' system practised effectively during King Fuad's reign and, as we shall see, applied with disastrous results in King Farouk's time.

Before we leave this chapter we may dwell finally on the more human side of the Anglo-Egyptian confrontation. One question that at once springs to mind is why were certain British representatives liked and respected, even though often charged with unpopular missions, and others disliked? An Egyptian diplomat offered me the following explanation: 'Il est difficile de recontrer un équilibre social chez les Anglais. Ils sont tellement obsédés par leur systême de classes qu'ils manquent les nuances nécessaires pour que leurs represent-ants puissent agir en diplomates. Ils sons "gentlemen" ou "épiciers", et nous ne nous entendons pas très bien avec les épiciers.' ('It is very difficult to find a balance within the ranks of the British. They are so obsessed by their class system that they are unable to develop the right appreciation of nuance which would allow them to be diplomats. They are either "gentlemen" or "grocers", and we do not get along very well with grocers.')

We should remember here that the Foreign Office had not at that time been completely taken over by the middle class and the service could still attract the sort of noble ambassador who was able to combine pressure with diplomatic finesse and so on without upsetting his interlocutors. This led to a kind of Jekyll and Hyde guessing game every time a new ambassador was named. Would he be a gentleman or would he be a grocer?

Over the subsequent years the British middle classes have to a very large extent managed to overcome their social inhibitions and the determined 'Englishness' of bourgeois pre-war ambassadors has declined almost to extinction. It would be a most courageous man who today strutted down Gezira Sporting Club race course, as did Lords Killearn and Lloyd, in full Ascot rig. Yet these and many other social snobberies were practised with relish and, to some extent, brandished in the faces of the khedives and kings of Egypt as a not-so-subtle reminder that the traditions of the great Queen over the seas were being observed here in her far-flung domain in the 'veiled protectorate of Egypt' as Lord Cromer is supposed to have described it.

6. Palace Politics

One of the first effects of King Fuad's educational planning was to isolate his son from children of his own age. Farouk's Egyptian education had generally cut him off even from other young princelings of the family, whose background was predominantly foreign, some having grown up in Istanbul where Egyptian royalty still owned large and splendid houses. Ottoman Turkey had been a fashionable holiday resort for Egyptian princes in the pre-war years. It was seen as a good place to deposit families – women and children – while the men sought the more daring life of Paris and the Riviera. Other young princes were sent to Britain, the idea being that an English education could be useful to one's career during that splended era of imperial autumn which preceded the Second World War.

It was fear of dynastic rivalries and princely ambitions that caused Fuad to keep fraternization with other members of the family to a minimum. Thus we have a picture of the lonely little Farouk and his sisters living out their Brixton Prison existence in the plush surroundings of Koubbeh Palace in Cairo and Montazah Palace in Alexandria, both remote and large establishments surrounded by high, unscalable walls, their entrances guarded by a proliferation of well-built and well-armed members of the Royal Bodyguard.

Outwitting the Naylor became a major preoccupation for the young king-to-be. He was fortunate in finding allies among the palace staff. Antonio Pulli, the palace electrician, an affable and discrete Italian who was to become an important confidant, made him counterfeit keys so that, while Naylor was deeply committed to her slumbers in the adjacent room, Farouk could sneak out and drink water to his heart's content in the small hours of the night. Sweets, likewise forbidden by British authority, were brought to His Highness by other members of the staff. By the time the young prince was ready for his military academy at Woolwich, he had at his disposal a small palace mafia of allies who were, with time, to be suitably rewarded. Antonio Pulli became Pulli Bey, Helmi the chauffeur became Colonel Helmi, and so on. Garro, the Italian barber, and Gavazzi, the Swiss-Italian keeper of the royal dogs, were likewise recompensed.

Farouk's time in England, however, brought with it the young man's first emergence as a politically significant figure when he attended the funeral of the late King George V as official representative of his father. More importantly, he was at the centre of the first palace intrigue to come his way, which was to carry long-term and serious consequences: the clash already described between the pleasant, social and tricky Hassanein Pasha and the crafty, highly intelligent and dangerous Aziz Pasha el Masry.

Farouk returned to Egypt from Woolwich none too soon, though the members of the royal family, represented by a brace of princes, constituted a threat less to the actual throne than to his peace of mind. While a majority of the princes might well look towards the possibility of kingship, the final decision always lay with the British. This meant that the king needed to be on the look-out in case too intimate a friendship should develop between some member of the family and the British Embassy. A comforting consideration was that most princes were Germanophile in their leanings and hence unlikely to enthuse the British Ambassador with their credentials for the highest office in the land. Nevertheless, a highly disquieting factor still existed in the British Ambassador's apparent personal hostility, which could lead, as it did some years later, to a serious threat to the King's position. But as things stood in 1936, no suitable substitute for the highly popular Farouk was available.

Meanwhile, overshadowing the whole issue, was a contention that Ibrahim Pasha had not been the son of Mohammed ali Pasha after all, and so Ibrahim's children and grandchildren were not legitimate heirs to the right to succession that Mohammed Ali had extracted from the Sultan of Turkey and his European associates by the *firmans* (decrees) of 13 February and 1 June 1841 when he was accorded the hereditary rule of Egypt. If this was true, then the whole line of the succession from Khedive Ismail to Farouk could be illegitimate. The counter-claimants to the throne ranged from Prince Mohammed Ali Tewfik, already mentioned, to the ex-Khedive Abbas Helmi II, who was living in Germany awaiting his chance of a come-back; to Prince Abbas Halim, a legitimate claimant, since he descended from Halim Pasha, a genuine son of Mohammed Ali; and to his cousin, Prince Said Halim, whose claimancy was a somewhat burlesque version. Yet of them all, Farouk remained the most appropriate, particularly since he was the only prince whose education had been tailored to an Egyptian pattern. Nevertheless this did place in his path, once he became king, a whole series of potential problems which might easily be developed by his enemies and opponents into dangerous situations.

Psychologically speaking, Farouk found himself caught between two awkward stools: preserving his 'face' as King of Egypt and the knowledge that he lacked the experience and know-how essential to effective rule. But the position and authority of his mother was a strong factor – unsurprisingly, since this conformed to the general role of the mother in Muslim society. So much nonsense has been written about the subservient position of the woman in Islam that many of the relevant facts have been obscured. Respect for parents, and in particular for one's mother, is a fundamental tenet of the Islamic faith. Muslims are from their earliest youth informed that 'the world is in the lap of the mothers'. And since filial devotion to mothers is a general feature in the world of Islam, most leaders will have in their background some outstanding mother-figure to whom obedience and respect are due both as a matter of course and as emphasized by tradition and faith. An outstanding example of this was Queen Shagaret el Dur ('Spray of Pearls'). The last of the Ayyoubite Queens and the first Mameluke Queen, she kept the death of her husband, the Sultan, secret to allow time for her son, who was absent in Syria, to return to Egypt. In the interim, she ran the country successfully enough to defeat the 6th Crusade in 1250, and to take the King of France prisoner.

Queen Nazly's statecraft, had it succeeded, would undoubtedly have consolidated the rule of her son. She firmly believed that he needed to maintain a close and friendly relationship with the Wafdist nationalist party in the person of its leader, Nahas Pasha, whose wife, Zeynab el Wakil, another vital and powerful lady, was her personal friend. Unfortunately this meant bucking a City Hall represented by the British chiefs in Kasr el Doubara and the various nationalist pashas and politicians who were already disturbed at the King's popularity. At stake was the policy of 'divide and rule' along with the careers of a variety of ambitious and unscrupulous politicos. Yet another element who could be relied on to upset any attempt at fraternizing with Nahas Pasha and the Wafd was the small coterie of pashas whose fortunes and futures were tied directly to royal patronage since they lacked popular support.

Among these, Ali Maher Pasha was the most influential. Farouk had relied on Ali Maher, as leader of the King's party under Fuad, for much of his early political education. If the pasha was able to teach him the elements of political intrigue, and no better teacher could have been available, then he was likewise able to use King Farouk's undoubted popularity, and to abuse the King's trust, in the service of his own enlightened self-interest.

Yet another new political factor was to emerge after King Farouk's marriage to Safinaz Zulficar: a group best identified as Queen Farida's family, whose leader, Hussein Sirry Pasha, her uncle, tended to compete with Ali Maher as representative of a royal political faction. Lacking any popular support, Hussein Sirry largely owed his rise to his family connections with the young Queen of Egypt. Here, too, we may pause to point out that Egypt had, since earliest times and in particular since Mameluke days, possessed a tradition of plots and counter-plots in which family connections, blood ties and various close and remote forms of kinship had played an undoubted role in the in-fighting between elements of the political scene. Cairo had something of the Italian Renaissance city-state in its political make-up. Montagues warred against Capulets and, as often as not, 'ancient strifes broke out to new mutiny'. Kinship therefore imposed its disciplines on its members, and in the process Farouk might hope that Sirry Pasha, being of his Queen's family, could be relied on to direct his principal loyalties towards the Palace. That this would prove to be a costly illusion would only emerge with subsequent experience.

These are but a few of the factional elements that, one way or another, sought to guide and use the inexperienced Farouk. They formed a patchwork of often competing influences, pulling His Majesty in various directions. I mention some here merely to throw a light on Farouk's personal response to his environment. As I have said, his was a 'kingly presence', closely modelled in appearance on his father King Fuad, whom the young man tended to resemble. Fuad looked and behaved like a king, and Farouk produced a reasonable facsimile of Fuad. But herein lay a problem. The act of adopting the kingly face did tend to spill over into his private attitudes, very often causing the young man to carry his public postures into his personal relations.

Farouk felt impelled always to seem to know better than his interlocutor, to be better informed, to be better advised. And since this was often far from the truth, such behaviour tended to create barriers between himself and the more honest among his entourage, who were not prepared to play the sycophant. On the other hand, these factors tended to favour the flatterer and the courtier. And here we come to yet another feature of the Egyptian scene. All through their history, the Egyptians, having had their fill of eccentric pharaohs and sometimes alarmingly sanguinary foreign rulers, have concluded that the only way their society can survive is through the simple device of corrupting the ruler, on the assumption that 'power corrupts and absolute power corrupts absolutely'.

Farouk's entourage were not new to the game, and it soon became obvious that the traditional habits of rulership were being instilled into him by his court. He developed a taste for the whispered intrigue, a liking for the absurdly extravagant adulation that was offered to him, and he finally succumbed to that most dangerous of political aberrations, a reliance on favourites. Yet this is to anticipate. At the outset of his reign, Farouk was still a schoolboy, open-minded, capable of taking

61

advice and honest enough to experience self-doubt. Had he been less isolated, had he been allowed to continue his studies in Woolwich, to develop friendships with those who were unimpressed by his royal personage, indeed, to have enjoyed some reasonable and genuinely disinterested human relations, he could well have followed a totally different path.

This was indeed his tragedy. Farouk was lonely, had few friends, and did not know how to make them. He would have had to climb down from his high horse to do so, and he was too afraid of his inexperience, possibly too ashamed, to make the effort. He remained a lonely king to the end. Those, like myself, who might have been his friend, were at the time either too young, too shy or too inexperienced to make the necessary move. The most honest among us were too embarrassed and made to feel awkward by him, and so, of course, the less scrupulous won the day. Since these latter were, without exception, grown-ups well versed in courtly wiles, we stood no chance. Our time, when it came, would be a while later.

7. A Royal Marriage

In November 1936 it became known that Farouk was in love with Safinaz 'Fafette' Zulficar, whom we have encountered already in our incursion into the Palace to meet the little princesses. The King's mother, Queen Nazly, had seen to it. The Queen, a well-preserved forty-year-old beauty, newly emancipated by the death of King Fuad, was full of energy and ready to embark on her first political role, and steer her only son through the rapids and shoals of the Egyptian political scene. She had sailed into the political arena like a 74-gun frigate, all systems at 'go'.

The first step was to get Farouk, still a 'pure' teenager, settled and safely married to an obedient well-mannered girl, a commoner like the Queen herself. There would be no autocratic princess from the royal family – and there were several delightful and high-spirited girls in the pool – for Farouk. Princesses, after all, are wilful, autocratic and eccentric, and would above all have been unlikely to submit to Queen Nazly's overrule.

Another consideration was that of the royal succession. The sooner a son could be born to the young King, the better. This was necessary to counter the latent threat represented by the claims of the ambitious and insidious Prince Mohammed Ali Tewfik, the septuagenarian Crown Prince whose constant wooing of the British Embassy activated, and probably justified, the apprehensions of the Farouk legitimists.

Safinaz, known to her family as Fafette, appeared to fit the bill most adequately. She was pretty, vivacious, ambitious and, Queen Nazly observed with satisfaction, well able to wield the feminine wiles and flirtations necessary to entrap the naïve and unsophisticated young monarch, fresh out of the hands of

General Aziz el Masry, the drill sergeants of Woolwich Military Academy and the residual influences of Mrs Naylor's nursery disciplines. Farouk, himself, was a sitting target, and there is little doubt that the great love of his life would be this first love, the soon to be Queen Farida of Egypt, for it was a tradition that monarch and consort must bear a name of the same initial. All that was needed was the green light from Queen Nazly. This was obtained through Fafette's mother, Zeynab Hanem, one of her ladies-in-waiting, a comfortable granddaughter of one of Egypt's Prime Ministers, Said Pasha, who came of sturdy Turkish and Greek stock.

Fafette held out every promise of being an ideal and hopefully retiring daughter-in-law. She behaved towards Her Majesty with respect, with the modesty and graceful deference becoming to her mother's mistress. The young couple, it was said, fell head over heels in love, though Fafette herself did not care for this version of the story in later years. She preferred people to believe that she only contemplated marriage to the King with considerable reluctance, and that she was subjected to a determined offensive by the young man before she finally agreed. Maybe this was true, but subsequent events suggest it is unlikely.

The announcement of the betrothal came after the investiture. The good-looking young King, the pretty young Queen and the majestically beautiful figure of the Queen Mother excited the popular imagination, and the Egyptians hailed the sovereign and his ladies with the natural intensity and whole-heartedness they exhibit on public occasions. Indeed, so popular was Farouk proving to be, that both the majority Wafdist Party and the British Embassy began to feel concern. Investiture Day saw Cairo in one of its major popular frenzies. Huge crowds thronged the illuminated streets, Farouk's picture was everywhere, and the sort of patriotism that sprang more spontaneously in those days than it does today overflowed; this was a Mafeking Night, a Queen Victoria Jubilee, a Bastille Day, all rolled into one.

At last Egypt had an Egyptian nationalist king, Arabic-speaking and married to an Egyptian commoner. A new chapter in the country's history was about to begin. A Treaty of Independence was, moreover, about to be signed in

London. As the fireworks burst in a multi-coloured rain above the palm trees of Gezira, the Egyptians felt that this was the beginning of a fulfilment to hopes, of a bright and dignified future, of a new era in the history of their ancient land.

The marriage itself was a grand affair. Several hundred guests gathered in the lush gardens of Koubbeh Palace to attend the evening party. Ministers, ambassadors and leading citizens rubbed shoulders with the princes and nabils of the Mohammed Ali family. Not since the opening of the Suez Canal had Cairo witnessed such a lavish occasion. The Royal Bodyguard, resplendent in its blue, gold and red uniforms, the tassels of its fezzes swaying to the music, went through its whole repertoire. The scent of jasmine, mingled with frangi-pani, competed valiantly with the many and expensive perfumes of Paris. The stars of stage and screen performed and, amid an appropriate hush, the great Om Kalsoum sang songs for the occasion. Another star of the show, making her début, was Tahia Carioca, the dancer. She was a cross between Hedy Lamarr and Elizabeth Taylor with her creamy white skin and a splendid mass of silky black hair. Her figure belonged to dreams and she won the hearts of her audience. She still lives today, an honoured figure of the Egyptian stage.

To get the full flavour of the occasion, one must be able to imagine the atmosphere prevailing on a star-filled moonlit summer's evening in Cairo. The night is velvet, the air sound-filled by a song of nature created by the environment. It is a heady, intoxicating, multi-dimensional mix of far-off music, of off-stage sounds, human and animal, of scent, rustle and summer murmur. The whole provokes a powerful, sensual response, for it is in a sense the sound of life: of thousands of living things from the cicadas to the frogs that rattle away in their remote canals, to the distant village weddings and the lowing of restless cattle, the braying of donkeys. All these and more fill the perfumed air. And then the voice of Om Kalsoum comes across, remarkable in strain, vibrating, intensely emotional.

I have seen adult audiences writhing in ecstasy at those sounds. Indeed, listening to Om Kalsoum for three or four solid hours is one of life's most remarkable experiences. By the end the audience is rolling about in ecstasy. It is the same with

Tahia Carioca. Her lovely figure, her body, the sexual attraction it exudes after three or four hours of watching her dancing, has the viewer completely carried away. Carried away, because as one follows this emotional, this exciting, erotic love-dance, a certain relationship develops between the dancer, the music and you, the viewer. You are dancing with her, you are actually making love to her.

These two ladies, officiates at the royal wedding, became legendary in the recent history of Egypt. Their fame, it is certain, will live on long after the political and national events that shook Egypt in their lifetimes have pretty well faded from memory.

8. First Troubles

The year 1937 marked the end of Farouk's adolescence and the official start of his reign. The hopeful schoolboy who had set out for cadet school in England less than two years earlier was now King of a turbulent and effervescent nation. He was also soon to become a married man, settled in what was hopefully a pleasant domesticity, and soon to be a father. His good looks, his innocence, his uncommittedness to this or that political party had earned for him a vast nationalist support which seemed to most observers to outstrip the popularity of the veteran nationalist party leaders of the Wafd.

Now, if ever, was the time for some clever and clear-sighted diplomacy on the part of Britain. A change of approach would be the logical conclusion, for the old game of divide and rule, besides its advantages, suffered from one major drawback. By dividing political factions and playing one off against another, you lost the friendship and confidence of all. Nobody likes a Machiavelli, since his whole outlook is, perforce, based on intrigue and dishonesty. Farouk was a malleable and well-intentioned idealist at this stage, his principal formative influences, as we have seen, being largely those of the Baden-Powell era. Had Britain accepted the need for change and nominated a young and clear-sighted ambassador, then the balance of power might no longer have been necessary, for Farouk, on the eve of his rule, spoke a roughly similar language to that of young England. Moreover, an important aspect of the young King's personality was an undoubted ability to exude a royal 'presence'. It was a gift recorded and observed by many, and it stayed with him to the very end.

Such are the manners and procedures of modern well-ordered societies, that cabinet ministers, ambassadors, cardinals and prelates will bow even to the youngest of kings with a deference and respect evolved over many hundreds of years of civilized history. For the politeness of diplomacy looks beyond the raw and innocent adolescent to the kingship the latter represents, and beyond that kingship to the people and country whose sovereignty the youthful ruler embodies. It is therefore surprising that the Foreign Office in London seems not to have appreciated this. On his investiture, Farouk became the sovereign of Egypt, and due respect for this role was accorded him by everyone except the British Ambassador, formerly the High Commissioner, Sir Miles Lampson. The way in which Lampson assumed the role and function of Ambassador surely transformed his status into something of a travesty. One suspects that, in the eyes of the Foreign Secretary of the time, Mr Anthony Eden, Egypt was still a 'veiled protectorate' requiring a 'veiled high commissioner'.

Being Ambassador was, in fact, a task that was rather badly fulfilled by the British envoy, whose blustering and hectoring arrogance was of the kind more to be expected from an envoy extraordinary of such as Idi Amin. For Farouk, the implication was clear. He was being treated as just another African cannibal king. The British were not interested in partnership or indeed in co-operation. They did not believe Egyptians to be their racial equals, but regarded them as an endemically subject people. Unfortunately, far too many of His Majesty's ministers and politicians went along with the situation and indulged in the humiliating pilgrimage to the British Residency in Kasr el Doubara in search of office or small favours.

The King was from the very outset of his rule subject to this form of persistent humiliation. The combination of an arrogant avuncular British Ambassador and servile Egyptian politicians instilled within the young monarch a somewhat hopeless and cynical detachment towards the mass of political figures who thronged the ante-chambers of the Palace at Abdin. Whereas his father, a wily and politically sophisticated man, sought to win loyalty by bribery or intrigue, Farouk, for lack of these useful but dubious assets, withdrew into the security of the Palace and the company of the small and unrepresentative clique of palace pashas and ministers.

Farouk's struggles were now beginning in earnest, for, in addition to the constantly complicated and turbulent political scene, a major battle was in the making much closer to home. This was a conflict of a type well known in the world: the conflict stemming from the feelings of a mother-in-law towards her daughter-in-law, the feelings of a wife towards her mother-in-law. Queen Nazly was, after all, a youngish woman. She had led a very frustrated life, having been more or less locked up during the period of King Fuad's reign, and now was suddenly projected into a different type of existence where she had total freedom. She could now do as she liked.

She was the mother of the King, was ambitious, was a strong-minded woman. She had selected the wife for her son, had overseen the marriage, and in fact directed the whole affair, having been the stage manager in the background. No one who has attained to this kind of position is likely to be ready to give it up in favour of someone they have always considered to be a minor figure and something of a puppet to be manipulated. But, Queen Nazly realized very soon after the marriage of her son, young Farida was not the subservient sort of little girl who was ready to follow her mother-in-law's path, project total admiration in her direction and accept being eclipsed by her. On the contrary, Queen Farida tended to play the Queen, and herein lay the seeds of conflict.

Queen Nazly, of course, was not ready to take this lying down and, since she had all kinds of resources at her disposal, she was able to bring about a very curious situation in Egypt. The Egyptian Constitution didn't really make much of a provision for a Queen Mother. A Queen Mother was seen as a has-been. Queens who have reigned in the shadow of powerful monarchs whose rule is over are usually happy enough to take a back seat and live in a comfortable palace for the rest of their lives. But this would not have been Queen Nazly's style, and so, by pulling the right strings, she managed to modify the Egyptian Constitution to the point where it registered the existence of a second Queen, the Queen Mother, who retained all queenly prerogatives and appeared to occupy (without this being too specific) some kind of position of dominance within the royal household.

It may be interesting here to look into the question rather

more closely. In a Muslim society, as we have seen, the mother plays a very special role. The European adage that states, 'The hand that rocks the cradle rules the world,' has its Islamic equivalent, quoted in the Koran, in the saying, 'The world is in the lap of the mothers.' Queen Nazly's concept of mother-in-law was precisely this: that she, as mother to the King and architect of his marriage, took right of precedence over the young girl who was her daughter-in-law. According to Islamic usage, it was a perfectly understandable and acceptable situation, but the Egyptian Constitution of the time was based on the Belgian one, in which the status of Queen Mother was certainly subservient to that of the consort of the reigning monarch. Thus, Farouk's wife should normally have come before his mother, but such was Queen Nazly's strength and personality that, in reality, it was impossible for Farida to dominate any society or group where her mother-in-law was also present. Farida's mother-in-law was certainly the more beautiful of the two. She was usually better dressed, and a taller, more graceful woman, and therefore, by her very presence, able to exude a dominance which the younger woman resented.

Farouk had to bear the brunt of these problems, and the confrontation between the two Queens carried political implications. Queen Nazly, the more sophisticated and wiser of the two, was in favour of a policy of closeness between the nationalist Wafdist leadership and the King. She felt that her son could find a devoted friend and supporter in the Wafdist leader, Nahas Pasha, whose wife, Zeynab el Wakil, was her personal friend. Nazly was fully conscious of Farouk's inexperience and highly sensitive to the intrigues of the British Residency aimed at keeping the King and the Wafdist party leadership apart. Farouk was too young to play the kind of game at which his father had been adept, and a truce with the party would have made much sense. Nahas Pasha was himself well disposed to befriending the young King and could be relied upon to develop a certain loyal devotion to the royal cause. Naturally, the balance of power that the British sought to maintain would have been seriously put out, and Queen Nazly here displayed an unusual political acumen, combined with a certain level of courage, for bucking the British Residency was undoubtedly a hazardous occupation.

Queen Farida, by contrast, was niece to the very able Prime Minister, H.E. Engineer Hussein Sirry Pasha, whose policies were markedly in harmony with those of the British, and whose loyalties fluctuated between fealty to the King and loyalty to Sir Miles Lampson. A *rapprochement* between Nahas and Farouk would have been, if anything, even less desirable to the Farida faction than to the British. But as it unfortunately turned out, the long arm of the Residency in Kasr el Doubara finally won the day. Queen Nazly's attempts to play at politics came to an end when she fell in love with Hassanein Pasha, a friend of the British, and embarked on a romance with that most pro-British of ministers. There were also other and possibly more powerful forces actively opposing her, including the Ali Maher group of pro-Palace pashas who, though sharing with Her Majesty an opposition to the British, were hardly likely to support a downgrading of their own status, which strongly relied on the continuing patronage of the Palace. They were, after all, the components of the Palace political machine put together by King Farouk's father, King Fuad, whose memory his son venerated.

For their part, the Wafdists did little to fall in with Queen Nazly's stratagems. As realists, they well understood the vested interest the British had in keeping them apart from the Palace. Elements of republicanism had also filtered into the corporate mind of Wafdist Ministers, but it was a republican-ism with a difference, the difference lying in the persistent egalitarianism of Muslim politics. Having avoided the conse-cration of dynastic rights, Islamic jurisprudence had, over the ages, shown an amazing tolerance for usurpers, revolution-aries and persons aspiring to kingship. Success in overthrowing this or that monarch was almost immediately followed by the legitimizing of the takeover by the *Shari'a* or holy law. Under the circumstances, no crowned heads could ever feel entirely safe. And because of the same lack of a monarchistic institution vested in the law, republicanism could likewise claim no special dispensation as a legal institution recognized by the *Shari'a*, so giving rise to the phenomenon of successful republican leaders behaving in a manner no less autocratic, no less self-protective, than their predecessors, the sultans or kings. This phenomenon has been strongly emphasized in recent years in many parts of the Muslim world, where presidential successors to kings, nawabs, caliphs, sultans and emirs seem to know the privileges of an absolutism far more absolute than that enjoyed by the older regimes.

Under the circumstances, a rallying of Wafdist ranks about Farouk was far from likely. Meanwhile Farida was proving to be a difficult wife. The young Queen, an intelligent and strong-willed girl, was well aware of the ambience in which she lived, and her clash with Queen Nazly was by no means her only worry. She also had to face the veiled hostility of her husband's sizeable family group, the descendants of Mohammed Ali, who could muster an innumerable collection of eligible and delightful young princesses and naturally felt that Farida was an intruder and that the King might have found his consort among the appropriate ladies of his own kin.

Queen Nazly, the commoner in the earlier marriage, had purposely pushed Farida forward to forestall and upstage any other candidate. Now Farouk might well be inclined to let his gaze wander in the direction of the many lovely young girls moving in his vicinity. It was not an atmosphere to encourage Farida's sense of security and, like many women in a similar predicament, she allowed herself to become both over-anxious and over-possessive. Attractive girls who might attract the King's eye were banished from the King's view. Many a proud beauty was placed at a distance on royal occasions at which they might have caught the King's attention. The ruse was especially evident at the great charity balls that were organized by the Oeuvre Mohammed Ali, an organization dedicated to charity and manned by the princesses of the realm.

A leading figure on these occasions, and one who played a significant role in the background of royal affairs, was Princess Shiveakar, who annually staged an immense charity ball in aid of the needy and the various charitable clubs supported by the Oeuvre Mohammed Ali. A major feature of these balls were the *tableaux vivants*, immensely lavish productions depicting scenes from harems or receptions at ancient courts. The decorations were magnificent and often authentic.

One memorable *tableau vivant* was played in the Nymphée

de Shubra, the provocative and descriptive name given to one of Mohammed Ali's pleasure palaces. It consisted of a large baroque water garden surrounded by pavilions and graced with artificial islands. In other words, it was the ideal place for the show. In Mohammed Ali's time, the nymphs danced and sang on the artificial islands in the lake or were rowed about in ornamental boats. Presumably they were scantily clad, and the Viceroy's fortunate guests, sitting on ornate cushions and sipping delightful drinks, could feast their eyes on what was probably one of the world's richest and most captivating collections of feminine beauty: lovely Greek captives from the wars of the Archipelago, Syrian girls from the mountains beyond the Lebanon, slim Circassian houris from the Caucasus and the delicate sloe-eyed girls of Egypt. It would have been enough to make a Hugh Hefner blink.

Her Majesty Queen Farida would therefore insist on being present at the dress rehearsals for Princess Shiveakar's *tableaux vivants* so she could carefully screen the young ladies and order the elimination of those who she thought might capture the King's fancy. Thus was many a fair beauty summarily dismissed. Princess Shiveakar did not take her tampering with equanimity but was outraged and outspoken at the interference with her arrangements. As a member of the royal family, she disapproved of the Queen, and the latter's high-handed interference made her Farida's most redoubtable adversary and ultimately her nemesis.

Shiveakar was an interesting figure. She was a scraggy, bony little lady with a prominent nose and no pretensions to beauty. Yet she had a redoubtable impact on the masculine sex. Her first husband had been King Fuad, Farouk's father, who divorced her and was shortly after attacked by the princess's highly eccentric brother, Prince Seif el Din, who shot him on the balcony of the Mohammed Ali Club, giving him a permanent squeak to his voice that lasted to the end of his life. A second husband had been my own uncle, Rauf Sabit. Her third was a polo-playing *seif'Allah*, Yussri Pasha; her fourth an unidentified Turk; and her fifth a brilliant party-giving man of good taste, el Hami Pasha Hussein.

9. The Palace, the Parties and the Blueshirts

The confrontation between the Palace and the nationalist parties – mainly the Wafd – upon which the game of balance of power hinged, received a serious jolt with the death of King Fuad and the advent of King Farouk. It became anybody's guess as to which was most popular with the Egyptian nationalists, the party or the monarch. Following the signing of the Anglo-Egyptian Treaty of 1936, a short-lived marriage of convenience did emerge between the young King and the benevolent nationalist leader, Mustapha el Nahas Pasha, who had succeeded the great Saad Zaghloul as Wafd leader. It only lasted a few months, however. Strong forces were working against the arrangement and an unavoidable rivalry emerged between the highly popular person of the young King and the Wafdists, whose claim to popularity found itself facing a serious, even a dangerous, challenge. Other opponents to any *rapprochement* between the King and the Wafd were to be found among the political allies of King Fuad, including Ismail Sidky Pasha, Mohammed Mahmoud Pasha and the highly intelligent Ali Maher Pasha. All these former Wafdists had by now left the central party to head smaller parties whose political strength depended largely on palace support, and there was always the British Embassy in Kasr el Doubara, for whom a Farouk alliance with Nahas might lead to undesirable political consequences. Farouk was barely on the throne before the machinery to split the throne away from the Wafd party was set in motion.

The name Wafd, or 'delegation', was originally given to the group of nationalist politicians who attended the London talks in 1918 and 1919, which eventually led to the foundation of the Fuad monarchy of 1923. Once that original function had terminated, they crystallized into a party that retained the name of Wafd, but which, with time, split into a series of sub-groups, headed by leading figures of the original Wafd. These included the Ittihadist party, the Sa'dist party and so forth. The main body of the old Wafd retained the title and inherited the considerable national support it evoked in the Egyptian public mind, which identified it with the original delegation and its universally supported objectives, both as leaders during the 1919 uprising against the British, the exile of Zaghloul Pasha and the final successful outcome. That the other parties could claim as legitimate a share in the name of Wafd as its official holders was lost sight of. On the two occasions when Egypt experienced free elections in this century, namely, in 1931 and 1951, the Wafdists were returned with overwhelming majorities.

Indeed, there have been many in Egypt, including the late President Anwar el Sadat, who believed that, given a similar opportunity, the Wafdists could again have returned to power half a century after their emergence. What is certain is that any Wafdist successes at elections were not to be ascribed to any special policy which they might be identified with, or to any specific party programme or social doctrinology. Their greatest single asset in the minds and hearts of the Egyptians remains the title 'Wafd'.

The palace opposition to the Wafdists was led, in the early part of Farouk's reign, by Ali Maher Pasha. A counter was needed to the Wafdist call for democracy and a democratic party government to carry forward the policies of Zaghloul Pasha, and this was found in another and more traditional sector, Islam. The ghost of the Pan-Islamic revival of the early years of the century had never been laid, and the idea of shifting the Islamic epicentre from Istanbul to Cairo was attractive to the anti-Wafdist establishment, led by Ali Maher and the able and venerable Sheikh Mustapha el Maraghi. It needed little imagination to justify having a go at reviving the Muslim activism of turn-of-the-century Istanbul. Farouk's Egypt could well pick up the threads where Enver Pasha and his associates had left them way back in 1912. To these would-be Muslim reformers, Farouk looked like being the ideal puppet Imam. He was young and persuadable and he had charisma on top of his other important qualifications. For one thing, he was the descendant and recognized heir to one of Islam's most effective modern reformers, Mohammed Ali Pasha, the founder of the dynasty whose bid to modernize Egypt had been imitated by the Ottomans and whose example had profoundly affected thinking throughout the Islamic world. For another, he was, on his mother's side, the grandson of Mohammed Cherif Pasha, who could prove descent through his father, the Sheikh el Islam of Istanbul, to the Prophet Mohammed himself by the line of the latter's grandson, el Hussein.

For the young Farouk himself, still a fresh idealist and nationalist, proposals of this kind were highly attractive and inspiring. Might he not aspire to become the great unifier of the Muslim world, the furtherer of the ambitions of his great-grandfather, Mohammed Ali? Was there not here a noble and historic mission whose fulfilment looked to be God-ordained? Sheikh Mustapha el Maraghi, the Grand Sheikh and rector of the prestigious Islamic University of el Azhar, had on the occasion of the King's investiture on 31 July 1937, delivered a statement of potent importance and significance. 'The only true constitution is the Koran and the only true constitutional monarch is the *Malik el Saleh*, the "pious and right-acting King".' The press picked up the sheikh's theme and hailed Farouk with an extraordinary adulation, especially focusing on the sayings in the *Hadith* of the Prophet Mohammed where he said, 'God will send to the Muslims at the beginning of each era, a renewer [a *Mogadid*], who will revive religion and reassert the holy ordinances.' 'Farouk's name itself is portentous,' said the sheikh. 'He is Farouk, the separator between good and evil.'

Here we have a full-blown recipe for a messianic king sent by the Almighty to lead his people in the straight path. He it is who will confront those forces of Anglicized colonial betrayal which lurk behind the British-inclined parties, those cowardly influence-peddling ministers who use the alien terminology of Western constitutional democracy to justify their ambitions and cause the people to stray from the way. In being introduced into this many-cornered political arena, young Farouk may be excused if he felt like some fairy-tale prince called upon to do battle with the forces of darkness. In his first speech from the throne on the occasion of the opening of Parliament in 1937, Farouk carried on the theme: 'I call upon my Cabinet to work for the realization of the hopes I have for my people to whose progress and well-being I here pledge my life.'

Confiding in me some years later, the King said, 'At the time, these circumstances induced in me a sense of mission, a feeling of destiny.' I could appreciate this, and I believe this background is important to a full understanding. Farouk was actually describing a sort of Arthurian elation within an Islamic context. In a curious way, his English-reading background played its part in stimulating his sense of dedication. We are in the realms of Tennyson's *Idylls of the King*, of T. H. White's *The Once and Future King*, of John Buchan's *Greenmantle*, of the whole Victorian mystique. Lawrence of Arabia had, in an earlier generation, responded to similar mythic urgencies. After all, there was little to choose between the Christian knight at his devotional vigils and the Islamic warrior at his prayers. Both obeyed similar ethics; both practised similar austere forms of Sufism; both responded to the messianic call in a spirit of selfless dedication.

From the angle of purely Egyptian politics, the Muslim path was likely to lead into some dangerous cross-currents. But it was, in essence, the logical counter to the democracy-brandishing nationalism of Nahas Pasha, the Wafdist majority and their British allies in Kasr el Doubara. The Wafdists were more Egyptian-minded than Islamic-minded, and their attitudes and inclination lay towards republicanism, or at least towards a British style of constitutionalism where the King would reign but not rule – a concept far removed from that of the 'pious and right-acting King'.

By encouraging Farouk to consider himself an Islamic renovator, Sheikh Maraghi, Ali Maher Pasha and, in the background, the future secretary-general of the Arab League, Abd el Rahman Azzam Pasha, and Aziz el Masry Pasha made of Farouk a potentially formidable political figure who commanded a substantial and decisive support among the politically conservative elements of a predominantly Muslim electorate.

Most significantly these developments also served to strengthen Ali Maher Pasha's position as the leading figure in Egyptian politics. Unlike his ministerial colleagues, with whom he shared a distinguished academic background, Ali Maher possessed an uncanny flare for public relations and publicity. He was fully aware of the importance of the press, and was at pains to create for himself a reputation for promoting imaginative reforms. He had, in 1936, launched a literary contest on the grand scale. The subjects proposed reflected the deepest kind of thinking and learned speculation, including such topics as the role of el Azhar University and Islam in the twentieth century; or the role of language, customs and religion as a foundation for national independence.

Ali Maher's clear intention was to seek to create a learned and intellectual infra-structure to support the concept of an Islamic system based on the Koran, led by a 'pious and right-acting King' and capable of facing the requirements and problems of the modern age. A panel composed of Egypt's foremost thinkers was organized, including, among others, a philosopher, Lufti el Sayed Pasha, a Coptic statesman, Makram Ebeid, who was to become Nahas Pasha's nemesis a few years later, Nokrashi Pasha, fated to be murdered by the Muslim Brothers in the late 1940s, Hafiz Afifi Pasha, and Tala'at Harb Pasha, the founder of modern Egyptian banking and economics. The patronage of Farouk was placed at the head of all this activity and Ali Maher, the King's most trusted minister, thus gained further status.

Just how this Islamic spirit would have approached the complex problems of present-day Egypt is hard to imagine. Would Ali Maher have accepted a reversal of the whole trend of modern Egyptian history in favour of the return to a Muslim fundamentalism? Would Farouk have cancelled the liberalization and modernization of the Egyptian legal system by a return to the Islamic *Shari'a*? Clearly this would not have been the case. Had the Islamization process succeeded, then obviously an application of compromise must have followed. Had the opposition to Nahas and the Wafd been allowed to make natural progress, then it may be assumed that there would have been a good chance for Egypt to produce an acceptable and benevolent twentieth-century Islamic state based on a rational compromise. The frustration of the Islamization movement, however, and its effective suppression during the Second World War in what has come to be known as the Abdin Incident of February 1942, forced it underground. The Abdin Incident will be described more fully in Chapters 12 and 13, but it amounted to a *coup d'état* by which the British promoted a corrupt and incompetent government, pleading the excuse of wartime expediency. By frustrating the elaboration in Egypt of a liberal Islamic system, inspired by the rational intellectual spirit of Islam, the incident was to have unfortunate repercussions well beyond the frontiers of Egypt. Most ominously, it sowed the seed for the rise of modern Islamic fundamentalism, whose most publicized recent exploit was the murder, in 1981, of President Anwar el Sadat.

Soon after he ascended the throne and, in effect, took office, the young King found himself totally dependent on the political ascendancy of his close advisers, of whom Ali Maher and Sheikh el Maraghi were the leading members. These latter, and their Wafdist opponents, were no longer prepared to maintain the truce that had prevailed between the Palace and the Wafdist party in the heady days following King Fuad's demise, the signing of the 1936 Treaty with Britain and the euphoria generated by the investiture and the royal marriage. A further complication was the revised status under the Treaty of the British Resident, whose role was reduced, so to speak, from satrap to diplomatic envoy. Sir Miles Lampson appears to have resented this down-grading and what seemed, for many Englishmen living in Egypt at the time, something of a decline in Britain's position in a country where plenty of other European nations were gaining substantial stakes.

Generating most apprehension at the time was the traditional French influence, but it was soon to be joined by an active Axis policy directed at winning the affection and admiration of the warm-hearted Egyptians. Both Hitler and Mussolini made special efforts in the 1930s to woo the young King. The former presented him with a magnificent wedding present of the usual Mercedes Super-SSK convertible, the super-charged Cabriollet. And Il Duce, represented by two outstanding Italian ambassadors to Cairo, Count Matsolini and his successor, the young and eager Fascist, Pelegrino Gigi, actively organized the large resident Italian community into ardent Fascist formations.

One may imagine the scandalized horror of Sir Miles Lampson at the spectacle of the parades of uniformed, black-shirted *Giovinnezzsa* and *Ballila* that were occasionally to be seen in Cairo. To make matters worse, Sir Miles Lampson's opposite number in the Italian Embassy openly officiated at these black-shirted parades, wearing the full regalia of Fascism and with his arm raised in the Roman salute, under the apparently admiring gaze of Egyptian personages. Egyptians have always liked a good show. The Italian operatic background, their enthusiastic expansiveness of gesture and heroic posturing, all went down well in contrast with the rather dull and grey frock-coated bulk of British officialdom. It was a matter of overstatement competing with understatement, of the Roman arena competing with Victorian Westminster, of the charismatic Caesars competing with the figure draped in mourning of her late majesty Queen Victoria. The pill must have been a bitter one for Lampson. He no doubt saw the Egyptians as ungrateful and fickle, the King as a transmogrified schoolboy rapidly becoming a youthful, dangerous and uncontrollable Oriental despot.

Farouk's first years of rule having witnessed a return to the old rivalries between Cabinet and Palace, the bickering over conflicting prerogatives was to continue. The Cabinet would complain, for instance, of the Palace's decision to nominate the Chief of the Royal Cabinet without prior consultation. The Palace would rejoin by delaying the confirmation of Wafdist ministers to the Senate or higher offices. Most decisive, however, was the scandal that broke over granting the concession for the electrification of the Aswan barrage when an article in a leading paper, *El Balagh*, by its editor, Abd el Kader el Mazny, called for the resignation of the Minister of Public Works, Osman Moharram Pasha. The article accused him of being the accomplice, with others, of a British firm represented in Cairo by one Colonel Grey, Osman Pasha having in effect been in the employ of this foreign firm. The British bid was meanwhile being energetically promoted by an Anglophile section of the Cabinet headed by Makram Ebeid

Pasha, who argued that, although the British offer was some £2 million above other offers, or nearly 40 per cent higher than its competitors, it should be accepted. Thereupon the Minister of Justice, Mahmoud Ghalib Pasha, and another Wafdist minister, Mahmoud Fahmy el Nokrashi Pasha, resigned from the Wafd. There followed the resignation from Parliament of Ahmed Maher Pasha and seventy-three other deputies and representatives.

The dismissal of the Wafdist Cabinet by Farouk was the main consequence of the scandal, but a third reason had also preceded his action. This was the Blueshirt affair. 'Shirt' politics were the fashion in Europe where Brownshirts and Blackshirts were taking to the streets, marching to military music, singing patriotic songs and roughing up unenthusiastic citizens. Two 'shirt' formations emerged at this time in Egypt, the Greenshirted 'Young Egypt' movement, Misr el Fatat, and the Blueshirted Wafdist youth formations. The former, being of National Socialist persuasion, appealed to the more activist elements of nationalist intransigence; the latter, controlled so long as the Wafdists remained in power, and vaguely official, were a good deal more numerous. Both groups expressed a certain level of hostile ambiguity where the monarchy was concerned, but neither professed an open republicanism, although the Wafdist leadership was known to lean in that direction.

The Farouk team was, as we have seen, developing an Islamic doctrinology to counter the imported theory of parliamentary democracy, and under the circumstances King Farouk's dismissal of his first government was not as high-handed as has been suggested. It was hard to see how a Westminster type of representative system could exist at a time when government-inspired Blueshirted roughs were embarking on a programme of street brawls and attacks on the property of opposition politicians. Matters reached a climax when a mob of Blueshirted Wafdists attacked and besieged the home of the respected Mohammed Mahmoud Pasha, a former Wafdist minister who now presided over the Ittihad Party.

At this point we may digress a little and record the curious fact that the British Ambassador in Cairo and Mr Eden in

London appeared to be putting their full weight behind the Wafdists, who were meanwhile behaving like Nazis. London even dispatched the veteran diplomat, Sir Ronald Storrs, to Egypt to advise the Palace discreetly not to dismiss the Nahas government. This action was something of a blunder, for there was, on the face of it, little to choose between this approach by Whitehall diplomats and the flirtations in Germany of Chancellor Hindenburg and Count von Papen with Adolf Hitler in the hope of harnessing unscrupulous thuggery to their own political ambitions. In Cairo, at that time, Nahas was no Hitler and King Farouk's team were a good deal more alert to the intricacies of political manoeuvre than were Hindenburg and von Papen.

National Socialism in Egypt had a thirty-year wait ahead before it would emerge with the Nasser regime. The demise of the Wafdists was followed by series of non-Wafdist Cabinets, starting with that of Mohammed Mahmoud Pasha and continuing with those of Ali Maher Pasha and Hussein Sirry Pasha, Queen Farida's uncle. This period, from 1937 to 1942, witnessed many convulsions, the most important among them being the outbreak of the Second World War. These events served to widen the gap between the British Ambassador and King Farouk, and war brought with it problems of interpretation for the 1936 Treaty between Egypt and Britain. The question of whether Egypt should declare war on the Axis was at the forefront, though in 1940 it seemed to the Egyptians that the chances of Britain winning the war were slim indeed.

'However much sympathy one might have for my allies,' Farouk said to me, 'I have to think of my country. Lampson refuses to accept our side of things and seems to make it a personal matter. We are not bound by the Treaty to declare war, and therefore I cannot see that I have even a legal or a moral authority for such a declaration. And what military contribution could we offer the British? Our army has already had to relinquish most of its weapons to the British Army. Our contribution to the war would be little more than symbolic. In return, we would feel the full brunt of German and Italian hostility by providing them with the justification that we are British puppets. I know that the German Ambassador in Paris, Otto Abets, has promised the former Khedive, Abbas Helmi, to restore him to the Egyptian throne from which he was evicted by Lord Kitchener. Lampson says I am plotting with the Axis! To be dethroned in favour of Abbas Helmi by the Germans because, in their eyes, I am a British puppet and he is the rightful heir to the throne, the victim of British imperialism? How absurd!'

There is little criticism which may be levelled at Farouk's role during the first five years of his reign. It was a difficult period, marked, in its first phase, by the Wafdist Blueshirt challenge to the monarchy, and in its second by the outbreak of war between Britain and Germany. We have seen how, in the face of the pseudo-democratic Wafdist challenge, the King's advisors hoped to offer an Islamic option. Now, however, the war introduced a more formidable element into this exercise in alternative forms of rule. Spearheaded by the British Ambassador, and strongly supported by the War Cabinet in London, the English began to tighten their hold over Egyptian politics. The Anglophile, Oxford-educated, pro-British Ahmed Hassanein Pasha was made chief of the Royal Cabinet. The British move was undoubtedly an expression of forcible pressure, in complete contradiction to the spirit of the relationship foreseen in the 1936 Anglo-Egyptian Treaty. It was also the thin end of a wedge which would finally precipitate the Abdin crisis in 1942, when the possibility of Farouk's being arrested and sent into exile was strong. Farouk's attitude in refusing to countenance a declaration of war was clearly justified from an Egyptian viewpoint, but his stance was nevertheless used by Lampson to support the contention that Farouk was an active sympathizer with the Axis powers.

Britain made the first move in 1940. This was a request by the Foreign Office, transmitted to Farouk through Lampson, to the effect that, 'The United Kingdom felt obliged to make strong representations to the King of Egypt for a change of government.' Ali Maher resigned on 24 June, and an Anglophile Prime Minister, Hassan Sabry, an Independent, was sworn in to form a new government. Mohammed Saleh Harb Pasha, the former Minister of Defence and a confidant of Farouk's, was dropped from the Cabinet, and Aziz el Masry Pasha, the Chief-of-Staff of the Army, was given six months' sick leave prior to being pensioned off. Abd el Rahman Azzam was likewise put out to grass.

With the supporters of the Muslim option forced to take a back seat, the seeds of eventual revolution against Farouk were also sown. Aziz el Masry's estrangement from and subsequent enmity towards Farouk led the general to plot against the King. Farouk had a shrewd anticipation of this betrayal-to-be, and the intensity of his feelings was such that, in a conversation with myself some time in 1945, the King said, 'Who will rid me of this Aziz el Masry? Someone who loves me could easily kill him by driving alongside his car and pumping it with machine-pistol fire.' Shades of Thomas à Becket!

Aziz el Masry Pasha represented a formidable opponent. The former Young Turk officer, the successful revolutionary against the Ottoman Sultan in 1908 and the founder of the militant Arab El Ahd party, the Egyptian-Circassian firebrand who was Aziz el Masry, could and did become Farouk's most intractable political enemy. If ever anybody could claim to be the instigator and inspirer of the Nasser rebellion when it came in 1952, it was General Aziz el Masry – a fact acknowledged by Gamal Abd el Nasser himself.

In later years, when he was still an active-minded but disillusioned old man, I had the interesting experience of holding various conversations with the general, for what was virtually a family relationship existed between him and the Sabits.

He spoke frankly: 'Farouk was a big disappointment. He lacked the discipline for any sort of sustained effort. Likewise he lacked the courage of his convictions. At a critical period in Egyptian history, in 1940 when the British began to interfere in the internal affairs of the country, when he could have opposed a British bullying, he preferred to give in. He dismissed Ali Maher and myself without any protest, and brought in Hassanein, who was little more than a British agent. Farouk had not the leadership or the guts to fight. That is why he lost his throne in 1952. Had he been as courageous as young King Hussein, he would have driven his car to Mustapha Pasha barracks and taken command there. At the time, the main bulk of the Army and the Navy was loyal and under the direct orders of his own officers. The handful of young Free Officers

84

Little Prince Farouk and his teddy bear, 1925.

Farouk and Fawzia at the seaside, 1926. The harbour at Montazah is in the background.

Fawzia, Farouk and Faiza, 1930.

Queen Nazly surrounded by Farouk, Faiza (standing behind) and Fawzia (sitting).

Queen Nazly.

Queen Nazly's English governess, Miss Katerina Regina Staunton, 1916.

Mme Sabit Pasha, the author's mother, and Queen Nazly at Deauville, 1930.

Miss Dorothy Ethelwyn Broadbent, 1941.

Queen Nazly's grandfather, Mohammed Cherif Pasha, founder of the National Movement in Egypt.

Prince Mohammed Ali Tewfik, heir-apparent, 1936.

A young Queen Farida in her wedding gown, 1939.

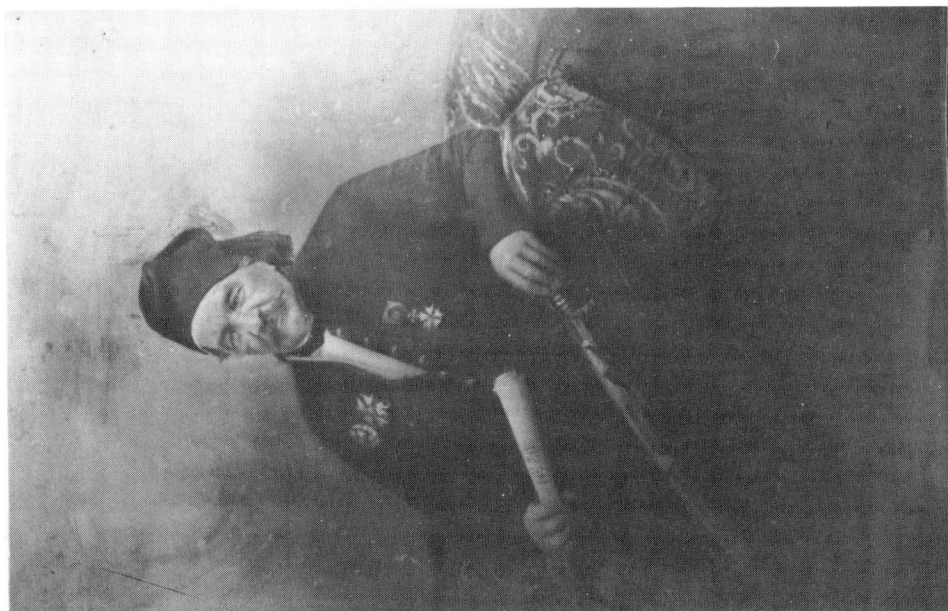

General Suleyman Pasha (Joseph Anthelme Sève), from a photo by Nadar, *circa* 1850.

The Shahpur of Iran greeting Queen Farida, 1939. The King is hidden behind his wife and Hassanein Pasha is to the right.

A group picture taken on the occasion of Fawzia's wedding in Teheran, 1939. From left to right, sitting: Princess Ashraf Pahlavi, Princess Shems Pahlavi, Queen Nazly and Fawzia. Standing: the Duke of Spoleto and Princess Alice Duchess of Athlone.

Empress Fawzia of Iran.

Fawzia shortly after her arrival from Teheran. She is here accompanied by her Iranian lady-in-waiting; on the right nearest to her is Hassanein Pasha; in the right foreground is the King's ADC General Nougoumy Pasha who was wounded during the Abdin Incident in 1942.

Princess Ashraf Pahlavi, Queen Farida and Empress Fawzia in Cairo, February 1942.

Princess Faiza, Farouk's second sister, 1960.

Fancy-dress ball held by Princess Samiha Hussein, 1943. King Farouk is dressed as an Arab, Farida is in Hungarian dress. The diminutive figure in Arab clothes next to Queen Farida is the fierce Princess Munira Hamdy.

Abbé Drioton, the noted archaeologist, at Luxor, December 1941.

The British Embassy in Cairo, 1940s. On the front step, from the left, are the Egyptian Minister of Foreign Affairs, Lord Killearn (formerly Sir Miles Lampson) and the author's father, Mahmoud Sabit Pasha.

A group of ambassadors. From the left: Suleyman Bey el Hour, an unidentified person, Abd el Rahman Azzam Pasha, Sharara Pasha, Omar Sirry Omar Pasha and Mahmoud Sabit Pasha.

The Special Police, 1941. From left to right: Abu Bakr Bey Ratib, Hamed Bey el Shawarby, Prince Amr Ibrahim, Cherif Bey Chahine, Mohammed Taher Pasha, Prince Mansur Daud, Wahid Bey Yusry, Prince Suleyman Daud.

General Leutnant Artur Wilhelm Schmitt, 1950.

in Cairo who seized power were virtually unarmed, and the tanks surrounding Abdin Palace lacked ammunition. Farouk could have smashed the revolt and Gamal Abd el Nasser would be in prison today. But he preferred to sit trembling in his palace. He betrayed the people loyal to him just as he betrayed Ali Maher and myself in 1940.'

Though these words had an undoubted ring of truth to them, it is only fair to examine circumstances more closely in the light of events unfolding in Europe: the Norwegian fiasco and the withdrawal from Narvik of the British Expeditionary Force, the clear evidence of Nazi military superiority soon to be followed by the even more inhibiting depression consequent on the fall of France. These caused even the most optimistic British to have reasons for apprehension, and it was conceivable that the Egyptians might feel that their ally and occupier was not going to win the war, such caution being induced by both sides amid growing pressures. Farouk, despite Aziz el Masry's defiant nationalism, was in the circumstances wise to accommodate a desperate British Foreign Office.

A further decisive event was the entry of Italy into the war, the Italian occupation of Libya meaning that the conflict was at Egypt's doors. Axis armies were now poised on the frontiers, and though Italian military bombast was still to be tested, nobody could seriously foretell the outcome of a confrontation with the British. The skills of Field Marshal Graziani and Air Marshal Balbo, and the apparently superior Italian technology in aircraft and armoured warfare, had been much touted in Cairo over the preceding months. The Italian Navy, which certainly possessed the sleekest, smartest and most sophisticated ships of the period, might easily dispose of the all too familiar and vaguely conservative British battle fleet based in Alexandria. The Royal Navy's capital ships, like the *Queen Elizabeth*, the *Valiant* and the *Barham*, belonged to an outmoded era of naval warfare, being veterans of Jutland and the Dardannelles. They seemed slow-witted nineteenth-century dinosaurs in comparison with the refined lines of the heavy Italian cruisers, the *Pola* and the *Gorizia*, or the ultra-sleek racehorse lines of the *Montecucoli* and the *Eugenio di Savoia*, light cruisers of Mussolini's naval forces. Malta, a friend predicted, would be taken in forty-eight hours, thanks to the

85

swarm of high-speed Isotta Fraschini-engined MAS torpedo boats concentrated at the southern tip of Italy.

It was possibly at this moment, with British prospects at their worst, that Farouk, conscious of his duty to his own people, determined to resist every attempt to drag Egypt into the conflict. It is true that the Italians were about to penetrate the western frontiers, yet they had clearly stated that their quarrel was not with the Egyptians, having no territorial or other ambitions on their country, but that they came merely to expel the British. Some voices in Egypt, notably that of Ahmed Maher Pasha, called for a declaration of war against the Axis, stating that Egypt must, as a sovereign country, respond with force when her territory was occupied. Otherwise it would seem that Egypt was a mere satellite of the British and held no opinions or personality of her own. Public opinion in Egypt took a different view, however. The Axis was winning the war. No Egyptian contribution or involvement could change things, especially since Egypt was respecting the 1936 Treaty and fully applying its terms for giving assistance to the British. Thus there was no valid reason why the Axis should be antagonized for a mere empty gesture and Farouk's decision against involvement was fully in keeping with public opinion.

A mistrust of British intentions also played a part in these decisions. Britain had all too often repeated her intention of withdrawing from Egypt without doing anything about it. It was unlikely that a victorious Britain would be inclined to evacuate the country. One could therefore conclude that an Italian or German presence might be no better than the British, and would certainly be no worse. Another aspect of the problem was the danger Egypt ran in the event of intensive Axis bombardments. The Aswan Dam in particular excited anxieties, with the prospect of Axis dambusters unleashing a nightmare flood on to the valley of the Nile with horrific consequences. An English commentator, George Kirk, has described the Egyptian attitude with accuracy:

It was unfortunate for the future of Anglo-Egyptian relations that the moment when the reality of war appeared on the threshold of the Middle East had also been the moment of collapse of Allied resistance on the European continent and the moment when Axis prospects of victory seemed to neutrals virtually certain. In these circumstances it was not surprising that Ali Maher's Government, seeking complete independence with the approval of King Farouk and of the greater part of the politically conscious stratum of the population, should have hesitated to commit themselves to Britain and should have sought instead to leave themselves a loophole of neutrality for renewing contacts with the Axis.*

A pattern was now to emerge in relations between Farouk and the British. So long as the fortunes of war were favourable to the Allies, relations remained cordial, and never more cordial than when Wavell's counter-offensive against the penetration of Egypt started on 9 December 1940, successfully expelled the Italians and established the British conquest of Cyrenaica, ending with the occupation of Benghazi on 6 February 1941. Farouk, ever-convivial, was soon on friendly relations with many of the senior commanders of the British forces, and his pleasure and gratification at Wavell's deserved victories were both evident and genuine. These friendly exchanges soon convinced important members of the British military establishment that Farouk was no Anglophobe, Axis-sympathizing monarch plotting the British downfall, as Sir Miles Lampson chose to believe.

Seeds of disagreement between the British Embassy and the British military were thus beginning to germinate. Close friendly relations between the King and high-ranking British officers, such as General Stone, GOC Egypt, General Sir Henry Maitland Wilson and Air Marshal Sir Sholto Douglas, were of a nature to disturb Sir Miles Lampson, who was well aware that criticism of the Embassy was prevalent in Cairo salons, and the King's part was often vociferously defended by many prominent hostesses whose views were accessible to influential British visitors. Inevitably, words and views would be transmitted to London, to circles possibly critical of the Foreign Office and its representative in Cairo.

*Survey of International Affairs 1939–1946: George Kirk, 'The Middle East in the War', Oxford University Press, 1952, pp 40.

British disappointment occurred at the beginning of 1941, when Rommel emerged with the Afrika Korps in Libya and inflicted stinging military reverses on the British Eighth Army in March and April. The taking by the Germans of Benghazi and their advance to the Egyptian frontiers gave an added urgency to the British Ambassador's desire to unseat Farouk. The King, apart from getting too friendly with the British generals, seemed to be pursuing a rigidly Egyptian nationalist line that ran counter to Sir Miles's ideas as to how Farouk should be behaving. One might wonder where the Italians came into this. The answer is that they did not. There was no evidence of any significant Italian political influence anywhere, except in the wife of the British Ambassador who, as a Castellani, came from a well-known Anglo-Italian family. The beautiful Lady Lampson was, however, a totally blameless and highly decorative lady. The British Ambassador's feeling towards the Egyptian King seemed almost pathological and a glance at *The Killearn Diaries, 1934–1946* will readily confirm this impression.

Clearly His Excellency had made up his mind that he should get rid of Farouk as soon as a convenient justification could be found, but such justifications were in reality rather hard to come by. The myth that the Palace was harbouring dangerous Axis agents was easily exploded when one met the gentlemen in question. Antonio Pulli Bey, the former palace electrician who had helped the young Farouk to bypass Mrs Naylor's blockades, was a harmless and rather gentle Egyptian-Italian far removed from the Ciano/Mussolini set. Garro was an Italian barber with even less political and diplomatic potential. Gavazzi, who looked after the King's kennels, was not an Italian at all, but a young Swiss from Lugano, still in his twenties and politically immature and neutral.

Lampson similarly suspected that the King had set up a clandestine radio link with the Axis, through which, in some unaccountable way, he was passing secret information. The absurdity of this farcical arrangement was obvious, since if Farouk did have any intention of engaging in any such operations, he would be unlikely to do it through the Palace; and since, for reasons already given, he would not in fact be likely to want an Axis victory at all. Yet Lampson was determined to have his way, as will soon be seen.

In the meantime, the internal Egyptian political scene remained quiet on the whole. There followed a succession of generally Anglophile ministers, and the death of one of these, Hassan Sabry Pasha, just after being decorated with the high order of Mohammed Ali and prior to his reading of the speech from the throne, brought to the premiership Hussein Sirry Pasha, Queen Farida's uncle and a strong advocate of close ties with Britain. Sirry Pasha was soon to be the conscious instrument of royal betrayal.

10. Royal Eccentrics

It has to be admitted that the eccentricities and related attitudes and outlooks of certain members of the royal family did much to provoke accusations of foreignness from the respectable, conventional Egyptian middle classes. That Egyptians considered the Mohammed Ali family eccentric to say the least was a matter of general knowledge. We may select at random two of the leading figures in this field.

I remember, for instance, the alarming but quite charming Princess Munira Hamdy, who lived in a splended villa on the banks of the Nile, adjacent to a tall newly built apartment house. Munira Hamdy was very short, barely five foot, and proportioned accordingly. She had a 'thing' about Lawrence of Arabia and was reported to have been secretly in love with him, though she had only met him once, many years before. In celebration of her strong emotion, Princess Munira wore flowing Arab robes, a *kufiya*, the Arab semi-turban popular in Saudi Arabia and Jordan, and an ornamental Hashemite dagger. Her favourite pastime was to patrol the streets of Cairo in her chauffeur-driven Rolls-Royce Sedanca de Ville, attended by a large and powerful Sudanese groom, on the look-out for gharry drivers who mistreated their horses, or other citizens who bullied dogs or kicked cats.

The princess was a contrary person, which meant that while almost the entire royal family was pro-German during the Second World War, she remained a firm Anglophile. Thanks partly to Lawrence, she was convinced that Hitler had evil designs upon Egypt and, during the advance of Rommel in the direction of the Nile Valley in 1942, began to arm herself. She had inherited from sporting relatives a goodly number of rifles and big-game guns, and these were made ready. She likewise managed to find, through the always available black market, some Tommy-guns and a substantial amount of ammunition, which she smuggled into her villa under the noses of the police. In the spring of 1942, as the Afrika Korps approached el Alamein, the princess waited.

One night she had an unusually vivid dream. A force of storm troopers had landed on the roof of the apartment block next door. Munira Hamdy sprang into action, sounding the alarm and marshalling her sleepy servants, the wide-eyed pretty little Circassian maids, the Sudanese *suffragis*, the gardener, the chauffeur, even the policeman who stood sentry at her gates. Rifles and ammunition were issued to everyone, and the princess personally aligned her people at the windows facing the building next door. When all was ready, the princess, herself manning an ancient Gatling heavy machine-gun inherited from her grandfather, gave the order to fire. A ragged fusillade broke out, shattering the peace of the Cairo night. The Gatling gun, having made alarming noises, over-heated and jammed, and so the princess seized a Thompson sub-machine-gun. The sound of small-arms fire echoed and reverberated throughout the whole area.

Soon the police were on the scene in the shape of the British Commandant, Russell Pasha. The Pasha was rushed into the princess's presence.

'*Finalement*,' she said in French. 'Russell Pasha, you are now here, you can see for yourself that the Germans have arrived and you are unprepared. What have you to say for yourself? Anyway, grab a gun and start shooting. This is no time for conversation!'

Russell, recognizing his inability to handle the fierce princess, went to the phone to call for Hassanein Pasha, whose diplomacy and subtle technique of speaking to princes were well known. Before long Hassanein had arrived in one of the royal limousines, wearing an overcoat over his pyjamas. It was four in the morning and bitterly cold, and alarm was spreading through the whole of the Giza quarter; police were cordoning off streets. The inhabitants of the apartment block, assuming that the Germans had indeed arrived and were for some unaccountable reason attacking their harmless building, were prudently taking refuge in the basement garage as the sound of breaking glass and collapsing mortar continued overhead. Hassanein, rapidly mastering the situation, put on a grateful smile.

'Your Highness,' he said in his best Master of Ceremonies manner, dodging a smoking Tommy-gun, 'I have been sent by His Majesty to congratulate you on this magnificent occasion. The enemy has surrendered and is now being disarmed by the troops. There is no further need for shooting. They have had enough. You have the Nation's grateful thanks.'

This appeased the princess, who turned triumphantly to her troops and said: 'We have won, Mabruk! We can be proud of ourselves today . . . But we must remain vigilant!'

They were all given a hearty breakfast and the blameless inhabitants of the scarred and battle-torn building next door crept discreetly back to bed.

Our second specimen member of the family, Prince Abbas Halim, one of the founders and leaders of Egypt's trade unions, was by far the most popular of King Farouk's cousins. A good deal older than Farouk, he was a handsome and dashing if somewhat controversial figure. Having been an officer in a crack German lancer (*Ulan*) regiment, he then joined the old Richthofen *Luftwaffe* and during the First World War saw service under Udett on the Eastern Front. Abbas Halim was a typical smart German cavalry officer. He had the bullet head and close-cropped hair of the breed, and occasionally wore a monocle, which emphasized his 'German-ness' even more. He was the sort of 'Junker' popularized by Erich von Stroheim. His accent, whether he was speaking Arabic or English, contained strong Potsdam inflections, and his appeal to the ladies was apparently irresistible. He had been a favourite of King Fuad, until they had a falling out and Abbas Halim was degraded by the King, who took his title away from him, princes not being hereditary in the Muslim world. Prince Abbas Halim thereafter threw himself whole-heartedly into the Egyptian labour movement, and diligently, with German energy and *ordnung*, set about creating and consolidating the Egyptian Trade Union Organization.

It was his stepson, 'Toats' Ismail Assem, with whom I would play as a boy, and I remember the many Wednesday after-noons and evenings when the labour syndicates would gather in the basement of their palace in Garden City. It gave me a glimpse of an entrancing world of subdued revolutionary plotting as workers of all kinds gathered in the vast basement. These were bus and truck drivers, marshalled by Abbas Halim's predominantly grey-clad, blue-bereted secretaries, presumably preparing for a revolution. We two small boys would be shown superior types of cosh, methods of defence and attack against the British-led police, guns of various calibres and demonstrations of how best to set tramways on fire.

Upstairs the prince, immaculate in his Savile Row clothes, a glass of Scotch in his hand, struck a truly inspiring figure in a study lined with hunting rifles and game trophies, including vast elephant-leg ashtrays and a full-sized stuffed lion disdainfully sprawling on the carpet. Toats would reverently show me a picture of his 'Pa' in the full-dress uniform of a *Kaiserlich Ulan* officer, and when no grown-ups were around, we raided the rifle cupboard and gazed with envy on the slim blue barrels of Mannlicher express elephant rifles, balanced Match Purdies, aristocratic Holland & Hollands, or the more military and plebeian Lee Enfields. Happily, no ammunition was readily available, and we had to content ourselves with looking and touching. In our eyes Abbas Halim was, quite naturally, something of a childhood hero.

Towards the end of his reign, in the spring of 1935, King Fuad had had enough of his socialist nephew and the police were unleashed against the prince's palace where we had played. Once the women and children had been evacuated, the city was treated to a siege of the palace. It lasted for several days, two of the bodyguard secretaries being killed in the resultant gunfire and the prince arrested and jailed. His wife, my friend's mother, Princess Tawhida Halim, a dauntless, romantic and dashing consort, took over a café opposite the window of her husband's cell in Cairo Central Prison. There she installed a large His Master's Voice radiogram and, to the tunes of Cole Porter, Irving Berlin and Ivor Novello booming across the square in front of the prison, kept a permanent party going. Sympathizers from all levels of the community flocked to the liberally appointed bar and buffet she installed there, and King Fuad, doubtless somewhat perturbed by the publicity the demonstration inevitably created, soon had the prince released on bail.

Abbas Halim did not limit his activity to the trade unions alone, but was an active pro-German influence during the years of Hitler's rise. He was received in pomp at the 1936 Olympics, attended the Nuremberg rallies with his old air-force buddies Göring and Udett, and was said to have been a confidant of the Führer himself.

After the Second World War broke out, Abbas Halim became a leading figure in the pro-German group of Egyptian princes, princelings, nabils, pashas and establishment personalities. The Halims were, as we have seen, rival contenders for the throne, opponents of the Ismail branch of the family to which King Farouk belonged. They had been active supporters of the nationalist element which backed the Arabi Revolt some sixty years before. Germanophilia was the natural corollary to Anglophobia, and to some extent a throw back influence to the sympathies felt in Egypt during the First World War with regard to the Kaiser and the Germans in general, the Kaiser, after all, having been the ally of the Caliph in Istanbul.

Not the least of British failures in Egypt was their inability to win over the Egyptian ruling establishment to a political truce, despite the fact that an appreciation of many things British seems to have been endemic; for the Egyptian aristocrats admired much that was British. They dressed in London, readily swallowed some of the more outrageous aberrations of British class snobbery, were proud to belong to an exclusive club, such as White's or the St James's, and were flattered to be friends with English dukes and other grandees. Indeed, with the latter they got on famously, fitting into the social patterns of Mayfair or, more energetically, the polo fields of Gezira and their posh cousins at Hurlingham, Bagatelle and Jaipur. This was nevertheless a ruling establishment which, when war broke out, fastened its admiration and hopes on the quite alien rantings and jackbooted militarism of a lower-middle-class Austrian housepainter.

Though socially, temperamentally and even emotionally closer to upper-class Britain, these scions of the establishment obeyed the loyalties of their nationalist Egyptian habitat. With the war, a new chapter in the Anglo-Egyptian saga had begun. As far as the British were concerned, the Germanophile Abbas was a marked man, but others of his family became prominent in a British-backed enterprise, the Special Police. This body started off as an auxiliary force to second the work of the Egyptian police under the nominal but highly limited supervision of the British Commandant, Sir Thomas Russell Pasha.

The Special Police were destined, in their initial conception, to become a glorified Air Raid Warden-cum-Home Guard along the British pattern. Colonal Boyd Cooper, an amiable ex-Indian Army Officer, appointed to be a kind of military Mary Poppins and adviser, was soon integrated into the heady social world of Abbas Halim and his friends. Their habitat was the smart Automobile Club, where life was a series of parties and gambling events, occasionally interspersed with motor-car rallies, such as the famous pre-war Rallye des Oases that had given the German Ambassador, Count von Stöhrer, and his Italian colleagues their valuable desert experiences. Count Almaszy, a rather shady Hungarian nobleman friend of Abbas Halim and one of his organizers for the rallies, subsequently became Rommel's desert adviser on the staff of the Afrika Korps.

'Good fellows, very British in their attitudes,' was Boyd Cooper's reported reaction to his new friends in the special unit. The Special Police started by adopting black SS-type uniforms and their interpretation of an air-raid warden's duties soon became all-embracing and fluid. The initially planned infantry force needed, they said, a flying squad. The members of this, since they would be motorized, would wear highly polished SS-type black boots and smart Himmler uniforms. They made a somewhat piquant reproduction of an SS unit.

It was not long before the mobile division, which started off with motor-cycles and private automobiles, was acquiring armoured cars from the Egyptian Army. The leaders of the body had decided, under the noses of the British, that they should make their force of air-raid wardens and home guards a paramilitary organization along the lines of the German SS, which, once the British had been swept out of Egypt by Rommel, would take over the transition and maintain law and order. To do this effectively, it might be necessary to clash at some stage with the British Army, and the assortment of princes and pashas who led the unit worked feverishly and with secrecy at the creation of an Egyptian SS force. Apart from acquiring armoured vehicles, anti-aircraft artillery training and the acquisition of guns were also undertaken, and even light tanks and Bren-gun carriers were quietly and unobtrusively commandeered with the complicity of the Egyptian Army. Had the British not been aware, through their efficient intelligence services, of these developments, a most dangerous situation might have developed in Cairo. Two months before the arrival of the Afrika Korps at el Alamein, the Special Police was disbanded by the British and many of its leading members put into detention.

Prince Abbas Halim, though not directly involved, was imprisoned again at this time together with Prince Omar Farouk, the last descendant of the Ottoman Caliphs. Prince Omar had committed the indiscretion of sending his old uniform as aide-de-camp to the Kaiser – he had been an officer in the crack Death's-Head (*Totenkopf*) Hussars – to the local *makwagy* (ironer) so that it might be pressed in time to receive General Rommel on his arrival in Cairo.

11. Luxor Christmas and New Year

The announcement comes one evening in 1941 on my mother's return from one of her almost daily afternoons at the Palace of Koubbeh. We are invited, she announces, to spend Christmas and New Year in Luxor. It is to be a kind of family gathering, where members of Queen Nazly's family will mix with those of Queen Farida's, though notably absent will be the members of the family of the late King Fuad. My sister Dodie and I are, of course, thrilled. Unfortunately the party will not include my friend Toats, presumably because he is the son of a lady who has become a princess and therefore belongs to another team.

The members of the party will, however, be very congenial, since they are all old friends. On Queen Nazly's team is my mother, my aunt Chahira and her husband, Hussein Sabry Pasha, Queen Nazly's brother, the urbane Hassanein Pasha, and the Queen Mother's ladies-in-waiting. And on Farida's side there will be Farida's mother, the Queen's chief lady-in-waiting, Zeynab Hanem, her uncle the Prime Minister, Hussein Sirry Pasha, his wife Nahed, their two daughters and Farida's little brother Cherif as well as a cousin, Ismail Mazloum.

We take off by royal train for Luxor from Cairo at the Koubbeh Palace station, arriving at the crack of dawn in Luxor, where the train goes into a siding to wait for the party to wake up and have breakfast. We now have our first sight of Farouk, heavily muffled and recognizable only by his size and bulk. He is pacing the platform, inspecting things and conversing with attendant station masters and their colleagues. This is typical of the King, who shares with his younger sister Fathia, or 'Atty', an energetic interest in anything that comes his way.

An entire floor of Luxor's Winter Palace Hotel has been

reserved for the royal party, otherwise the establishment carries on business as usual with a full quota of visitors and tourists. This being wartime, most of the other residents are British officers with their wives and diplomats on leave from Cairo. There is a vague American or two, an archaeologist, Egyptologists and a smattering of Egyptians from Cairo and Alexandria. The atmosphere is completely relaxed. The King and the two Queens behave as if they were run-of-the-mill tourists on holiday. Not that this prevents them being treated like special exhibits. Wherever they go, well-bred groups of people sitting in the lobby or on the expansive hotel balconies or in the garden, follow them with their eyes or self-consciously try to ignore them.

A large dining room of the hotel is reserved for the royal party, and here we become witnesses to the deep-seated clash that exists between the contrasting personalities of Queen Nazly and Queen Farida. The pretty young consort is convinced that Queen Nazly purposely provokes her and needlessly humiliates her by treating her like the junior member of the royal team, constantly upstaging her whenever the occasion presents itself. The high-tension points always come at meal-times, when, having assembled around the dining-room table, the entire party, including the King and Queen Farida, have to await the entrance of the Queen Mother, the latter being a spectacular technician at the staging of entrances. And since she has the personality to go with such demonstrations, she has no difficulty in stealing the show, much to the young Queen's mortification.

Queen Farida does not take this phlegmatically, but seeks refuge in what one might call a diplomatic illness. This confines her to her bedroom during mealtimes, though in between she is as energetic and as healthy as anyone. As a special treat, we young people are allowed to take our meals in Farida's bedroom, which is situated immediately above the dining room where the rest are seated. Here we gather, and the Queen posts scouts at the top of the staircase to calculate the exact moment of Queen Nazly's stately entrance down-stairs. We are then ordered to stamp on the floor, dance and make noises in a childish demonstration against the grown-ups. Things do not stop here, and during a week of constant visiting of temples and tombs, when we are accompanied by such illustrious personages as Howard Carter and the bouncy and enthusiastic Egyptologist, the Abbé Drioton, the feud continues.

The tension, however, is hidden behind a veneer of almost ritual politeness: the sort of social hypocrisy that the Florentine Medicis and Machiavelli might have practised in less enlightened times. The atmosphere of court intrigue is universal. Since my sister and I belong to Queen Nazly's family, we have to be careful what we say about Queen Farida, and the same applies to the others. A sort of Montague and Capulet situation begins to emerge. It is uncomfortable and does much to convert what might have been a charming holiday into something of a Renaissance drama. Howard Carter is a forceful and vital personality, but grumpy and rather dour with people, tourists being his pet aversion. Carter can nevertheless be a charming and interesting man when he is not thundering imprecations on the Egyptian government's Antiquities Department, with whom he has a long-standing feud.

'I know,' he says to us, 'where Alexander the Great is buried, but I shall not tell anyone about it, least of all the Antiquities Department. The secret will die with me.'

And apparently it does, for a few years later this distinguished and world-renowned archaeologist will pass peacefully away, an escapee, some think, from the curse of the Pharoahs.

The Abbé Drioton, on the other hand, is short, tubby and dynamic. He wears a fez at a rakish angle over his strict religious garb and is given to rapid agile gestures. Excitably French, we conclude, being dutiful pupils of Miss Broadbent and having absorbed Anglo-Saxon attitudes about such matters. Yet the abbé has a pickwickian gleam in his eye, and is liked by all as a contrast to the rather proconsular austerity of Howard Carter. Thanks to the presence of King Farouk, we are shown around the Valley of the Kings, and in particular the tomb of Tutankhamun, by Howard Carter himself. A memorable and distinguished occasion.

In the evening our party, led by the royals, sits in the grand hall of the hotel in the immediate vicinity of the other guests.

There is a band and dancing is on the programme. We sit and wait but nobody dances. It becomes clear that the other guests are too shy to start, presumably expecting the royal party to set the example. So every night of our stay I am detailed to take one of the princesses as a partner and open the ball. For me it is a shameful and humiliating operation. As I am likewise a hopeless dancer, this is remarked and orders are issued: 'Teach Adel to dance properly.' And so part of the holiday is spent being taught by a succession of ladies-in-waiting without their succeeding, as far as I can make out, in making anything of my stumbling steps or curing the unpleasant tendency of my feet to tread on the dainty toes of royal partners.

What with court intrigue and tension and dancing lessons, life is not too easy for myself or my sister. We do not really manage to get on with Queen Farida's relatives. They, doubtless overcome by the fact that their sister or cousin has become a Queen, tend to take on airs which, in people of their age, make them bumbtious and, we feel, unjustifiably self-assured. Dodie, my sister, is a close buddy of the princesses, and their outlooks and interests and mine naturally diverge considerably.

I have been given by Queen Nazly as a birthday present a sparkling new Rolliflex camera and have been quite bowled over by the idea that the supreme ambition of my life is to become a crack international press photographer. Luxor is at this time a photographer's paradise, and with such foreground subjects as the King and the Queen, taken from the inside, so to speak, the challenge seems enormous. I am told, however, that the King objects to being snapshotted, so censorship is imposed but does not prevent me from securing some very good pictures.

But it goes without saying that the whole event is over-shadowed by the quarrels of the Queens. And certainly the main victim in this is the young King himself. Caught between the complaints of his wife and the triumphant personality of his mother – both strong women, both beautiful, both competing at practically every level of femininity – the King is at a disadvantage. Farida, unfortunately for her, is losing the battle to the older woman. Though she has her youth and freshness on her side, her opponent, Queen Nazly, has experience and the maturity of a beautiful and dominant older woman. It must be exceedingly unpleasant for Queen Farida. She fears isolation. She knows that hostility exists with regard to her on the part of many – a hostility veiled and camouflaged by the deference and flattery traditionally projected towards monarchs. This must be making her feel even more insecure.

The King, though he is to all intents and purposes a devoted young husband, a delighted father of the charming little doll-like Princess Ferial, is still a young man, vastly inexperienced in the pleasures and temptations of womankind in general. And there are on stream some most delectable examples of the species. An older and wiser woman might conclude that a certain controllable and tolerable infidelity would be the best safety valve to protect the marriage and act accordingly. But Farida is no Pompadour and she rashly indulges in jealousy and possessiveness, which is the last thing she should be doing.

There being several pretty women in the hotel, and Farouk presumably having a roving eye, she mobilizes her young brother and her cousins to keep their eyes open and report to her any possible infractions in this department. The King, however, doubtless upset by the quarrels of his womenfolk, has little inclination to indulge in anything. Indeed, he is so overcome by the situation that he arranges to leave the party on the pretence that he needs to make an inspection tour of a remote oasis of his kingdom.

We do not see him again on the trip. But grave events are in the making. He will soon be facing what will possibly be the most significant crisis of his reign: the British *coup d'état* of Abdin in February 1942, a bare month and a half after the Luxor New Year festivities.

12. The Abdin Incident

We now come to one of the most remarkable incidents in Anglo-Egyptian relations, Sir Miles Lampson's foray against Abdin Palace in February 1942. But first let us consider the scene. Life in wartime Cairo had become rather a nervous tension-ridden form of existence, though war had relaxed normal social conventions. This led to an unprecedented permissiveness in the life-style of a British community of officers, their wives, secretaries and other members of Cairo's British wartime establishment. Cairo had, after all, become headquarters to one of the main Allied war centres, the communications link between Britain, India and the Far East. In the basement of a tall and modern block of flats, Grey Pillars, in fashionable Kasr el Doubara, a telephone and telegraph centre was installed which linked with Whitehall in London the front lines of the armies as far away as Burma. The age of electronic warfare was with us. Civilian, military and administrative personnel of all kinds lived in the apartment houses of Gezira, Zamalek and Garden City as well as in the outlying districts of town.

Cohabitation was the order of the day, and promiscuity inevitably followed the enforced desegregation of the sexes. Sexual dramas were frequently resolved by the adjacent battlefield, which eliminated husbands or boy-friends by the simple expedient of death in action or other less lethal demands of war. The women left behind worked mainly in jobs for the army or other war-created services, and were easy victims in a situation where extra-marital relations represented escape from anxiety or consolation for the instant bereavements which followed official announcements. Men were dying not so far away in the deserts around Egypt. Their wives meanwhile were often dancing in the brightly lit Egyptian capital, their beaux of the moment maybe brother officers of their husbands, snatching a few hours' leave away from the battlefields of Gazala, Tobruk or el Alamein.

The human problem was poignant and a new code of emotional behaviour emerged. You have just heard this afternoon that your man has been killed. Should you or should you not go out dancing this evening? The convention requires that you should not, yet your dancing companion of the evening may die next week, so how can you deny him a few moments of pleasure? You, too, may be in need of consolation or a temporary forgetfulness. It required a certain level of moral courage and social bravery to carry on as many did. In such small personal incidents a new outlook emerged which was to have a profound and far-reaching effect on British attitudes; but that is a subject for the psychologist or sociologist. The fact remained that life had to go on, and business as usual was the motto. In Cairo there was a way of living of unprecedented intensity, its content highly emotional, for the city was the first to feel the toll of death and wounded from the desert battlefields of the Western Front. Cairo was also a city rife with rumour, spy-fever and nationalist plotting, and it was against such a background that King Farouk had to face his first major crisis.

The begetter of the Abdin Incident was none other than the British Ambassador, Sir Miles Lampson, the larger-than-life proconsular representative of the modest and quiet King of England, George VI. We have encountered Sir Miles before and know he was no retiring or publicity-shunning figure. He had nevertheless accepted with apparent resignation his effective demotion from the high status (as High Commissioner) of co-sovereign of Egypt with the late King Fuad to that of accredited representative (as Ambassador) to Fuad's son King Farouk. From being a virtual ruler, he had accepted the discipline attendant on being demoted to the role of diplomat, a profession for which Sir Miles was temperamentally hardly suited. It was rather like asking the distinguished actor Sir Laurence Olivier to play Cinderella to a juvenile ugly sister. The idea, given the circumstances, was not inappropriate, for

Sir Miles was soon to play another type of Hollywood role in a scenario straight out of the mind of Mack Sennett.

Farouk was a great source of frustration to Sir Miles. The 'Boy' was always doing the wrong thing: provoking the Embassy, consulting with unsuitable anti-British Egyptian ministers or, worst of all, generally behaving as if he were the real king of the country, treating the British Embassy as an unpleasant but to-be-endured necessary evil. Remarks of this nature, attributed to Lampson, were continuously being reported in Cairo. Then, to make matters worse, for some months prior to February 1942, Farouk was seen hobnobbing with various British generals and air marshals who seemed to like him personally and were not ready to swallow all of Sir Miles's critical opinions. Farouk also lacked the knack of showing the deference to the 'British Raj' that was displayed by other Middle Eastern monarchs. This was a deference which sometimes took such peculiar forms as adopting curious feathered headdresses and uniforms directly inspired by the demagogic whims of Victorian field-marshals, whose figures were certainly more appropriately stately than those of the diminutive Arab kings who sought to imitate them.

Sir Miles's dislike of Farouk led him along some strange paths of imagination. The King, he thought, was obviously plotting against the British Empire. He was harbouring Italian spies. He controlled an intelligence network that supplied Hitler and Mussolini's armies with vital military information. His co-conspirator, the Vichy French Ambassador, Monsieur Jean Pozzi, was using the French Embassy as a base for intelligence operations and supplying these valuable services to the Axis powers. It is easy to picture the British reaction: 'How intolerable! Farouk has to go! But first let us get rid of Monsieur Pozzi.' His Excellency, Monsieur Jean, was one of the most unlikely desperadoes you could imagine. A tall, stately, elderly Frenchman, he was the epitome of a French diplomat, with the manners and polish that only a veteran of the Quai D'Orsay could muster. Certainly he did not come from the same mould as Lampson, and no doubt regarded the representative of His Britannic Majesty as something of a rough diamond.

Pozzi did not belong to a breed that was likely to be

especially impressed by the Englishman. He was, in any case, far from being an Anglophobe, belonging, as he did, to the generation of Frenchmen who had been comrades-in-arms with the British during the First World War, when he was a liaison officer between the British and French armies. If anything, he was bitterly anti-German, and to suggest he served the Axis was a total absurdity. He had been made Ambassador under Daladier and remained at his post after the French defeat in 1940 without protest or resignation, simply because he was a professional diplomat with no political ambitions. Indeed, the important French community in Cairo was divided into pro-Pétain and pro-de Gaulle camps. The split was between those who upheld a metropolitan, legitimist government and those who, aroused and angered by war and defeat, saw their duty or interest as being to support an expatriate revolutionary movement.

That a certain amount of Anglophobia should also exist within the French community was, however, natural. The countries, though allies, had always been rivals in Africa. Two years earlier, on 3 July 1940, the Royal Navy had 'treacherously' surprised and attacked the French Fleet while it was at anchor and immobilized in the harbour of Mers el Kebir off Oran. For the Egyptians, particularly for King Farouk, the preservation of a French presence in Cairo was essential. France had played a distinguished part in Egyptian history, and could justly claim an honourable share in the processes that brought Egypt forward as an international independent entity. She was also a counterweight to the excessive British encroachments on Egyptian sovereignty and a friendly voice in the community of nations. The Egyptian objections to a British request that the French Embassy be closed and the Ambassador be expelled were well expressed by no less a personage than the former veteran Prime Minister, Ismail Sidky Pasha, in the National Parliament:

There is no clause in the Anglo-Egyptian agreement which calls for a subject procedure towards a state which is not at war with our great ally. If the suspension of diplomatic relations has been inspired by the spirit of the treaty, the moment chosen is not a pretty one. Information continually being received from London indicates that the Vichy government is resisting strong pressures from the Germans. It may even be said that it is keeping up the struggle against Nazism, which is incompatible with the idea of a France collaborating with the forces of the Axis. We have received no information that Egyptian residents in France have been subjected to measures of any severity or any ill-treatment on the part of the French authorities. Our representative at Vichy has not been in any way hampered by French officials in the discharge of his duties. Moreover, the French Legation has never taken up an attitude of opposition to the interest of the two Allies. Finally, by suspending relations with France, the Egyptian government has not taken into consideration the privileged situation enjoyed by that country here, in view of the services she has rendered, and is continuing to render, to Egypt from the cultural, financial and political points of view. These services go back to that remote period when France so powerfully aided the founder of the reigning dynasty to wrest Egypt from Ottoman domination and secure its effective independence.[*]

The whole matter came to a head during the King's absence on the memorable desert trip he undertook to escape the quarrels between his mother and his wife. Queen Farida's uncle, the current Prime Minister, Sirry Pasha, called a Cabinet meeting under strong pressure from Lampson and, over the objections of his Ministers, bulldozed through a motion to withdraw diplomatic recognition from the Vichy government. Such action against a friendly foreign power, affecting the status of an ambassador duly accredited to the King, could not, under the constitution, be done legally without the royal sanction. Sirry's action was clearly out of order and presumably directly engineered by the British Ambassador.

Inevitably the King, on his return from his extended desert tour, made his objections known. He was outraged at this high-handed action by the Cabinet and suspected behind it the

[*]See Jean Lugol, *Egypt in World War II*, SOP Publishers, Cairo, p. 306; also quoted in *La Bourse égyptienne*, 8 January 1942.

influence of the British Ambassador. These feelings were unanimously shared by the King's advisers and ministers. There followed several days of Cabinet crisis that ended with the resignation of the Sirry Cabinet. The Ambassador, clearly regarding this as a direct challenge to British authority, now decided on the favoured solution in such circumstances, a piece of gun-boat diplomacy. It is possible to see the drift of Lampson's motives here. If Farouk were allowed to get away with it, then the whole of the British position of puppet master to Egypt's politics would be threatened with dangerous loss of face.

Harold Macmillan in his war diaries described Lord Killearn, the former Sir Miles Lampson, as 'a man of considerable personality – strong, unscrupulous and entertaining. He has served our interests well in Egypt and plays the Government against the King and the King against the Government very satisfactorily.'* A man such as Killearn was hardly going to take Farouk's defiance lying down. Cairo was about to witness one of the most tremendous examples of overreaction to be organized since the days of Queen Victoria, namely, a punitive expedition in the grand style, in the spirit of Napier, of Magdala, of Roberts at Kandahar and the many other glorious occasions that punctuated the great Victoria's reign.

The scene on the morning of 4 February 1942 is Cairo, the greatest British war centre outside metropolitan Britain at a time of total war with the Axis. Over a million British soldiers are in Egypt. Some thirty airfields and landing strips surround Cairo, manned by the Royal Air Force. These are the bases for hundreds of aircraft – bombers, fighters and reconnaisance planes. The harbours of Egypt are home for a vast armada of warships which includes such floating fortresses as the dreadnoughts, His Majesty's Ships *Queen Elizabeth, Barham, Valiant, Royal Sovereign* and many more. There are enough ships, indeed, to fight the Battle of Jutland all over again. Never in history has so much military muscle been available to subdue so modest an objective as an undefended royal palace

* Harold Macmillan, *War Diaries: Politics and War in the Mediterranean, January 1943–May 1945*, Macmillan, London, 1984, p. 393.

and a king who waits quietly at his desk in his office to receive the representative of all this power.

Yet Sir Miles Lampson apparently feels that he needs an escort of over a regiment of men, backed by tanks and guns, to invest Abdin Square, and it seems that only lack of space prevents a greater concentration. Had Abdin Palace Square been large enough, Sir Miles might be marshalling a force of 100,000 men or more! With guns and tanks! These, after all, are readily available from the plentiful supply immediately to hand. Escorted by a group of senior officers, revolvers at the ready, the British Ambassador, perhaps trembling inwardly, enters the wide-open doors of Abdin Palace. Casting the civil practices of diplomacy to the winds, he thrusts aside two chamberlains who come forward to greet him politely and advances on the King's study. He bursts in, to be greeted by a smiling King who asks: 'What is the matter, Sir Miles? Are you afraid of something? Do not worry, you are quite safe here.'

There follows a brief exchange in which the King quite rationally implies that, since the British have force on their side, he will not be foolish enough to make a stand or prevent the British from once again overruling the terms of the 1936 Treaty in which respect for Egyptian sovereignty is a basic guarantee.

'You want Nahas? Have him,' is the King's response to the demonstration.

The above account of the Abdin Incident is based on King Farouk's personal description of the event, told to me some time later. The King added: 'I knew perfectly well, since Lampson was notoriously indiscreet, that he was looking for an excuse to depose me. Had I shown any sort of resistance I would have been playing into his hands. I had therefore given strict orders to my Guard Regiment to stay in their barracks, which were situated across Abdin Square. The guards covering the immediate palace approaches were ordered to behave normally and greet the Ambassador with the usual courtesy. The chamberlains were instructed to do what they always do when a friendly Ambassaor comes to visit. The only incident occurred when my Sudanese ADC, General Nougoumy, unable to restrain himself at the sight of drawn revolvers on the part of the British, drew his own gun. A trigger-happy British colonel shot him in the hand before he could use it.'

So ended the absurd and undignified Keystone Kop-style comedy of the storming of Abdin in February 1942. The need existed to protect ambassadorial prestige, and behind it British prestige, and the Residency was quick to cover up the details. Yet time has passed, and even today there seems to be no definitive account of this ludicrous event. It is a well-established fact that not all of the British were in agreement with the Ambassador. No less a person than General Stone, the Officer Commanding troops in Cairo and an unwilling actor in the farce, strongly dissented and only agreed to participate with his forces after the Ambassador had demanded a direct order for him from London. (The source for General Stone's attitude, reported here, was a private personal account he gave to Madame F. Zulficar, a close friend.) Stone was shelved by Churchill, the British Prime Minister, shortly afterwards, and had to last out the war in unrewarding jobs – a waste of an excellent general.

To the unbiased observer, King Farouk may be regarded as having come out on top in the encounter. True, he was, as a ruling monarch, temporarily laid aside while the government of Nahas Pasha was given power through British authority. Nevertheless the designs of the British Ambassador were ultimately frustrated and within a few years Farouk would stage a vigorous come-back.

To say we were appalled at the British action against the King would be an understatement. The King's policy with regard to the war and the treaties with Britain was looked on with approval by a majority of Egyptians. Egypt respected the 1936 Treaty with Britain and scrupulously obeyed its conditions. It had contained no obligation to declare war.

The quarrel over the status of the Vichy French Ambassador at a time, when de Gaulle himself had scarcely emerged and was certainly not yet recognized by the Western Allies, was an essentially trivial issue. This was an incident enormously exaggerated by the British Ambassador, who was looking for an excuse to get rid of the hated 'Boy', a fact that emerged very clearly with the publication of *The Killearn Diaries* in 1972. The blundering of the Egyptian Prime Minister, Hussein Sirry

Pasha, Queen Farida's uncle, who should never have acceded to British demands, created a *fait accompli* placing Ambassador and King in direct opposition within an atmosphere of highly charged political tension.

At the very moment of the Abdin Incident, Rommel, forced earlier by the Auchinleck 'Crusader' offensive to fall back on the Gazala line, west of Benghazi, was counter-attacking and had begun the great advance that was to reach el Alamein, within a hundred miles of Alexandria, a few weeks later. Benghazi fell to the Germans on 29 January, barely a week before the Abdin Incident, and the British Army found itself in full retreat towards the Nile. The much-vaunted 'Crusader' offensive was broken and in Cairo the peril became clear. The British could not afford to lose face and so the whole ridiculous show of force could be justified in the light of a British imperative.

At the time of the incident, I was on the night shift of my job as a government newspaper censor. We were, in effect, fulfilling the provisions of the 1936 Treaty and diligently controlling a somewhat unruly press on behalf of our British allies. Egyptian press censorship was at that time a joint Anglo-Egyptian operation that came under the authority of the Egyptian Ministry of the Interior. My immediate chiefs were Hassan Bey Yussef, a diplomat soon to become a pasha and Chief of the Royal Cabinet, and his deputy, a charming and erudite Englishman, Professor Robin Furness. Furness, recently an Oriental secretary at the Embassy, was a man of considerable literary standing. He was also a Greek scholar of some renown and had been a translator into English of the widely read and appreciated poems of the Greek poet Cavafi.

Furness was tall, apparently austere and rather solemn, and he rarely answered questions rapidly, but took a considerable time to ponder his replies. When they came they were to the point and revealed a quick-witted, dry and humorous trait. He was completely loyal to his personnel and often found himself defending these in the face of angry notes from the British Embassy. I had occasion to be grateful for this characteristic. I had earned the anger of the assistant editorialist of the *Egyptian Gazette*, a lady by the name of Morley Brook, an American who was married unhappily to an Egyptian. As a result she tended in her daily column to be less than diplomatic so far as the King and his country were concerned. As a censor, it was my job to delete the more polemical of her writings, and this caused angry remonstrations. 'That awful Egyptian censor,' she would cry, 'is interfering again!' This would be followed by a passionate complaint to the editor, Jeffrey Hoare. The latter, no doubt shaken by the lady, would shoot off a strong complaint to the British Embassy, who passed the buck to Furness. I would then be called in by the professor to explain my position. His method was quiet and unruffled.

'Adel,' he would say after a long pause. 'The Embassy has sent me this letter. Could you read it and give me your views?'

Needless to say, my views would be listened to with a total objectivity and fairness. Poor Morley Brook had to continue to submit to the unmentionably humiliating interferences of the censor.

So far as we were concerned, the evening of 4 February began quietly with an undercurrent of nervous tension. We, in the press, were aware that some sort of crisis was in the air. The comings and goings between the palace and the Embassy in Kasr el Doubara had been noticed. But just what it all concerned was known only to a few political figures. It was therefore something of a shock when news began to come in of unusual British military activity in the immediate vicinity of the King's Palace. Rumours were soon circulating. The King had been deposed, was the first to hit people's minds. There had been a bloody encounter at the foot of the stairs leading to the King's office. Chamberlains and ADCs had been killed. Lampson himself had been wounded in the hand. A British tank had been set on fire in the Abdin Square. The Royal Bodyguard had been besieged in barracks. And so on.

The problems facing us as night censors of the press were, first, to find out exactly what had happened, and secondly how much of the news could be released to the press. Questions phoned through to the Chief Censor, Hassan Yussef Bey, were answered briefly without any details. Yes, there had been a crisis, but now it was all over.

'What instructions do we have, Hassan Bey?' we asked.

'I'm sorry,' said Hassan Bey. 'I'm no longer Chief of Censorship and cannot give you instructions. You must just fend for yourselves.'

Professor Furness was unavailable – tactfully, one felt, since he was clearly no fan of Sir Miles. So we censors had to decide for ourselves what must be done.

Luckily, many of my colleagues were eminent journalists pressed into service by the Ministry of the Interior when war broke out. Among them was a nationalist, Mohammed el Ghamrawy, who had vowed to wear mourning so long as the British occupation lasted and who was always dressed in black. Another was Tewfik Salib, a distinguished Copt of the *Mokkattam* newspaper. Our anchor man at the Ministry was Abbas Ragy, a confirmed Anglophile and secretary to the Anglo-Egyption Union. Another censor was an irascible Greek, Marco Bey, who looked like a retired field-marshal with violent waxed moustaches. He was the brother of one of Cairo's khedevial police generals and seemed to treat all members of the Greek press in Cairo like so many potential drug traffickers. A more mysterious censor was a Mr Ohanessian, who seemed to be lost amid confusing Armenian politics which led to eternal quarrels between the lively but confronting editors of Cairo's two warring Armenian newspapers.

I was the youngest of the group, but by virtue of the fact that my papers were the English-language *Egyptian Gazette* (the unofficial voice of the British community and therefore read by all self-respecting Englishmen from General Auchinleck down to the lowliest of literates among the other ranks) and the pro-Gaullist French-language *La Bourse égyptienne*, I had to watch my step. Luckily the consensus of opinion among my fellow censors was to play things cautiously and without furore. We would wait for some sort of official pronouncement before allowing anything through. We were intently conscious of the mood of the British and had no wish to provoke a declaration of martial law, which could have followed had the newspapers communicated the story to the inflammable and highly nationalistic public. Naturally, we would have liked to have proclaimed the outrage from the house-tops, but wiser counsel prevailed.

In any case, on the following day the nomination by the King of Nahas Pasha as new Prime Minister was announced and brought with it the usual organized demonstrations of loyalty on the streets. A significant incident occurred when, out of sheer force of habit, the organized demonstrations starting off from the Midan Ismailia (now el Tahrir Square) chanted, 'Down with the Wafd!' to the consternation of the cheer-leaders, who could be heard crying 'No, no! Up, up with the Wafd!' There followed a typical piece of Egyptian political flexibility, stemming no doubt from a healthy cynicism and a deep-rooted mistrust of all government. It needed just a few hundred feet of progress along the street for the words to be changed, and by the time the demonstration went by the Club Mohammed Ali (now el Tahrir), a hundred yards down the road, the crowd was dutifully crying, 'Long live Nahas, *yahya el Wafd!'*

And so passed one of the most dangerous moments in Anglo-Egyptian relations. The country was now moving rapidly towards the crisis of June 1942, when Rommel would reach el Alamein. The British had begun to tighten their security system in accordance with the seriouness of the situation.

Two incidents seem worth recalling here, the first a personal one. Shortly after the Abdin crisis my close friend Toats came to me and said: 'I have a special message for you from my Pa. You have been chosen as one of the élite shock troops of the new movement that he has started, the *Nizam Gedid* [New Order]. You will be issued next Wednesday with uniforms and weapons and will be assigned an important job. I can't tell you exactly what, but probably you will have to kill one of the Wafdist ministers. This, of course, is a great honour, and you cannot refuse, since you would then unfortunately have to face a tragic consequence. We are doing this for Farouk, and it is your duty to obey.'

Mercifully, it was the day after this that Abbas Halim was arrested and put away by the British. Otherwise, who knows what could have happened? We were a somewhat wild and rather break-neck group of youngsters who would probably have opted for that particular path to glory. You only die once, after all.

Another candidate for the British detainee lists was Abd el Rahman Azzam Pasha, who had earned the suspicion and dislike of Lampson mainly because he was a nationalist and a friend of Ali Maher, and had voted in Parliament against an Egyptian declaration of war on the Axis. Azzam's name was consequently put on a list of Axis sympathizers to be detained by the British military authorities in the event of an emergency. Unbeknown to the Ambassador, Azzam was on Mussolini's death-list because of his involvement with the Libyan resistance against Italy some years before, and so he had approached General Sir Henry Maitland Wilson, a friend for some time, and asked if he could rely on British Army protection in the event of the Italians advancing into Egypt. Wilson had given him an assurance that he would be evacuated in good time and need not worry. Thus, when he came to read through the Embassy list, Wilson was surprised to see Azzam named as an Axis sympathizer. He therefore informed the Ambassador rather dryly that he would not be able to detain Azzam since this would interfere with arrangements already in hand to evacuate him and protect him from the Axis powers. The story of this incident, given me by Azzam Pasha himself, is typical of the slap-dash way in which a section of British security did their business at a time when personal antipathies very often motivated official action.

High feelings against the British prevailed in Cairo for some time after the Abdin affair. Most affected were those Egyptians who had enjoyed close social relations with British acquaintances, and there were many cancelled friendships. Most unfortunate of all, the British reputation for fair play suffered immeasurably and induced a criticism of things English that would take many years to dispel. Lampson himself may well have had to pay the price of his mistakes. His candidature to become Viceroy of India was turned down and Farouk eventually emerged as the unchallenged sovereign of Egypt.

Part Two

Iranian Interlude

13. A Dynastic Alliance

Ambassador Jem of Iran was a portly, short and cheerful man. He was a friend of my father, Mahmoud Sabit Pasha, who was at the time Chief of Protocol at the Ministry of Foreign Affairs. This job was a Mary Poppins sort of function, the Protocol Department being a main section of the ministry to which diplomats brought their problems. The Ambassador's daughter wants a driving licence. The Protocol Department must fix it. The Papal Nuncio has been seated in the wrong place at the Grand Lama's dinner party. Call in the Protocol Department. The translation of the Treaty of Eternal Friendship with Ruritania is imperfect. Protest to the Protocol Department. When, back in February 1939, the Iranian Ambassador announced his arrival at my father's office, my father and his staff braced themselves for some sort of crisis. But this was not the case. Mr Jem had come to sound out my father as to whether the son of the great Shah-in-shah, Reza Pahlavi of Iran, might be acceptable as a suitor for King Farouk's eldest sister, the Princess Fawzia. The request was duly forwarded to Farouk, whose reply was characteristic: 'They are Shi'ite Muslims.'

When his advisers advised that this was not a serious obstacle to a marriage, the King said, 'Iran is far away. Will Fawzia be happy there?'

Clearly His Majesty was not enthusiastic about the idea, but at last he gave his answer. 'It is up to Fawzia herself to decide, and I will go along with her decision.'

Fawzia was in those days virtually a prisoner in her mother's houseboat on the Nile. She rarely went out, and when she did she was surrounded by ladies-in-waiting and retainers. At a time when all other young girls were enjoying a relative freedom, Fawzia, by virtue of her position, was closely hemmed in. Marriage must have looked like a happy escape, a thrilling adventure with the Crown Prince of Iran, a young man a little older than herself. She was unaware that this young man, the Shahpur Mohammed Reza Pahlavi, was very much in love with a lovely Iranian girl, and that the betrothal to the sister of the King of Egypt was being forced on him by his father. And so her answer was, 'Yes,' to marriage.

An overjoyed Jem forwarded the glad tidings to Teheran. And soon the request was made public and the Shahpur was on his way to Cairo on 15 March 1939. He was a slim, slightly built young man with a long and serious face and what seemed to be an inbred tendency to frown at everything. He wore a high-collared military uniform of a rather unpleasant shade of khaki and crowned the whole effect with a peaked cap of vaguely Balkan style. He might have been a Bulgarian cavalry officer of the Georgy Dimitry school of tailoring. We were told that Iranian princes were instructed to frown on everyone except their peers. This, of course, did not go over too well with the somewhat free-wheeling Egyptian court. The two Queens and King Farouk were disarmingly unceremonial in their attitude and were each blessed with a strong sense of humour, which in Farouk was expressed in gusts of energetic laughter. The Egyptian royals were fundamentally democratic and put on no airs with their subjects. The King, in particular, would project his jocularity at everyone, from palace grooms and chauffeurs to his ministers and high dignitaries of the realm.

There followed several spectactular parties and garden gatherings where the princesses and the palace competed to celebrate the betrothal. Cairo makes a splendid setting for a huge garden party, and the lawns and flower-beds of Koubbeh Palace were illuminated with thousands of multi-coloured lights as the uniformed throng milled about in the lush gardens. Through the multi-coloured, bemedalled, bejewelled and beribboned crowd of high and mighty personages, diplomats, ministers, soldiers and their wives, the young Shahpur wandered stiff-necked, escorted by chamberlains and ADCs, bestowing muted frowns which might have passed for heavily suppressed smiles on the hundreds of welcoming

118

faces of *le tout Caire*. Fawzia looked pretty and rather virginal, and a bit bewildered at the unaccustomed hub-bub. Queen Nazly, in a splendid white sequinned dress, crowned with a tiara and accompanied by a cloud of similarly dressed ladies-in-waiting, floated elegantly amid the sea of guests, a graceful, beautiful vision rarely achieved by real queens, but often present in fairy stories. The young princesses, trailing their mother, added a touch of vestal beauty to the scene. Only Atty, bubbling over as usual with excessive energy, darted about collecting the innumerable little gold coins that were being showered on to the audience, this being an ancient and quite charming wedding custom in those circles which could afford it.

Certain outstanding guests could be discerned in the throng. These carried with them an air of shared power, being proconsular and commanding. The undoubted leader among them was the bulky and towering Sir Miles Lampson, His Britannic Majesty's Ambassador to Farouk and, in some people's eyes, the actual sovereign of the country. Lady Lampson, a flashy and very attractive Anglo-Italian beauty, was a fitting consort for the proconsul, who in moments like these could be the soul of conviviality and friendliness. One felt, even so, a certain constraint, for in Islamic fashion no drinks were offered except a variety made up of the usual highly sugared, highly syrupy juleps. The Ambassador had, quite sensibly, fortified himself with a few whiskys before leaving the Embassy, and had no intention, unless otherwise compelled, of delaying too long his abstinence from liquid sustenance.

Another figure, dressed in the full regalia of monarchical Fascist Italy, was Count Matzolini, the Italian Ambassador, a sparkling European diplomat of the Ciano school. He was urbane and vaguely triumphant, for these were the great days of Mussolini when Italian ships raced about the Mediterranean in the full bloom of their graceful grey lines, ocean greyhounds from the Trieste yards that had built the prestigious liners of the Lloyd Triestino. (Recently the *Rex* had won the Blue Riband for the fastest crossing of the Atlantic to New York, a trophy once monopolized by British Cunard.) Thus Matzolini could preen himself in this reflected glory, proud to be representing a latter-day revival of Roman imperial power. And here as well was the German Ambassador, Owe-Wachendorf, soon to be mysteriously liquidated by the Gestapo. He wore the frock-coat and down-played elegance of Central Europe.

Alongside these Europeans the Egyptian ministers looked more sharply intelligent, though they were on the whole small in stature and physically unimpressive. Ali Maher, Mohammed Mahmoud, Nahas Pasha and their peers were hardly pin-ups, but they did impress with another kind of show. Their blend of outward urbanity, quick-mindedness, wary insight and brains could very often overtake and out-distance the rather slower-on-the-uptake Europeans or Anglo-Saxons. They were the kind of people who had saddled British colonial diplomacy with the theory that Egyptians were wily and devious and the only way to handle them was to avoid arguments and let gun-boat diplomacy decide.

The Egyptian politicians were highly educated and often brilliant students, not only of the Cairo University but also of French and British faculties. Mentally they were the equals of the run-of-the-mill diplomatic bureaucrats who, more often than not, represented the intellectual manpower of foreign embassies in African countries. They had grown up amid the constant clash of Egyptians with Britain, and were veterans of the 1919 uprising that had ended in a victory for Egypt, if independence and a constitution could be so termed. Thus, behind the spangles, the tinsel and the coloured lights, something of a veiled confrontation existed, cutting across lines of genuine, friendly relations between the two parties but nevertheless concealing explosive situations and potentially incandescent consequences.

The marriage of the Shah's son to the sister of King Farouk of Egypt quite naturally excited comment and provoked suspicious imaginings in the minds of the political officers of the British military and diplomatic ante-chambers. The old Shah was known to be pro-German and to have adopted all manner of Germanic ways. Many buildings in Teheran carried a touch of Hitlerian and Albert Speer influence. Göring's Air Ministry, a monumental and massive building which, when it was built, excited the imaginations of Nazi leaders, seems to have been the pattern chosen by the Shah for the equally majestic Officers' Club in Teheran. To many minds, Iran was a potential ally of the Axis.

Just what King Farouk's pretty sister could have done about this seems to have bothered no one. Did the Egyptian establishment greet the marriage with enthusiasm? Did the panegyrics of Egypt's press media represent the real thinking of the Egyptians? A bemonocled prince of the royal family gave an answer which struck a note of truth and cynical sincerity. Observing the frowning young man and his retinue of ill-dressed ADCs, His Highness remarked, '*Des parvenues.*'

The festivities in Cairo were followed up with a ceremonial visit to Teheran by Queen Nazly and her daughters, who were warmly received in the Iranian capital by the Shah. The latter was nevertheless unhappy with Queen Nazly's free and easy ways, with her habit of throwing expensive parties, of displaying a degree of feminine emancipation that could only be dangerous in Iran where male chauvinism was strongly entrenched, where the Iranian Empresses held court as a rather grim trio of elderly women, His Imperial Majesty having married several times into the better tribal families of Persia. This Queen was a Kadjar of the old reigning family, that one a Bakhtiar, which meant she was daughter of a powerful and unruly tribe. The last thing needed here was for the Queen Mother of Egypt to come and spread seditious ideas about feminine emancipation.

The ladies of the Iranian court may well have been compelled by their 'progressive' sovereign to wear the gowns and accoutrements of Lanvin and Chanel of Paris, but underneath the elegant clothing the shadow of the *chador* (the Persian veil) remained ever-present. His Imperial Majesty had been known to banish subjects who provoked his displeasure to the grim hospitality of the several fortress prisons ringing Teheran, where even disobedient ladies of the court could find themselves hemmed in by rough grey walls. As she left her daughter behind in Teheran, Queen Nazly could hardly have avoided feeling a sense of apprehension at the kind of life she might lead in this ancient country that lay at the mercy of the uncouth, rough-and-ready rule of a former trooper now an Imperial Majesty.

14. Imperial Visitors

On 21 February 1942, a few days after the Abdin Incident, King Farouk's sister Fawzia, by now Empress of Iran, accompanied by the Shah's twin sister, Princess Ashraf Pahlavi, arrived on a private visit to Cairo. The first party given in the honour of the imperial couple was at el Marg, the abode of the most senior of the Egyptian princesses, Princess Neemat Mokhtar, by her daughter, Madame Amina Togay, wife of the Turkish Ambassador. The ball was organized in honour of the young Empress in this palace situated to the north-east of Cairo. It was a sumptuous affair. It was also the King's first sortie into the public eye since his withdrawal after the Abdin crisis.

The Marg Palace was a gracious building set in a palm-tree rich garden. Coloured lights blinked among the trees and the party gave every promise of being a good one. We had never seen Fawzia look so glamorous. Iran seemed to have transformed her into something out of an exotic Oriental fairy-tale. It was the period, of course, of Hollywood's greatest impact on fashion, make-up and the general upgrading of female beauty. The current reigning star was Vivien Leigh. She had recently appeared, with Robert Taylor, as the lovely young ballerina in that sad nostalgic film, *Waterloo Bridge*.

Fawzia had an element of Vivien Leigh about her, but it was laced with something else, something indefinable and mysterious, delightfully artificial and a little brittle. I only realized what it was when, many years later, I dined with the lovely second Empress of Iran, Suraya, in Munich. Suraya exhibited an identical aura of brittle, priceless and mysterious femininity. It was the result of a process whereby the Persians, great and sensitive lovers of beauty, transformed their women into moving visions of loveliness. It was a process requiring a special kind of voice: a pretty, artificial forming of words with a kind of lilting, waterfall sound, like crystal water pouring daintily into a cut-glass goblet. The make-up was expert but plentiful, and emphasized the fictional artificiality of the girl. The Fawzia who reappeared in Cairo was no longer the tomboyish Fawzia we had known. She was a creation combining the modern arts of the Hollywood glamour factory with the ancient sophistication of the girls of Hafez, Sa'di and Omar Khayyám. It was a heady and dangerous mixture, and I fell madly in love with the unobtainable.

Princess Ashraf, the Shah's twin sister, was a slightly built brown-complexioned girl who was full of energy, humour and dash and the antithesis of her rather morose brother. Ashraf had *joie de vivre*, was clearly very intelligent and, like many bright people, something of a tease. She was to become the inadvertent blockade breaker of Queen Farida's security cordon around Farouk, and her arrival was to mark the start of the young King's emancipation from the powerful female influences of his wife and mother. It happened literally on the first day of the arrival of the Iranians when a tea party was arranged on board the King's sumptuous Nile yacht, the *Kassed Kheir*.

The yacht was then moored off the southern tip of Gezira Island at the foot of a small ornamental royal rest-house, subsequently to become the headquarters of Nasser's Revolutionary Republican Council. The afternoon was balmy with a late February crispness in the air. Trees and gardens graced the surrounding shore-lines. In the distance, on the other side of the Nile, could be seen the dome of the Kasr el Ainy Hospital and Medical Institute, which looked vaguely like the British Admiralty buildings in Greenwich. Further to the north was a dazzling tribute to Art Deco, the Semiramis Hotel. Suspended in the crisp air, the distant roar of traffic crossing the recently built Kasr el Nil Bridge could be heard as the wash of Thomas Cook's Nile steamer, the SS *Memphis*, its decks crowded with tourists as it sailed by towards Luxor, slowly rocked the royal yacht at its moorings.

Ashraf decided that King Farouk was to be her target for the day, and before long the two were exchanging jokes and

123

ribbing each other. Ashraf's natural good humour and the King's equally quick repartee soon created an atmosphere of tease and jollity. I cannot personally say that I found Princess Ashraf beautiful, attractive to many as she may have been. She might well have produced raves in Sweden or Northern Europe, but to us she represented a type of beauty with which we were fully conversant. She could have been an Egyptian girl. She was small-boned, had fine aquiline features, a wealth of black hair, fine dark eyes and delicately formed small brown hands.

Her chief attraction was her personality and I detected nothing to suggest that King Farouk saw in her more than a pleasant tomboyish companion. She was certainly no rival to the lovely Queen Farida, whose jealousy was inexplicable under the circumstances. Ashraf was a natural flirt and had probably been well briefed about Farida's jealousy, for she was clearly and somewhat maliciously provoking the latter. Since Ashraf was an imperial Iranian princess and honoured guest, Farida was willy-nilly forced to play the uninterfering onlooker, for once unable to banish a possible rival from the scene. Matters peaked when Ashraf managed to lock herself up in a cabin with the King, from which sanctuary we could hear loud laughs and feminine squeals. Farida, in a state of high fury outside, pretended to notice nothing and continued to take tea. But she was quite unable to hide the anger and tension she clearly felt.

The next few days were heady and tiring. Party followed party. Every princess, and there were a score, had to give an evening ball for the visiting Empress and the Shah's sister, the style having been set by the first party at Marg. The King, clearly intrigued by Ashraf and suddenly enjoying a new-found freedom from his wife's domination, besides realizing that, for the first time, no official reason stood in the way of his having fun since he was shelved by the British, threw himself heart and soul into the party spirit.

Some of the loveliest women in the world were in attendance on him. Heading an impressive, heady and dazzling collection of beauties, all competing for His Majesty's attention and favours, were the beautiful brunette Princess Mahivesh Tussun, a lovely Circassian girl married to Prince Said Tussun;

the blonde and slightly Valkyrian Fatima Tussun; and three splendid Ottoman imperial princesses, Nesl Shah, Hamzadeh and Habatullah. In fact the feeling of sympathy for the young King's political tribulations dominated people's attitudes and provoked a general mobilization of effort to console him and indirectly express support and sympathy. Everyone therefore entered into the party spirit, and social pleasure blended with what was conceived as duty to the sovereign.

Needless to say such sentiments made each party go like a bomb. Dancing would continue into the dawn, oblivious to the war not so far away in the desert. Youth and beauty joined hands with their elders to contribute to the festivities. One saw ancient pashas, their fezzes at startling angles, waltzing to the strains of Strauss. The young were served with more fashionable musical fare, such as the 'Raspa' or the 'Chica Boom Chic', made popular by Carmen Miranda, the Brazilian bombshell of the moment, or else the 'Bump-sa-daisy' or the 'Palais Glide' from war-time London. One danced to the music of Harry Roy and his Savoy Hotel Orpheans, to Harry James and many other great bands of the day, to the tunes of 'Roll Out the Barrel' or 'White Cliffs of Dover' and many others.

Slow tangos were highly popular. The more daring danced cheek to cheek, for these were still sentimental and romantic times. People were still some way from the hard and brassy sexual availability of women which we now experience. We identified dancing with holding your girl in your arms. We didn't believe in keeping her at arm's length or in striving to make intimate conversation through a cacophony of noise like that produced at an electronic disco. Romances started on the dance floor and communication between dancing partners could assume dimensions unknown and impossible to recreate in the world as it is today.

15. Empress in Distress

The news from Teheran late in 1944 was disquieting. The young Empress of Iran, Farouk's sister, was reported to be gravely ill. My father, Mahmoud Sabit Pasha, who was expecting to be posted as Ambassador to Turkey, was on the King's orders rerouted to Teheran. A few weeks later we were *en route* for Persia, travelling by car via Jerusalem, Amman, Baghdad and Hamadan.

Arrival in Teheran was exciting that evening in March 1945. We were carried away by an inexplicable euphoria. I learned later that it had something to do with the altitude, some 6,500 feet above sea-level. This had a kind of 'benzedrine' stimulant effect, the sort of feeling German paratroops experienced under the influence of pep drugs on the eve of operations. At first, as we drove into the city from the north, we saw nothing of special interest, though here and there we noticed glimmerings of gardens artistically laid out with crescent-shaped pools and lunar landscaping of the kind which inspired Omar Khayyám. The rest was sandstone and deserted and forbidding mountain peaks: an Eastern-style vision of an inferno.

Teheran itself is set in a plateau, ringed half-way round by sulphur-breathing mountains, and on the southern and eastern sides by low barren hills that lead towards endless deserts. Of the Golden Road to Samarkand we found no trace that evening. The streets were filled with shabby people who shuffled along wide Mussolini-style avenues before disappearing into medieval alleyways. One stepped without pause from the twentieth into the fifteenth century.

Everywhere was the smell of mutton-grease, a highly prized culinary ingredient for the Persians. This, mixed with the odour of unwashed humans, was a powerful deterrent to any adventures down dark medieval alleys. Albert Speer's imprint was also evident. Besides the Teheran Imperial Officers' Club, the immense 'New Order' building modelled on Hermann Göring's Air Ministry, the National Bank of Iran was likewise a splendid example of latter-day Teutonic architecture. All of this lent a peculiar blend of splendour and squalor to the Teheran scene.

Splendour and squalor were the 'yin and yang' of Persia under the Pahlavis. The one could not exist without the other. For completeness the two images had to merge. Perfect man had to be good and bad, rough and gentle, ruthless and compassionate, judge or executioner and martyr in a cosmic equation closely tied to our whole understanding of the constituent elements of existence. One could understand how, in this atmosphere, some of the world's greatest esoteric mystics had thrived: Hafez, Sa'di, Khayyám, Rumi and Shams Tabrizi, those poets who 'sing to know your heart we know not why'.

I wondered how Fawzia had been coping with this strange land and its mysterious people. She was no Gertrude Bell or Freya Stark – those doughty, curious and romantic English-women. Farouk's sister was ill-equipped to understand, let alone handle, an Iranian entourage. Her Egyptian ladies-in-waiting had long since abandoned her, and the delightful Iranian beauties who replaced them were lovely and inscrutable, difficult to place as friends or enemies. The departure from the scene of the old Shah (he had abdicated in favour of his son when the Allies occupied the country in 1941, and died in South Africa in 1944) had had a profound effect on the nobles of Teheran. Their alarming ex-trooper Emperor was no longer there to torment them, and their ladies might even revert to the *chador* without being confined to one of the sinister fortresses.

Reza Shah's own three wives, all Empresses in their own right, had been wedded to him for political reasons, since they belonged to the three most powerful tribal families in the country, the Bakhtiars, the Kashgai Kadjars and the Karageuzlus. These could be expected to regard the Egyptian Empress as an unwanted interloper, a heretical Sunni princess imposed on Iran by the eccentricities and 'snobbish' pretensions of an *arriviste* 'tyrant'. The three elderly ladies held court, we were told, in an atmosphere of drunken and uninhibited orgy. One of the Empresses was a consummate businesswoman. She had bought up all the Swiss watches on sale in wartime Baghdad, and so enjoyed a monopoly on the watch sales business in Teheran. Citizens needing to know the time were consequently compelled to pay enormous prices for even the cheapest of Swiss time-keepers and alarm clocks.

Poor, innocent Fawzia was singularly ill-equipped to face such formidable wheeling and dealing. The Shah, her husband, was a man of charming manners but not the most assertive and masculine of husbands. He lacked the iron will and adventurous spirit of his twin sister Ashraf. Furthermore, he was much under the spell of Monsieur Alphonse, his former Swiss valet, a kind of imperial major-domo – part Richelieu, part Sancho Panza. He was not much of a prop for his Empress, though he loved her dearly, or so they said. But we were about to see for ourselves how the land lay in Teheran.

The Egyptian Embassy, where my father was now Ambassador, was a large, ancient and vaguely pretentious building set in an untidy garden, its wooden eaves inhabited by an army of birds, bats and creatures of the dark, which rustled, rumbled and squawked in a most sinister manner during the long Teheran nights. An earlier ambassador, the magnificent Nashaat Pasha, had installed – doubtless because he was transferred from Berlin – luxury bathrooms in the Albert Speer tradition, with lovely crystalline and coloured wash-basins and baths large enough to drown an emperor. The one trouble was that no covered water system existed at the time in the Persian capital, and so muddy, slushy water had to be pumped up from the convenient ditch outside the ambassadorial main gate. If His Excellency needed a bath, clean water had to be purchased from the British Embassy's mobile water carrier. The British Embassy was lucky to possess a well of pure water in their embassy garden, and the Foreign Office Bureau of Works, a thrifty and pennywise organization, had provided the diplomatic establishment in Teheran with neat barrows mounted with water tanks which could be hand-drawn about town, offering pure water for sale at a reasonable price. The British Embassy water-barrows were a picturesque feature of Teheran during the 1940s.

Within an hour of our arrival at the Egyptian Embassy, we were honoured by a visit from Empress Fawzia. She came alone and unaccompanied, and to say we were startled by her appearance would be to put it mildly. This was no young and beautiful woman, and certainly not what we had expected to see. It was a bony, cadaverous apparition of the type made familiar by the horror pictures of Belsen. Fawzia's shoulder-blades jutted out like the fins of some undernourished fish, and she looked ill, which was not surprising, since she was, we learnt, recovering from a double bout of jaundice and malaria. There followed a tearful reunion, for we were the first close members of her family she had seen for years. Everyone was naturally overcome, the Empress most of all. But my sister Dodie and my mother, having come through the first shock, were soon embarked on answering and asking questions. Fawzia was obviously delighted, but my father and I were, as mere men, rather tongue-tied.

We talked late into the evening, and although we were tired from the endless driving through northern Iran from Hamadan via Kazvin, the emotions and tensions of the occasion allowed us to lose any sense of time and fatigue. After Fawzia had left, some stock-taking was clearly in order. Obviously something was seriously wrong with our young princess. Could the rumours be true that she was being slowly poisoned by the Persians? For us, the Iranians were an unknown quantity, and we were ready to believe anything. It was, of course, essential for the King to be informed of the situation as soon as possible.

Things had changed considerably in Iran since the elimination of Reza Shah in 1941, when sovereign authority was effectively transferred to the occupying Western Allies and the Soviet Union. Any political advantages that union with the Egyptian monarchy might have given the Pahlavis, an upstart dynasty, had been to Iran of no value that anyone might have noticed. The war had swept aside any original considerations, and even made them look frivolous. The redoubtable old Shah had been ousted with ease, and the problems of Persia had taken on the time-honoured form of confrontation between the Russians and the British (now strongly supported by the

129

Americans). Our arrival in Teheran occurred at a time when, aided by the Soviet Union, the Tudeh party, composed of survivors of Reza Shah's persecutions, was establishing strong roots in the Russian-occupied territories of northern Persia.

Iran as we saw it forty years ago might well be regarded as the rather showy crucible out of which its present face was formed. It was a place mysterious, ancient and dangerous. Its people were devious, subtle and complicated, and had for centuries practised the dark arts of political manipulation on a level fully capable of inspiring and encouraging a Machiavelli. Their political virtuosity went far beyond the limits of Florentine deviousness in having successfully mastered the art of harnessing self-destruction and martyrdom to political ends. Shi'ism applies the kamikaze technique to statecraft with remarkable success.

Iran now being a field of encounter between the super-powers, the Iranians had to submit to the humiliation of alien occupation and alien quarrels against a background of new-era technology. Though the modern world of computers and megabyte memories, of Zoids for children, was still in its infancy, we were on the threshold of Hiroshima and Nagasaki. With the fall of Berlin, the technical dominance of the West had overwhelmed and eliminated the Nazi war machine. The victories of the Red Army, on the other hand, owed more to the kind of indomitable human spirit of man in the mass that the Russians seem to be so good at organizing. On the Eastern Front the war was won by men who lived in the recent memory of the Revolution of 1917, led by generals who had fought battles against the Tzarist Whites. Timoshenko, the Ukranian cavalry general, was a latter-day Cossack straight out of a painting by Repin; Zhukov, Koniev, Rokossovsky and many others were all figures out of an Eisenstein epic or a Moussorgsky symphony. One had a sense here of Russian history, of a bloody, murder-punctuated saga in all its human dimensions and Promethean intensity.

More popular with the Iranian élites were the Americans, who had deployed some 30,000 Sea Bees for the business of transporting the weapons and goods of war to Russia. Their prestigious achievement was the construction of a railroad and the splendid Lend-Lease Highway, a marvel of modern

130

road building linking Basra to the Urals via Kermanshah, Hamadan and Tabriz. Some three million tons of war materials were carried to the Red Army via this route in an unending stream of large US trucks and tank transporters bearing ammunition, guns, tanks, aircraft and other stores – an impressive demonstration of American productive capacity and know-how. The road, generally running parallel to the old caravan routes to Samarkand and Bokhara, roughly followed the track of the ancient Persian invasion routes to Mesopotamia and Baghdad. It was reminiscent of the campaigns of the American Civil War, when Yankee ingenuity and industrial efficiency built the vast military railway transport system that played a decisive role in Sherman's campaigns against the Confederacy. Here, in Iran, the same Yankee know-how, allied to the ancient skills of the road planners of Persia, gave similar support to the Russians in 1943. In Teheran, the US aid and the good times that seemed to be offered by the 'American way of life' won over the Persian élites, more impressed by the comforts and pleasures offered in this quarter than by the rigours of the spartan and sacrificial virtues of the embattled Russians.

The British, for their part, introduced a measure of aesthetic sophistication into these international confrontations. The great social event here was the British Ambassador's 'Wistaria Party', given upon the evanescent flowering of the Embassy wistaria, an event occurring on one evening in the year. The timing of the party therefore required a high degree of horticultural virtuosity on the part of British diplomacy. For here, where forward planning and preparation of the celebration presented peculiar difficulties, skills were needed that surpassed the conventional abilities of less seasoned diplomats from other countries. This particular British gesture, with its Asiatic undertones, its tribute to plants and plant worship, its implied concern and admiration for gardens, was of a nature to endear the British to a garden-worshipping Iranian society. That the master-minds of Whitehall were aware of these appeals and on the job is suggested by the fact that other members of the British Embassy frequently embarked on long, solitary walks in the hills and dales of Teheran's country suburbs, to muse on the poetry of Sa'di and ponder the philosophies of Shams Tabrizi and Rumi in the delightful glades of Gulhaq.

As for the Iranians, it needed little prescience to interpret their outlook. This proud and ancient people held on tenaciously to their culture and the inbred feeling of superiority that characterizes the Persian ethos. They had been defeated and humiliated by powerful alien forces, and frustration had set in. They were dissatisfied with their leaderships. The Pahlavis lacked, in large measure, the panache and autocracy of former Shahs. Though they had respected and feared Reza Shah, the upstart tyrant, his son was not of the same clay. The dynasty was, to say the least, unimpressive. Empresses who traded in Swiss watches between orgies and a ruler influenced by a Swiss janitor had little to commend them to this proud and humbled people. It might be fair to conclude that the seeds of a revolt which was to bring about the rule of the ayatollahs were already being sown.

In March 1945, while the Soviet Union was energetically aiding the Tudeh party in its bid to promote separatism in the north-western part of Iran in Azerbaijan and Kurdistan, life in Teheran was dominated by a palpable malaise. The fall of Berlin had infected the Russians with a kind of 'Superman' syndrome. On the sidewalks of Teheran, large members of the occupying Red Army, made larger by the immense ankle-length greatcoats and bulky Tommy-guns they carried, were to be seen shouldering citizens and occasional American GIs off the pavements.

At the time we were there the Soviet Embassy, which occupied a large compound in central Teheran, threw a 'Victory Party', at which Teheran's wartime establishment of Allied generals, ambassadors, Iranian ministers and lesser mortals milled around lavishly overladen tables offering mountains of black and grey caviar, blinis and other Russian goodies, to be washed down with gallons of Russian champagne, vodka and sweet Caucasian wines.

After night fell and the guests had departed, Teheran could hear the sound of machine-gun bursts breaking the stillness; presumably as persons disliked by the Russians were liquidated on the embassy lawns. People frequently disappeared unaccountably. Attempts to trace them were discouraged by the generally powerless Iranian Imperial Police. There was an impression of an underground war raging between the various rival big-power intelligence services, their Iranian supporters and other undefined but dangerous groups.

Against this backdrop, an intensive social life thrived. Any excuse was good for a party. The Iranian official establishment, the diplomatic corps, and even the Papal Nuncio threw themselves wholeheartedly into the whirling celebrations. I attended one such function given by the Shah. The occasion was a showing of the latest Humphrey Bogart movie to reach Teheran, courtesy of US Lend-Lease. It was given at the new Imperial Palace, a modern construction built in the elaborated Bauhaus style appropriately favoured by MGM movie houses. A brilliant gathering of guests thronged the royal foyer in true Hollywood *grande première* style. Evening clothes and uniforms were worn with sparkling and colourful miniature decorations, ladies were in ball dresses, scents from a liberated Paris perfumed the air and tiaras dazzled the eye. Assorted military personages in feathers, plumes and peacock accoutrements lent a carnival tone to the proceedings, the whole making an extraordinary hotchpotch of colour, sound and light in which the ghosts of parties long past, of state balls at the Hermitage, in Vienna or at Potsdam, of formal occasions in Paris, of Command Performances at the Folies Bérgères and Covent Garden, seemed to be looking on at a remarkable and rather Satanic travesty of Western grand occasions. It put me in mind of the mechanical *Totentanz* ('Dance of Death') tableau of Lübeck cathedral, where a long line of revelling dancers makes its way to the foot of the cathedral's magnificent baroque staircase and into the arms of the sinister, cowled and skeletal figure of Death.

The position of Fawzia in all this socio-political turmoil was, to say the least, ambiguous. Underneath the usual polite protestations of undying friendship a certain reserve could be detected with regard to the Egyptians. The Iranian official establishment had been disturbed by King Farouk's cavalier behaviour, after the death of Reza Shah, when he reportedly intercepted the Shah's property on its way back to Teheran from South Africa via Cairo, and appropriated a ceremonial sword to add to his collection of military memorabilia.

Furthermore, within the Islamic context, Cairo was the great resolutely Sunnite capital, and as such Teheran's most serious rival in the Sunni/Shi'ite international confrontation. Farouk's new friendship with King Abd el Aziz ibn Saud was also disturbing, Iran having tenuous and latently explosive dissensions with the Saudi Arabians. These dissensions usually surfaced during the annual pilgrimage to Mecca, when Shi'ite pilgrims frequently engaged in hostile and insulting demonstrations against the Sunnis. Thus the presence of an Egyptian Empress in Teheran made little sense and there could be serious concern for her safety. The Shah, though amiable and well-meaning, had to contend with explosive pressures at home, and though he might still genuinely wish to preserve his marriage, it was doubtful whether he was able to provide his wife with the reassurances and safety to which she was entitled.

My father reluctantly decided to advise the King that a termination of the marriage was prudent, and it became my job to inform the King of the situation. The matter was one of extreme delicacy. Above all, the Iranians had to remain completely unaware of the way the wind blew. Not even the Egyptian Foreign Ministry was put in the picture, and the official programme of events that transpired was that the Empress, accompanied by an impressive retinue, would be visiting her brother in Egypt for a short holiday. Fawzia herself had to be persuaded to travel to Egypt. Her weakened condition and state of near exhaustion had induced in her an apathy in which taking any initiative became something to be avoided. My sister's task here was to work on her and convince her that to travel would be both beneficial to her health and a potential source of enjoyment.

I thereupon flew to Cairo and was immediately received by Farouk, who cross-examined me closely about the state of his sister's health.

'I knew it would never work out,' he said. 'The marriage could not have succeeded between Fawzia and the Shah. These Persians are savages besides being Shi'as – look at the way their pilgrims behave in Ramadan! I was always against the marriage, but since Fawzia wanted it, I did not say anything. It was against my better judgement that I consented.'

Farouk was indeed sincere in this. At the time of the engagement, Sheikh el Maraghi, the Grand Sheikh of el-Azhar, had been sceptical. A gap existed in the diverging spiritual outlooks, and already the Iranian version of Islam was being looked at with some concern. It was violent and suicidal in its martyr complexes; secretive and revolutionary in its brooding attitudes; irritating in its poses of superiority. The easy-going and highly intelligent Egyptians were a world away from it in thought and deed.

'Adel, you must return immediately to Teheran,' the King said. 'Tell Mahmoud Pasha that he must organize Fawzia's return to Egypt with or without the blessings of the Shah. We will send the Shah an official invitation, and we will have everything ready to receive her here. Above all, keep every-thing secret, and I shall place you in charge of the operation when she arrives.'

I flew back to Teheran to find my father had enrolled an Iranian ally. This was Hussein Ala, the Shah's Minister at Court, a distinguished old-school diplomat and a close confidant of the Shah. Ala had even suggested that Fawzia should visit her brother and expressed concern as to her state of health. He was in the forefront of those Iranian veteran liberals who did so much to create modern Iran and build up a satisfactory relationship with the United States. He was a short, dapper man, whose attitude and bearing fully lived up to the kind of person a traditional Persian diplomat ought to be. It was Ala who acted as go-between for the Shah and my father, and as a result the matter of an official visit by the Empress Fawzia to Egypt was organized with the maximum efficiency and most cordial exchanges. The Shah himself expressed his pleasure, and the Court busily recruited the members of Fawzia's entourage. A mission was organized, to be headed by an Iranian tribal aristocrat, the quite delightful Mohsen Karagozlu – a convivial and civilized personal friend who enjoyed some sort of family connection with the Shah. Another member was the formidable Madame Arfa, an older English lady who was married to one of the Shah's generals.

With hindsight, it seems likely that Fawzia's departure from Iran was regarded by those in the know as likely to become permanent. The dissolution of the marriage, though it seemed at the time a remote possibility, could well, in the eyes of the Iranians, be regarded as politically desirable. They were too subtle and tactful to reveal such inward thinking, but it needed no special perspicacity for them to foresee such an outcome.

16. At the Villa Antoniades

The scene now shifts from Teheran to Alexandria, where the King chose the Villa Antoniades to house his sister, after her arrival at Nuzha Airport close by. The Villa Antoniades is situated in Nuzha Gardens, the former Ptolemaic suburb of Eleusis, and was once the home of a rich Greek cotton broker who gave it his name. Mr Antoniades had been a friend of the Khedive, to whom the ladies of his family were generous with their favours. It is supposed that these intimate friendships led to substantial material returns. At all events, a grateful Mr Antoniades bequeathed his villa to the city of Alexandria.

The gardens of Nuzha provide exuberant examples of classical nineteenth-century landscaping. Heroic marble statues of gods, heroes and nymphs compete with scarlet gladioli and roses, with ponds and pelicans, headily odoriferous flower-beds, noble tree- and statue-lined vistas, and band-stands and greenhouses. All this splendour is characteristic of Alexandria, a city which was for many years the home of cotton tycoons – a kind of Egyptian Newport, R I, where an alien and very wealthy aristocracy of mainly Greek and Levantine 'pashas' lived it up in a dizzying atmosphere of business, brokerage and fancy-dress balls.

Feverish efforts had been made to prepare the villa for the Iranian Empress's arrival. Farouk himself, with his usual meticulous attention to detail, supervised everything. Having been given the honorary title of head of his sister's household, I was now plunged, rather unhappily, into these preparations. His Majesty was particularly concerned at the possible reactions of Queen Nazly. He had kept the Queen Mother in the dark about the Teheran situation and only announced the imminent arrival of his sister a day or two before it was due to happen.

'I hope everything goes well,' he said to me, mopping his brow. 'You never know with my mother.'

Without realizing it, I was about to embark on a crisis in my relations with Farouk, to become a victim of the intrigues of courtiers and the complex interplay of jealousies and hostilities that accumulate around a monarch. But more of this anon.

Madame Nahed Rashad, an intelligent and dominant lady who was a close friend of the King, was made Chief Lady-in-Waiting. Her husband, the beefy Dr Yussef Rashad, a kind of unofficial medical presence, was charged with hovering constantly in the background. The King's sister, Princess Faiza, and her husband, who had been hoping to take off for Europe, were instructed to their dismay to remain in Egypt and help out with the entertainment of Fawzia. My job, meanwhile, was that of a kind of marshal, co-ordinating activities and generally making myself unpopular with the 'prestigious' helpmeets who resented the interference with their plans to go abroad for what was actually part of their nuptial celebrations.

Fawzia arrived amid the usual pomp at Nuzha Airport and was greeted by her brother in a high state of emotion, intensely sensitive to her physical maladies. He was shocked to see her emaciated condition.

'She is in a terrible state,' he said to me later. 'I expect you all to do the utmost to cheer her up and bring her back to normal.'

He was clearly resentful of the Iranians and blamed the weakness of the Shah and the negligence of the court in Teheran. An official sit-down tea party inside the villa had been organized for the arrival, and here an incident occurred. The King summoned me to tell me that, as he collected coins and examples of foreign currency, he would like to buy Iranian currency from the delegation of honour.

'That should not be difficult,' I said, 'because just now Mr Mohsen Karagozlu pulled out a wallet that positively bulged with Iranian money. I'll go and ask him.'

I went to Mohsen who, doubtless viewing Farouk with some suspicion, was clearly not too happy with the request. Perhaps since it was the King who asked, usage might have expected him to give the money to His Majesty. Obviously having no intention of indulging in such a courtly gesture, Mohsen turned to me and said: 'But I have no money with me!'

'But Mohsen,' I said, 'I just now saw you pulling out a wallet full of money.'

'No, no, you must be mistaken!' And he pulled out another rather shabbier wallet and showed it was empty.

I went back to Farouk to report. The King was furious

'Adel, go and tell the guards to body-search all the Iranians to find out if they have money on them.' Here was a job for a chamberlain to handle, and fortunately one was available in Mahmoud Bey Yunes. He immediately took over and was able to talk to the King, persuading His Majesty to settle for a compromise. All at once the indoor tea party was converted into a garden party on the beautiful Nuzha lawns. Following heroic comings and goings by an army of servants, the hundred-strong party was transferred to the gardens. Meanwhile, as the celebration continued, the Iranian luggage back inside the villa was diligently searched. In this Farouk acted pretty much as Henry VIII might have done in similar circumstances – completely in keeping with monarchical absolutism.

The Empress went through a period of depression after her return. She smoked excessively and seemed to have little appetite. My sister was her companion, and indeed lived with her at the Villa Antoniades, where the King was also constantly present. Queen Nazly had swept into the picture with her usual charisma, greeted her daughter effusively, embraced her son with grand and motherly gestures, remarked with distress on the apparent ill-health of her daughter, and in no way showed irritation at having been so tardily informed of her arrival. I could see Farouk's relief. He had been expecting a dramatic emotional scene.

The incident showed Nazly to be an intelligent and subtle woman. Though she was inwardly angry with her son, unlike Queen Farida she well understood that he must be protected from the humiliation of being criticized in the presence of others. One might have personal resentments, but one must respect and protect the King's image. Nevertheless, we did not after that see much of Queen Nazly, who withdrew to her summer villa in Ramleh, expressing a dignified disengagement regarding the problem of her imperial daughter.

17. The Zohria Set

Fawzia was now to be drawn into the orbit of the colourful and energetic world of her sister Faiza and her Turkish husband, Bulent Mohammed Ali Rauf. They had only recently married and the post-honeymoon celebrations, centred at Rokn Farouk, a picturesque royal kiosk on the Nile at Helwan, south of Cairo, had been going on for over a month and were expected to last a good deal longer. Guests arrived at Rokn Farouk at any hour of the day or night to find full preparations for their reception. During the night hours, Faiza and Bulent took turns at entertaining until breakfast. Fawzia now joined the action.

Cairo was at that time in the full throes of post-war demobilization, and had become a kind of colossal staging area where regiments withdrawn from the fighting fronts of Europe were routed through demob procedures. Among these were officers from the prestigious British Life Guards regiment, who had intimate knowledge of the ways and rules of royal courts. There were likewise noble English girls who worked for the military and diplomatic services in Cairo. These, we found, made appropriate companions for Egyptian royalty. Faiza and Bulent included many of them on their guest-lists, which on one occasion gave rise to an amusing incident.

Faiza, in her capacity as President of the Egyptian Red Cross, had a full schedule of work which required a certain amount of diplomatic socializing. One day she had to return the visit of the English wife of the President of the National Bank, Sir Frederick Leith-Ross, at a time when none of her ladies-in-waiting were available. A friend, Lady Margaret Fortescue, whose father was Earl Fortescue and whose mother was Lady of the Bedchamber to Queen Elizabeth, volunteered her services as lady-in-waiting to Faiza for the day. To the horror of the British community, and in particular to that of the bourgeois members of the British Embassy, Margaret Fortescue accompanied Faiza to Lady Ross's and went through the normal routine of a lady in attendance.

We were told that the incident had been received with distress in some British circles, where it was presumably felt that Lady Margaret was letting the side down by serving a 'native' princess. Despite this, many affinities existed between we Egyptians and these well-born British, and by recognizing that Egyptian royalty deserved a status comparable with that of the European monarchies, Margaret was, in effect, doing a good job of public relations for her country.

Faiza's 'court' was at the time a heady collection. By comparison with their European equivalents, the Egyptian 'establishment' young, being of mixed Egyptian, Circassian, Turkish, Albanian and Levantine stock, were a highly individualistic, headstrong and slightly anarchical crowd. Unlike the Europeans, they were a bare generation or two removed from a feudal society which tended to flout laws and trample on convention. In many cases, their individualism led to a sometimes quirky eccentricity, such as the young Egyptian Prince Ismail Hassan, who had a mad and passionate love of mounting suicide scenes from Italian opera in the small hours of the morning. On one notable occasion, Ismail and one of his cousins set up a KGB-type operation on a harmless White Russian, Michel Bibikov, breaking into his apartment in the middle of the night to 'arrest' him, and in the process spraying Tommy-gun bursts out of his window into the street below.

Bibikov, himself a close friend of the princess and her husband, was likewise eccentric. Apart from being a specialist in the determination of the sex of geese – for which skill he drew a salary from the city of Lausanne – his 'thing' took the form of excessive drinking, which led to delirious nightmares in which he would be attacked by giant ants. Since he did not wish to give up drinking, he decided to interest himself in ants. His late nights were spent studying their habits and following their way of life in portable glass-topped ant colonies, which soon littered his hotel bedroom. Learned books and documents would be consulted, and soon Bibikov became a leading myrmecologist, which earned him membership of the prestigious Entomological Society of Britain. This, in turn, led to talks and lectures which brought him recognition as a leading world expert on ants. Other eccentrics included my cousin Fayed, among whose special skills was his habit of cartwheeling across the Champs-Élysées and other major thoroughfares around the world.

Another character was the Alexandrian Gabriel de Saab, a Papal Count, whose peculiar objective was to be the complete Renaissance Man, with one foot in the field of agriculture and the other in the world of culture and music. In pursuit of this end, he was engaged in composing a particularly dull Gregorian symphony, consisting of long-drawn-out monkish resonances, and in keeping a financially distressed German symphony orchestra and its conductor alive. He would practise conducting with this orchestra, usually at lunchtime engagements in minor Swiss hotels. Such cultural activities were offset by a programme of buying Swiss cows to breed in the deserts of Mareotis.

Yet another colourful character to appear in Faiza's entourage was none other than Donald Maclean, who arrived in Cairo with his charming American wife, Melinda, to take up the post of counsellor at the British Embassy. They were a model young couple, good-looking and 'with it'. They had barely landed in Cairo before they were whisked away to one of Faiza's parties. The British first secretary at the time had asked the princess if he could bring them to the party straight from the airport so he could be introduced to the good life of Cairo from the word 'go'. This was done, and the Macleans never looked back. They were soon very popular with the Cairo 'jet set', among whom they could number many friendships. By no stretch of the imagination could any of us have discerned a Moscow-orientated agent behind the smart British façade. Neither was Maclean's behaviour suggestive of underhand operations. Indeed, his lack of caution and his flaunting of diplomatic decorum on top of his indiscretions might be regarded as factors to discourage any reasonable espionage agency from employing him.

It was indiscretion and wild behaviour that eventually caused his downfall in Cairo. He was hastily bundled out of

Egypt by the British after having wrecked the flat of an American girl in the smart suburb of Zamalek in a moment of uncontrolled abandon. That he should after this escapade have been reinstated in the Foreign Office as Chief of the American Desk seems as astonishing as anything else in his story.

The British contingent was more typically represented by officers from the élite regiments. These put over a curious blend of responsible conservatism and eccentric anarchy. No longer the uptight Victorians of an earlier age, obsessed with the needs of sartorial one-upmanship – shirts by Hilditch & Key, shoes by Maxwell, suits by Poole – this new breed made eccentricity smart, unusual clothes being a mark of distinction promoted by the aristocrats of the LRDC (Long Range Desert Group). Sloppy bush-shirts topped shabby, vaguely tinted corduroy slacks, and shoes called Desert Boots were worn, or, alternatively, 'brothel creepers', originally made by an obscure desert village cobbler at Hammam, down the coast on the way to Alamein. On top of all this they sported splendid brightly coloured silk scarves by Sulka. These 'in' officers, with their banana-republic clothes, were quite naturally attracted to the sophisticated salons of Cairo, where Paris fashions thrived and the good life had continued in spite of war and the menacing shadow of Adolf Hitler.

Derek Cooper, the leader of the Life Guards contingent, was a highly characteristic blend of an aristocratic 'Ouida' type of officer seasoned with a pinch of John Buchan charisma – tall, fine-looking in the nineteenth-century fashion, with a drooping cavalry moustache. His second-in-command was Major John Greenish, a fearless, rather break-neck leader who seemed fitted, but apparently not destined, to command Her Majesty's Life Guards, a job requiring, in addition to military virtues, expertise in ballroom dancing, a way with the ladies and a devoted loyalty to the throne. A broken marriage and a one-sided divorce (he and his wife being a Catholic couple) lost him his chances of this prestigious command. Other more junior members of the Life Guards were portly, quiet and horse-loving Jeremy Tree and the lanky young Marquess 'Sonny' Blandford. The appearance and character of the former contrasted sharply with the latter's youthful ebullience.

Another frequent visitor to Zohria, Faiza's permanent residence, was Michael Cubitt of the Rifle Brigade. Large and handsome, and also a Catholic, Michael was a poet and a vulnerable romantic. He leaned rather dangerously towards introspection, Sufism and esoterica of various kinds. He was unjustly accused by an Egyptian officer of being Faiza's lover, and expelled from Egypt without ceremony. But possibly the wildest of the military gentlemen was John Grice, who wore 'Bishop's' pips on his sloppy and unpressed Household Cavalry tunic and engaged in gun-running, was mad about cars, and traversed Cairo like an untidy comet, leaving in his wake a trail of abandoned cars and forsaken women.

The glamour department itself contained some outstanding ladies. Competing somewhat unfavourably with the extremely beautiful Faiza, they nevertheless held their own. Margaret Fortescue possessed a kind of 'young Mrs Thatcher' look. She had the charisma and dominant personality to go with it, and her most persistent admirer was Tommy Wertheimer, of the ill-fated King's Dragoon Guards, a confirmed cosmopolitan, a pillar of the Champs-Elysees Travellers' Club and the son of an expatriate Hungarian countess famous for her London parties. Another charmer was the exotic Maharanee of Palanpur, an Australian who had married her maharajah, wore saris and was more Indian than the Indians. Another Indian lady was the Maharanee of Jaipur, who combined Western sophistication with a rather dauntingly awesome Oriental aristocracy. There was also the delightful, beautiful and charming Shelagh Barker, official hostess of the prestigious British Community of Alexandria, itself an offshoot of the community of British merchant princes of the Levant. Shelagh, the wife of Michael Barker, a scion of the Alexandria Barkers, officiated for her father-in-law, Alwyn Barker (President of the British Community in Egypt), on such grand occasions as the annual British Benevolent Ball. And there were the lovely half-Russian Tatiana Preston, who sang heart-rendingly sad songs from Tzarist Russia; the dark-haired María Pilar Serrano from Chile, with her superb Amazonian profile and her mysterious blue-background paintings of black Nubians; and the two American 'bombshells', Peggy Wheaton and Letha Little, recent products of Vassar College, with all the self-assurance

144

and feminine potential that this represented. These and many others faced the formidable competition of the Egyptians, outstanding among whom were the princesses themselves, Mahivesh Tussun, Nesl Shah, Han Zadeh, Fatma Tussun, Ulvia and Nevine Abbas Halim, Leyla and Mona Sami, Eliane Valsamides and many others.

It might well be asked how it was that these groups contained such a high proportion of foreigners and why there were not more Egyptians. The answer, of course, was that foreigners came and went, being transients with no intention of laying down roots and without political ambition. Consequently they could be regarded as 'safe' companions – as, in fact, latter-day Mamelukes. This community of young people lived it up, and because life in palaces was, when all was said and done, something of a drag – especially since the King forbade too much public exposure of his sister – people had to devise home-based amusements beyond the usual party and dinner engagements.

Faiza's house, Zohria, from which the set operated, was just beside the Gezira Sporting Club. It was thus splendidly sited for 'dropping in for a drink' occasions. Having once been the home of Field Marshal Wavell, Zohria still preserved a certain aura of latent power. Bulent had spent a fortune on redecorating the rather 'chintzy' interiors of its former British occupants. The combination of oak panelling from stately homes in England, furniture from Paris, a Velázquez and some Corots, alongside Ottoman bric-à-brac of quality had produced an interior in which Boldini and other Edwardians might have felt at home. A white-haired British butler presided over a team of smart Egyptian servants – spotlessly white-coated, black-trousered, fez-wearing presences who ministered to the guests with quite admirable discretion.

At the end of that summer of 1945, the King decided the time had come for Fawzia to return to her palace home and abandon her official Antoniades residence. Her unfortunate Iranian delegation of honour stayed on at the residence until the total disappearance of their Empress convinced them that their return to Teheran was desired. I felt very sorry for them. They were treated badly and made to feel that Fawzia's experiences in Iran were resented. But I was unable to do

145

anything about it, since I myself was by then in disgrace and banned from the Palace. This was the result of an unfortunate intrigue against me and my sister by palace courtiers who were jealous of our position regarding the Empress. We had a painful interview with the King in which both myself and my sister spoke our minds with a quite unusual bluntness that shook poor Farouk, who had never been spoken to in such a manner before. We were, in consequence, banned from the Palace.

Queen Nazly summoned us to hear our account of the event, and advised me to see Hassanein Pasha. I met the old fox in his bedroom at the Winter Palace Hotel.

'Adel,' he said, 'I must give you a word of advice. Do not try to mend your relationship with Farouk. I know that once he has turned against somebody, it is for good, and you should resign yourself to this.'

He spoke like an old palace intriguer, a man interested in isolating the King, that fatal isolation which was ultimately to cost Farouk his throne. Fortunately, I chose to ignore the advice, and was able to re-establish close relations with Farouk less than six months later.

Meanwhile, Fawzia had duly left the Villa Antoniades and returned to live with her brother, Faiza had been allowed to go to Europe and Nahed Rashad had become Fawzia's lady-in-waiting. The question of Fawzia's divorce from the Shah now surfaced, for His Imperial Majesty desired the return of his wife. When he realized that she wished to end the marriage, he courteously and with impeccable manners if some resignation accepted her decision. So ended the saga of Fawzia. After her divorce was made official in 1948, she married Ismail Shirine, who will figure with some prominence later in this book. The King took the opportunity of his sister's divorce to do the same with Queen Farida, thus ending his own marriage in the same year as his sister's.

We might here permit ourselves a commentary on Farouk. He was a fundamentally insecure person, he lacked the ability to project an unbiased judgement on the persons around him, and he lacked that highly prized virtue a King should possess, namely, the ability to select the right sort of collaborator or minister. He too often tended to place his own immediate

146

entourage above everyone else, which in the long run had disastrous consequences, as will be apparent from this book. He was surrounded by ambitious people who placed their own personal interest above that of the King and the country, and who did their best to fend off any person who showed signs of winning His Majesty's confidence.

Yet, aside from their power-seeking aspects, courts have traditionally tended to seek their amusement beyond the immediate bounds of their royal restrictions. If you had magnificent deer-filled forests, you hunted, taking the ladies and your courtiers along with you. People like François I or Henry VIII were graceful, prestige-orientated, horse-riding stag-hunters. The Saudi princes of today go falconing, Marie Antoinette played at being a shepherdess, and so on. The tedium of court life engenders such occupational escapism, a form of chemistry which worked strongly on the imaginative, energetic and slightly eccentric court of Faiza at Zohria, and took the form of ambitious excursions into amateur movie making. This was encouraged by the presence of serious film-making persons in her entourage, among whom was my wife, Frances Ramsden, who had starred in Harold Lloyd's 'come-back' film, *The Sins of Harold Diddlebock*, retitled *Mad Wednesday* for its British release. Frances had, in addition to starring in her first film, also studied movie production at the hands of one of Hollywood's most famous directors, Preston Sturges.

Another *habitué* of Zohria was a scion of Newport society, Harry Cooke Cushing III, who had a Vanderbilt mother and brought with him a whiff of the old Scott Fitzgerald charisma. Harry joined wholeheartedly in the movie-making activities, and before long Zohria began to take on the aspect of a mini Hollywood studio. It being the King's sister who presided over these activities, movie-making equipment, from huge generators to travelling cranes, was readily made available, and the big studios were kind enough to offer every facility. Faiza's husband Bulent made an ideal director. A large and friendly man, he had a knowledge of human psychology and a capacity for projecting highly emotional pressures, which enabled him to manipulate people in general. These qualities, allied to a Machiavellian cynicism, made him into the kind of movie

147

director who could persuade the most obtuse actresses into becoming Sarah Bernhardts.

Our star, my cousin Fayed Sabit, a short and slightly crippled man who was a born mimic, possessed an acute and rather deadly sense of humour. With him we created the character of 'super detective' Professor Stromboli, a kind of burlesque Hercule Poirot. Stromboli was also a man of action in the style of Errol Flynn. In our epic production *Oil and Sand*, a Middle-Eastern-based adventure story, Stromboli and his secretary (my wife, who follows him and types for him on board a camel) take on a wild desert sheikh with his hundred warriors, superbly played by Prince Mahmoud Namouk, an heir to the Ottoman throne and descendant of Suleyman the Magnificent. Poor Stromboli is defeated, taken prisoner, trussed up like a chicken and left to die in the blazing desert sun. He manages to burn his bonds with his spectacles and escapes to rescue the daughter of the American millionaire oil man.

Of course, our 16-mm Bell & Howell camera would have been dwarfed by full-sized movie-making equipment, but the challenge was such that we decided to shoot each individual section in a different style of film-making. Thus the scene of the desert sheikh's harem was straight from what could have been a historical epic on the life of Prince Dmitri Donskoy, who held back the Mongol 'Golden Horde'. It mingled with pure Eisenstein for the wild orgy scenes, in which a lovely girl is delivered rolled up in a carpet and deposited at the feet of the sheikh and his jealous harem girls to dance an erotic 'Dance of the Seven Veils'. This latter dance was to have been performed by Rita Hayworth, who was visiting Cairo at the time with Ali Khan, but unfortunately they had a quarrel and left the country.

The film ended in grand style with a ball shot in the true Hollywood manner as a climax to our epic movie-making. It was set in Faiza's palace, and to bring a touch of realism to the affair, the princess sent out invitations to the Diplomatic Corps to invite them and ask them to come in full-dress official attire. The ambassadors and attachés thus prepared for what they assumed was some important function, little realizing that they were about to fill the roles of film extras. The occasion was the sort of lavish display that Hollywood used to mount in the good old days; one could easily have expected to see Nelson Eddy, Jeanette Macdonald, Douglas Fairbanks Jr, Maurice Chevalier or Greta Garbo making surprise appearances. The ladies wore superb ball dresses, the men authentic decorations, white tie and tails, uniforms of famous regiments. It was all like a ball from *The Merry Widow,* with a full aura of authenticity. The diplomats were the real thing, ambassadors were real ambassadors, princes and princesses were real princes and princesses, and the hostess was a lovely royal personage of the Mohammed Ali dynasty.

Little did we think that this was to be the last ball given by royalty in Egypt, the swan-song of the régime of khedives and pashas of a dynasty famous for its fêtes and parties, its social occasions and lavish panache. One sad note was sounded. Farouk was not invited and he did not attend. The Zohria crowd did not care for him. They saw him as a spoil-sport. Bulent Rauf vetoed my suggestion that the King ought to be there – perhaps incognito, disguised like Haroun el Rashid or in the uniform of a minister.

'If he comes, he will spoil things as he usually does,' said Bulent. 'People will feel uncomfortable. Ambassadors will be self-conscious and the women might even get out of hand. No, we can't have him.'

It was just another of that series of endless betrayals that Farouk was to suffer before his abdication.

Part Three

King in Being

18. 'Big Egypt' *versus* 'Little Egypt'

'They had forgotten that I was the descendant of the great Mohammed Ali!' an elated Farouk said to me.

We were dining in that autumn of 1944 in the gardens of the old Shepheard's Hotel in Cairo. On the previous day Farouk had expelled the Nahas government by what might be described as a royal *coup d'état*. The startled Prime Minister, Nahas Pasha, had woken up to read the morning paper and learn through lurid red headlines that His Majesty had graciously accepted the resignation of his Wafdist government. A courteous letter of thanks, signed by the King, accompanied the imposed resignation.

'At least my *coup* was a bloodless one, whereas Mohammed Ali had to massacre nearly three hundred people,' said His Majesty.

We learned that the King had sent a company of the Royal Bodyguard Regiment to invest the Parliament buildings. One might add that the British garrison in Cairo must at the time have numbered several hundred thousand. The British, who might normally have been expected to intervene on behalf of their nominee premier, made no move. Farouk's *coup* had taken place at a time when the war in Europe had to all intents ended and the British were preoccupied with matters and conflicts closer to home. Killearn was away, his career already on the slope of retirement.

The *coup* marked a turning-point in Egyptian affairs. The 'Little Egypt' political outlook was about to be discarded and a determined bid set in motion to seize Egyptian leadership in Arab politics. The dismissal of Nahas Pasha and the virtual disappearance of the tutorial and humiliating interference of Lord Killearn from Egyptian politics meant, in effect, that

Farouk became, for the first time in his reign, actual leader of his country, while the high officials of the Palace, Hassanein Pasha, Hassan Yussef Pasha and the rest, became shadow ministers of a super-government.

With the dissolution of the power triumvirate represented by the Wafdist Party Cabinet, the British Ambassador and a weak and largely shelved Palace, Farouk took over the privileges and powers of the Cabinet, upgraded the Palace and began to enjoy a far better relationship with the British Embassy as its role as a kind of political headmastership receded. The truth was that the British, heavily engaged on home-based problems and with Mr Attlee's Labour Government in the wings, were neither inclined nor willing to keep the old imperial trumpets sounding in the land of the Pharaohs.

What were Farouk's intentions against this happy background of regained political power? First, with regard to internal politics, he called for a closing of party ranks, for the formation of a national multi-party government from which the Wafd was excluded. His efforts were hampered by the petty squabbling of the party leaders, though they finally rallied to form a government headed by Ahmed Maher Pasha, head of the pro-Palace Sa'dist party. A notable member of the new Cabinet was Hafez Ramadan Pasha, head of the Nationalist party, which had hitherto stood aloof with regard to Cabinet positions. Now an old political factor was to re-emerge with some strength. This may best be described as the confrontation between what could be called respectively the 'Big Egypt' concept and the 'Little Egypt' concept.

Roughly speaking, the 'Big Egypt' concept stemmed from ancient political outlooks. Since the earliest eras of her history, Egypt had, in the words of Professor Arnold Toynbee, been a 'universal state', namely, a state whose influence and authority sometimes reached beyond its natural borders. The term implies more than the over-used cliché term 'imperialism', for the universal state applies other values to its impact beyond the political and material ambitions of latter-day imperialism, these pointing to cultural, spiritual and intellectual leadership. Egypt, as a universal state, could look back on a host of incidents and events supporting the appellation. In Pharaonic times, for instance, concern for the security of its Nile sources had fuelled a determined drive towards the creation of a southern empire. Other instances were the countless incursions from Egypt into Palestine, Syria, Cyprus and Rhodes, and the penetrations into Anatolia. Yet another example was to be identified in the intellectual and scientific dominance of the old Mediterranean world by Ptolemaic Alexandria. Pharaonic and Graeco-Roman Egypt became the meeting-place of the Egyptian Afro-Semitic civilization and its more recent fellow, the civilization of Greece. This coming together produced a socio-political phenomenon that presided over the launching into history of what we today choose to call 'Western civilization'.

In more recent years, the same political chemistry continued to work. In the Islamic context, Egypt was again to become the seat of empire for several centuries. It was from Cairo that the Fatimids bid to create a Shi'ite empire of the Middle East; from here, too, the armies of Islam broke the back of the Mongol tidal wave and expelled that other invasion of Islamic lands termed the Crusades. The Mameluke Empire, based on Cairo, stretched for a while in the fourteenth and fifteenth centuries from Asia Minor to the south Sudan. In the nineteenth century, Mohammed Ali, Farouk's ancestor, repeated the pattern, sending Egyptian armies as far as Kuwait, Greece and Asia Minor. Indeed, in 1835 and 1839, the Egyptians inflicted crushing defeats on the Turks and advanced to within two days' march of Istanbul. Khedive Ismail likewise engaged in an ambitious drive into Africa. I mention all these historical incidents to show that the big-power outlook represents a 'historical constant' in the Egyptian political mentality.

What then of the 'Little Egypt' idea? This was largely a product of the Ottoman victory over the Mamelukes in the sixteenth century and the transfer of the Islamic Caliph to Istanbul. For over two centuries, Egypt became a tributary to the Ottomans. Though several rebellions against Turkish suzerainty occurred, notably that of the Circassian Mameluke, Ali Bey el Kebir, in the eighteenth century, it was Mohammed Ali who conducted the most effective rebellion against the Turks.

Successive Egyptian victories over the armies of a declining Ottoman Empire provoked the massive intervention of the

Western European super-powers and Russia. Throughout the nineteenth century, the bid to create an Egyptian empire was pursued by the successors of Ibrahim Pasha, but they all failed in the face of European intervention, Ottoman weakness and, eventually, British occupation in 1882. Out of these disappointments emerged the 'Little Egypt' outlook. This was in essence the conclusion that Egypt could not go it alone, but needed to ally herself to a major power in order to survive. With 'Little Egypt' policies imposed on the country by circumstances, 'Big Egypt' notions survived in the ranks of the nationalist opposition to the British.

'Little Egypt' outlooks were fundamental to the policies of such personages as the Armenian Nubar Pasha, the Jewish-originated Riaz Pasha, the Anglophile Mustapha Fahmy Pasha, the unfortunate Boutros Ghali Pasha, who was murdered in 1906 for his sponsorship of a modification to the Suez Canal Charter that sought to extend the British presence on the waterway. During Farouk's reign, possibly the most glaring example of 'Little Egypt' policy was that followed by the Wafdist Party in wartime. It could be argued that they had little choice in the matter. Their critics, however, accused them of an excessive concern for their British-sponsored interests. And the British interest in imposing a 'Little Egypt' outlook was clear.

To Azzam and Egyptians of his generation, who had in their youth supported the cause of Islamic revival and unity promoted by the Young Turks, the dream of a unified Islamic entity, governed by a central parliament in Istanbul, or latterly in Cairo, was persistent. It carried with it undoubted advantages and it promised a new life to the Islamic cause, long used to interference and manipulation by the super-powers of Europe.

It is against this background that the unravelling of the subtle movements in Egyptian policy regarding Arab unity need to be observed. Farouk was to become an essential player in this 'great game', as the Victorians might have called it. Thanks to his Baden-Powell, *BOP* background, it might justifiably be concluded that here, in Farouk, was a stirring of that same imperial call which had motivated the British builders of Empire. The naming of Azzam Pasha to the secretary-generalship of the Arab League was Farouk's first move in his bid for Egyptian hegemony. From the outset, I personally became a confidential go-between for Azzam and Farouk, with whom I had immediate access through an arrangement with Pulli Bey, the King's man in confidential affairs.

In outline the master plot evolved by Azzam Pasha was simple. Through his wife he had direct access to the Saudi Arabian monarch, Madame Azzam's father being Khaled Abul Walid, a Libyan resistance leader who had become an adviser to King Abd el Aziz ibn Saud. He was also a close personal friend of Prince Feisal, the heir-apparent. A first stage in the move towards unification was to be centred on the League of Arab States. This was an era of regional representation, and Egypt had been one of the signatories to the 1945 San Francisco Conference setting up the United Nations. Nobody could object to the formation of an Arab regional organization built along similar lines but serving more local needs. Indeed, the UN Charter tended to encourage such formations. Care would, of course, be taken to hide any possible religious or racial connotations.

But, in the words of Azzam: 'One need not be a genius to see the Islamic dimension behind the Arab League's creation, although we shall never admit it. The overwhelming nature of the Islamic factor in Arab affairs must in the end make the League a Muslim one. In any case, both the Jews and the Christians are in essence Muslims, since in our vocabulary being a Muslim essentially means submitting to the One God.'

Azzam's theories were clearly laid out in a book that he wrote and published at that time in several language editions (including Turkish), variously titled *Al Rissala el Khalida, Ebedi Risaleti* and *Divine Message*. That Azzam and Farouk saw in the Arab League an instrument progressively to bind member nations into a growing unity until this emerged into a unified federal state, was apparent. Less evident was the latent desire to apply an Egyptian dominance. Yet the intention remained, and the setting up of a latter-day Caliphate undoubtedly existed in the hinterland of Farouk's thinking. The religious bond, with its attendant political disciplines, would come later.

157

Egypt meanwhile continued to represent a factor of disquiet for British policy-makers. Azzam Pasha, in a conversation with me, made this comment: 'Few foreign governments can command the intelligence and depth of planning of which British diplomats are capable. Downing Street looks very far ahead, and possibly that is why they tend to look upon us in Egypt as rivals. It is a fact that when they [the British] are compelled to leave the Middle East, only Egypt will remain to fill the vacuum created.'

We now come to the tactical aspect of the 'great game', which took the shape of an Egyptian/Saudi alliance. Relations between the Wahabites and the House of Mohammed Ali had been strained for many years. In the 1820s, Ibrahim Pasha's armies had crushed the Wahabite uprising and delivered its leader, Abd Allah en Abd el Wahab to his execution in Istanbul. Now Azzam was to mobilize his special skills with the Saudis and through these to forge what was in effect to be a Saudi/Egyptian political axis.

Back in 1944, King Abd el Aziz ibn Saud had visited Egypt to meet President Roosevelt and Mr Churchill in the oasis of Fayoum. Lord Killearn (he had been created a peer the previous year) indulged in one of his petty discourtesies with regard to Farouk. The King was simply ignored, Saud's visit being conducted in the strictest secrecy and Farouk only learning of the event after it had occurred. Before long, however, King Farouk, attended by Azzam, went on a pilgrimage to Mecca, where the ageing Saudi monarch received him as a son and accepted the King's invitation to visit Egypt officially. This visit took place in March 1946, and from then on a special Saudi/Egyptian relationship developed. By achieving a grouping of the Arab world's largest urban nation and its largest and most powerful tribal nation, Azzam had forged a political instrument of considerable strength and promise.

There was, of course, more to the new-found relationship than met the eye. Saudi Arabia was the country where the world's most impressive crude oil fields were situated. More important, its petrol was the subject of a major clash between British and American oil interests. From having been virtual outsiders in the Middle East oil business, the Americans had arrived and installed themselves in Saudi Arabian concessions on a large scale. Particularly irksome to the British was the fact that these American intruders in what was formerly a wholly British sphere of interest, had negotiated with the Saudi government deals that were a good deal more generous to the Arab side than anything being given to Iranian and Iraqi client nations by the British firms. It was therefore a challenge to Egyptian diplomacy at the time to take full advantage of this Anglo-American discord. Relations with the Saudis meant recruiting the American oil lobby in Washington into the political confrontation between Britain and Egypt.

Such were the moves preceding the Egyptian bid to enrol the United Nations on Egypt's side against the United Kingdom at Lake Success, New York, in the early summer of 1947. But lack of lobbying and debating experience within the corridors of the world body by the somewhat raw Egyptian delegation, headed by Nokrashi Pasha, failed to gain a sympathetic UN vote. Nokrashi stated the Egyptian case with impassioned brilliance, but the necessary operation of behind-the-scenes bargaining with other delegations lacked inspiration and enlightened backroom diplomacy.

In another area, that of Palestine, Arab diplomacy was certainly more efficient. Azzam Pasha was here involved in the Arab League's most important job. He led and co-ordinated the Arab bid to prevent the recognition and creation of the state of Israel by the United Nations. In this we were assisted by two non-Zionist American Jews, Joe Levy and James Batal, who actively helped our public-relations efforts. Thanks to them, I learned much of the ways and means of modern American lobbying and promotion, and we were able to mount a good press and publicity operation for the Arab cause. In the background to the Arab programme hovered the giant figure of Dr Judah Magnes, the philosopher and humanist Dean of the Hebrew University in Jerusalem, who was one of the leading advocates of binationalism.

The Arab proposals were remarkable for their rational content and liberal implications. Briefly, they consisted of a demand for the lifting of the British Mandate over Palestine, on the grounds that the mixed Muslim, Christian and Jewish communities were ready for self-government and should be given a chance to decide for themselves on such major issues

159

as unlimited immigration and the building of a separate Jewish entity practising racial and religious discrimination. They proposed the formation of a state in which a full proportionate representation at every level of government would be shared by the three communities. In addition, they proposed that an international guarantee be operated by the United Nations to preserve the cultural and national identities of the Jews, Christians and Arabs in the structure of a new state of Palestine. The alternative, the Arabs argued, would be war, the Arab threat to go to war on behalf of the Palestinians being officially communicated to the US Secretary of State, General George Marshall, in June 1947 by Azzam Pasha, who had been mandated to do so by the Arab League General Assembly. Azzam had gone on to say in the same interview that such a war would be one to be likened to the Crusades and could continue for generations; views that the Arab delegations repeated at the UN General Assembly. Such was the strength of the Arab diplomatic offensive that they very nearly succeeded in frustrating the vote for the creation of Israel, despite the unusual circumstance of both an American and a Soviet vote of support. Washington was obliged *in extremis* to twist the arms of two small banana republics, who, under a threat of US economic sanctions, gave the resolution for the creation of Israel in the United Nations its two-vote majority.

In conclusion, we might invoke the words of Shakespeare in *Richard II*: 'This royal throne of kings ... this earth of majesty, this seat of Mars ...' for Egypt has been these things and more. Dreams of empire have come easily to her rulers: the Pharaohs, Alexander of the two horns, the Roman Marc Antony, and after these the Muslims, who from an Egyptian base conquered Spain and reached Poitiers in France. Later still, there were the Fatimids, who dreamed of establishing a Shi'ite empire; and Saladin, who battled with the Crusaders for possession of Jerusalem and won. He was followed by the Mamelukes of the irresistible cavalry charges, who overwhelmed the Mongol hordes at Ain Djalout and hewed out an empire stretching from the cataracts of the Sudan to the cold foothills of the Caucasus. In more recent times, Napoleon Bonaparte dreamed from his palace in Cairo of an empire to include Persia, India and the Levant. An honourable mention must also go to Farouk's forebear, Mohammed Ali, and his redoubtable son and general Ibrahim, who conquered Arabia, smashed the Greek revolution, marched to the doors of Istanbul. All these and many others, who now sleep at the foot of the Mokattam Hills or in the western pyramids of the desert, still sound their distant trumpets of adventure, conquest and war.

The British from Victoria's Lord Ponsonby onwards were well aware of this history. After all, they, too, had tasted the wine of imperial conquest and were well aware of the rivalry that could emerge in the areas of their tenancy. They had systematically played watchdog over the ambitions of Egyptian rulers and, when necessary, taken appropriate action to frustrate their designs. We need look no further than the events surrounding the building of the Suez Canal. The waterway, once built, made Egypt a splendid base for the eventual subjugation of India. In this lay a strong justification for the occupation of Egypt in 1882, giving Britain an essential facility for the building of an African empire.

The great proconsuls, Cromer, Kitchener, Allenby, Lloyd and finally, of course, Killearn, did much to clip the wings of Egyptian leadership. We in Cairo believe that Gordon was sacrificed on behalf of a British stake in the Sudan through reconquest. The growth of leadership within the Egyptian community was likewise frustrated. Cromer saw to this by bringing from Delhi Mr Dunlop, an educator of *babus* and Indian civil servants. He it was who preached the politically obedient conformism which continues to hover over Egyptian teaching institutions to the present day.

19. The Arab League and the First Arab-Israeli War

There was another dream of Empire which could be discerned in Farouk's time, and it has already been hinted at elsewhere in this book. It could be seen in the efforts of Ali Maher Pasha, Sheikh el Maraghi, Aziz el Masry Pasha and others to lay the foundations for a modern Islamic state. Here, too, Killearn worked to put a stopper on things. Farouk, as we saw, was asked to dismiss Ali Maher and Aziz el Masry in 1940. With Farouk's return to power at the end of the Second World War, the scene underwent a dramatic change. The King was free to turn a new page in his bid for hegemony, a process designed to make of the Arab League a new super-power.

To achieve this end, a certain mastery in favour of federalism was required. Egypt on her own might not be able to tip the scales. A tribal and traditionalist Arab element was essential to complement and complete the evolved and progressivist urban Egyptians. The alliance with Saudi Arabia fulfilled this need, and that, in turn, led to an Egyptian-Saudi dominance within the voting of the General Assembly of the League. Anthony Eden's dream of an Arab League to serve as the handmaiden of British policy in the Arab countries faced a severe awakening in October 1946 when, at a memorable meeting of the Arab League Council in Cairo, this 'instrument', promoted by the Foreign Office, voted a condemnation of British policy with regard to Egypt. Lebanon and Syria, who might have been expected to remain neutral in the conflict, voted with the Egyptians.

Azzam Pasha, the Secretary-General of the Arab League, outlined the policies the league intended to follow. 'We stand,' he said, 'for the self-determination of all peoples, and will do all in our power to bring this about. We will even stand by the side

162

of the German people, since self-determination is a universal principle . . .' These sentiments were shortly to be put into effect when the General Assembly of the Arab League issued its recognition of and support for Sukarno. Before the Dutch government had ended its conflict with Indonesia, the Arab League was the first group of nations to recognize the independence of an Asian land so far removed from the Middle East. It was reported at the time that Nehru was much disturbed at this intrusion by the Arabs into India's backyard.

Another initiative of the kind, though closer to home, were the secret negotiations carried out by Azzam Pasha and the Italian Ambassador, Count Fracassi, at Glymenopoulo Alexandria in late 1947, when a deal was made with the Italians whereby they sided with the league to support the move for Libyan independence and the lifting of the British Protectorate at the United Nations in exchange for Arab support on behalf of Italian interests in Somalia.

An undercurrent of clash with the West was to be discerned in all these activities. Largely because of residual Rooseveltian idealism, America could initially be relied on to be sympathetic to such Arab attitudes, but with time and the emergency of the pro-Zionist Truman administration, the Arab lobby in Washington began to lose ground. The death by suicide in 1949 of the US Secretary for Defence, James Forrestal, a staunch opponent of Zionist ambitions in the Middle East, clearly indicated Zionist strength. Forrestal died in a state of depression as the result – it was assumed – of his failure to frustrate the formation of a state of Israel and the intensive campaign of denigration and slander directed at him. Here, indeed, was a true indication of the power of the Zionist establishment in Washington. It was strong enough to overrule American national interests as well as Forrestal and his army advisers. The Zionists were therefore to be regarded as formidable elements in the power game.

The Arab delegation at the United Nations was no match for the Zionists, who not only were able to impose themselves but also managed to muzzle a not insubstantial opposition within the Jewish ranks. It was a matter of some concern to see that a strong anti-Semitism existed within the American community, a phenomenon likely to spawn an election-motivated pro-Jewish backlash. I had an amusing experience at the time. Being in charge of press relations, I was surprised to find that those newspapers owned by traditional 'WASPS', namely the White Anglo-Saxon Protestant Americans of the largely anti-Semitic establishment, were markedly pro-Zionist, whereas the *New York Times*, owned by Jews, was far more balanced in outlook, and the tabloid *New York Mirror* was quite amazingly pro-Arab though its ownership was New York Jewish. This mystery was partly explained when Azzam recalled a conversation he had had with an elderly gentleman on the train on his way back from Washington. It transpired that the old gentleman was the owner of the *Mirror* and had, like many before him, fallen victim to Azzam Pasha's eloquence.

'We have threatened war,' said Azzam Pasha. 'It is essential that we prepare for war. The threat of war, if taken seriously, may well lead to an acceptable resolution and compromise. Our peace offer ensuring the political rights of Christians, Muslims and Jews in Palestine is rational, logical and, in the end, perfectly acceptable to the three communities, including the Jews. It could be the basis of an international understanding. Such an understanding is possible if we can convince the UN nations that we will be determined to fight for it. If we do not prepare for war, we will lose all credibility and a solution favouring the Zionists will be imposed upon us.'

He asked me to stress this viewpoint to the King. When I asked for an interview, His Majesty instructed me to come to Abdin Palace. He received me in one of the first-floor rooms, a place vaguely unfurnished, white-walled and containing plain, stark furniture.

'Well, what do you think, Adel?' he asked after I delivered Azzam's message.

'It sounds logical, Your Majesty,' I replied. 'Some people seem to think we mean war. Even General Spears felt he should try and dissuade us.'

The Francophile General Sir Edward Spears had been visiting Cairo, and I described to the King the conversation that had taken place at a lunch party given by the head of the National Party, Hafez Ramadan, at which all the leading ministers were present. Spears had asked them if they agreed to go to war: the answer was yes. Spears then offered a warning. 'Gentlemen,' he said. 'When you go to war, one of two things will be revealed – your strength or your weakness. My feelings are that it will be your weakness.'

'I know this,' Farouk said. 'I am being pressured to give up the idea of war, but I feel that Egypt would be dishonoured if she abandoned the Palestinian commitment. We have no alternative but to honour the policy we have initiated. As for the other Arab nations, I shall have to convene a conference of their kings and presidents in order to co-ordinate policies and achieve a united front in the face of this situation.'

During our conversation, which took place in 1948, the King made no mention of the deal negotiated between King Abdullah of Jordan and the Israelis. Maybe he knew nothing about it.

Farouk's role in promoting the 1948 war has been much debated. He has been criticized for being a warmonger, for pushing the country into a war for which she was ill-prepared; indeed, for being the main architect of the disaster. I therefore think that the record needs to be put straight. Long years of subservience to Britain had dulled the minds of Egyptian leaders, a symptom of this being the inability to correlate policy with consequences and subsequent action. To threaten war is no light manoeuvre at any time. Words are either empty or they are to be taken seriously. No nation can afford to be frivolous in its threats or in the speeches of its ministers. Farouk was perfectly justified in following through with the policies laid down by a majority of Arab states. Indeed, the Palestine war was the first major test of the effectiveness of the Arab League, and the reputation of its members was here on trial. Perhaps Farouk's error was largely to have relied on the good faith of his allies. He lacked the bazaar mentality that was able to distinguish between reality and hyperbole. In effect, he was fooled by King Abdullah of Jordan, and in general the Egyptians were betrayed by their allies, whose participation in the common front was either negligible or downright treacherous.

To say, as some have done, that he should have known that his army could not possibly win a battle with the Jews is likewise wrong. The Egyptian Army of the time was well-trained, well-organized and high in morale. This has been testified to by the Jews themselves. In the line-up with Israeli regular forces, such as the Palmach and the various terrorist groups, the army should have given a good account of itself, fully justifying the confidence Farouk placed in it. Why therefore the defeat? The first answer is that the army entered Palestine with barely three days of logistic stores. By the time it reached Gaza, it had run out of ammunition. No efforts had been made by the High Command during the entire nine months that had been available to prepare for a conflict, the Palestine case having been debated in 1947. General Heydar Pasha and his staff of incompetent officers in fact did nothing to prepare for war. By the time a UN embargo was imposed on arms shipments, it was too late.

It is difficult to account for all the clear evidence of inept logistic planning. Obviously it would have been easy to organize a major purchase of ammunition for the artillery, which, in any case, used standard British calibres. Vast quantities of surplus materials were being disposed of by the British government at the time, and there could have been no reason to deny the Egyptian Army a complete stores build-up of everything it might need, from Bren-gun ammunition to 6-inch naval shells and trucks which were at the time being sold on the civilian market for some £100 Egyptian apiece. On Egyptian territory in the Suez Canal military zone, stores sufficient to supply an army of over a million were present, and the British were willing to sell them.

While I was screening officer at the Arab League in charge of arms dealers, I was informed by the British that two train-loads of ammunition for the Egyptian Army had been made ready in Fayed on the Suez Canal and they only needed Egyptian locomotives to draw them into the possession of the Egyptian Army. This was ten full days before the embargo was applied, but needless to say, nothing was done about it. Under no circumstances could Farouk be held responsible for such things.

In another area of military preparedness, one might point a finger at the ineptitude of the staff-work involved. In an age when, only recently, war had begun to be conducted by armoured divisions whose tactics were a war of movement, of bypass, of encirclement, the Egyptian Army generals ordered

166

a manner of fighting popular in the late nineteenth century. They sent in teams of infantry with fixed bayonets – these then being mowed down by well-entrenched Jewish settlers armed with heavy-duty machine-guns. The next step was a blatant misuse of artillery, where, again, valuable ammunition was wasted bombarding the fortified and entrenched Israelis. Another absurdity was to encircle Israeli settlements, thereby forcing the settlers to fight to the death, whereas the provision of a possibility of withdrawal could have provoked flight.

At all events, the German General Schmitt's reaction was interesting. 'Mr Sabit, why worry about a little semi-civilian settlement, quite incapable of mounting a flanking attack against your army. Had your officers decided to ignore and bypass them, they would have arrived in Gaza with ammunition and the settlers would probably have straggled back to their lines. Indeed, unprepared as it was, the Egyptian Army was certainly relatively far more powerful than the Afrika Korps when it first took on the British.'

20. The Causes and Consequence of Defeat

The 1948 war with Israel was possibly one of the worst-managed wars in modern history. It was an extraordinary production, conceived, prepared for and put into effect by an international team of kings, presidents, prime ministers and politicians, all obeying different loyalties and several secretly ready to betray one of the others for opportunist reasons. In all of this Farouk was to become the innocent victim, and his country, Egypt, was to pay the highest price in men, money and other costs of war. Egypt lost several thousands killed and wounded, together with its prestige, and the King eventually lost his throne.

But let us start at the beginning. Despite repeated warnings from the Arab countries that the event would unleash a chain-reaction lasting generations, the Western world, aided surprisingly by a Russian vote, bulldozed *in extremis* the creation of the state of Israel through the United Nations. The necessary majority in the General Assembly for voting Israel into the Assembly of Nations was secured, at the last moment, by American pressures on the two Latin-American mini-states who were unable to stand up to super-power arm-twisting. Israel, as soon as it was in existence, was a direct challenge to the members of the Arab League, who had individually threatened war in the Security Council debates on the subject. Thus they had committed themselves to armed reaction, and they really had no choice except to honour these commitments, however rash they may now appear to be in hindsight.

My liaison role between Azzam Pasha and the King was strictly discreet and informal, but I nevertheless found myself in the middle of events. Azzam asked me to stress to His Majesty the need to take effective military action, since

Egypt's reputation was directly involved. I was to remind the King of his conversations with Azzam and to endeavour to counter the effect of certain negative opinions which might be advanced to persuade His Majesty into remaining inactive. The King was surrounded by a mob of palace sycophants and toadies whose loyalties could be bought and whose opinions reflected many non-Egyptian interests. Assisting the negative side mightily was the disclination of the army top brass, led by the Minister of Defence, Heyder Pasha, seriously to anticipate or prepare for open warfare.

Farouk was therefore faced with something of a dilemma. Azzam's team was calling for a serious preparation for war, which, apart from purely military considerations, required a high degree of Arab solidarity and purpose. Against this, Farouk faced the urgings of other palace influences who reflected the tendencies of other Arab monarchs, notably King Abdullah of Jordan, who was actively engaged in wheeler-dealing with the Israelis in the shape of Walter Eytan and Mrs Meir, to achieve a Jordanian-orientated partition of Palestine. It says much for Farouk's personal integrity that he was able to resist these powerful pressures and go along with the honourable course proposed by Azzam.

Azzam's line of argument was relatively simple. The Arab states which had solemly expressed their commitment to a Palestine war of liberation in the Security Council needed to be reminded that they were duty-bound to honour such commitment. Azzam urged Farouk to use his influence and prestige with the other Arab leaders to get them to fall into line with Egypt. The imminence of war similarly required that the Arab armies should prepare for this eventuality and needed to be backed by an appropriate mobilization of resources. Azzam argued that no formal declaration was necessary and suggested the opening of an intensive guerrilla campaign in Palestine as well as channelling all possible Arab resources into building and equipping an overwhelmingly powerful Arab air force. In the light of this, it is ironic to record how, despite Farouk's efforts, the army group headed by Heydar did so little to ensure beforehand that the forces entering Palestine were adequately provided with a sufficiency of ammunition and other military stores.

169

It may be mentioned in passing that not least among the Arabs' unexploited resources was the bitter anti-Irgun and anti-Zionist feeling existing in the British Army. In attempting to administer the Palestine Mandate, the British had, after all, found themselves, so soon after the defeat of the Nazis, bearing the brunt of the Irgun's pioneering terrorist tactics. Had irregular international forces been raised, as Azzam had suggested, there is no doubt that many British officers and other ranks would have joined the Arabs.

Another interesting aspect of things at the time was the sudden arrival on the scene of scores of international arms dealers. One of my tasks in the Arab League was the screening of the arms dealers who came to offer their wares. These were a colourful and interesting gang. They included Otto Skorzeny, the Nazi commando colonel who had rescued Mussolini after the Fascist collapse in Italy, and who now offered us an entire German U-boat with half its crew for one million dollars. There was also Pat Domville, a former chief of RAF intelligence in the Balkans. Domville was the son of an Admiral Domville, who had headed an Anglo-German friendship society at the beginning of the war.

Another member of this arms-dealing fraternity was an ex-Turkish ambassador, Lufty Satvet Tozan, a dapper and soberly dressed senior-citizen type. He considered himself to be an aristocrat in arms dealing. 'Adel Bey,' he would say, 'I am not interested in deals under one million pounds!' He had been Turkey's Ambassador in Sofia during the war, and had worked with Pat Domville in arming Michaelovitch and the Chetniks in Yugoslavia. The fortune he amassed from these deals had gone judiciously into purchasing shares in the Swiss armament firm of Oerlikon and the French Hotchkiss company. As an influential partner in these companies, Tozan enjoyed an impressive capability in delivering certain basic military goods. He lived quietly in an expensive villa over-looking the Lake of Geneva, where, between occasional forays into the arms market, he led an exemplary life within the norms of Swiss citizenship and precise Swiss habits.

And then there was the American, Harry Blank, married to a glamorous Tunisian singer, Hassiba Rushdi. This couple seemed to be truer-than-true versions of the kind of people you would expect to meet in a Bogart or Hitchcock movie. All these and others were a colourful band of professional, or sometimes occasional, arms dealers, embargo dodgers and get-rich-quickers, with the odd Israeli agent infiltrating the Arab systems. This type of adventurer has on the whole disappeared today, pushed out of business as clandestine arms dealers have been taken over by the CIA or other cover organizations which serve super-power interests.

The goods offered to us were varied, ranging from Skorzeny's submarine through Mulberry harbours to the immense array of war goods being peddled clandestinely by shady and hard-to-identify gentlemen. The stores themselves came from as far away as Japan and Korea, where the aftermath of war had left vast residual stock-piles, or, indeed, from closer to home, for substantial caches of equipment were to be found in Greece and its islands as relics of the war against Nazi Germany. Many of these had lain mouldering in the Mediterranean sunshine or sea-washed coves, and when some of this material, purchased in good faith by a hurried programme of arms acquisition, was found to be unservice-able and dangerous, it provoked accusations of corrupt arms dealings. Even the King was indirectly denounced and his Palace searched for evidence. None was ever found.

But when all was said and done, the 1948 war against Israel was lost through a combination of the ineptitude of Egyptian generalship, the unreliability of Arab allies and, of course, the betrayal of Arab kings. Farouk, as principal architect of the war, had to bear the brunt of recrimination. A cover-up, engineered in part by the incompetent army leadership, actively addressed accusations against His Majesty and Azzam Pasha. But had a serious preparation for war been made in time, the army would have had no difficulty in amassing sufficient ammunition and logistic stores to engage in a long campaign. As matters turned out, and partly because of the unwise wastage of ammunition and artillery shells on subsidiary and unimportant targets, the Egyptian forces ran out of ammunition on reaching Gaza at the very outset of the campaign and were forced to remain inactive at a crucial point in the advance while arms dealers of every kind were con-tacted frantically to supply the necessary stores. Meanwhile the Israelis had been given a valuable respite to build up their military storehouse, which they did with their usual efficiency and their proverbial capacity to mobilize friendly support all over the world.

The experience made Farouk acutely aware of the short-comings of his army, and so the reform and rebuilding of the forces became a key factor in his agenda. On the other hand, Heydar Pasha, the Minister of Defence, was busily eliminating those officers, such as Nasser and Anwar el Sadat, who had distinguished themselves in the war and who might have the ability to get through to the King with their criticism. This was done by the simple device of banishing them to garrisons remote from Cairo, or by a whispering campaign depicting them as dangerous political revolutionaries. When the challenge to Heydar did come, it was to originate from quite another quarter.

Heydar Pasha was no war leader and his career in no way fitted him for the task. He was chosen for his loyalty to the King, having at an earlier stage aborted what appeared to be an attempt on the King's life by charging the alleged assassin down with horse and sword. He imposed an over-centralized discipline on the forces and endeavoured to conduct the war from the comfort of his armchair in Kasr el Nil barracks. It was said, though it scarcely seems believable, that not even the artillery commanders could open fire on an advancing enemy without the authorization of a confirming phone call from Cairo. Post-conflict attempts to analyse the causes of defeat were frustrated by the energetic cover-up that endeavoured to lay all blame on the politicians.

Another factor for defeat was the serious deficiency in the army at staff level. The campaign strategy, as applied by the Heydar Pasha team, was apparently inspired by the nineteenth-century tactics of Egypt's wars in the Sudan. Competent leadership did exist in the shape of Aziz el Masry Pasha and others, but these were regarded as politically unreliable and were never consulted. There is little point in dwelling on the details of the humiliating negotiations with the Israelis in Rhodes. Proud Egypt had suffered disastrously at the hands of an amateur Jewish army. The defeat was doubly humiliating since the King had been completely misled by the braggadocio of the generals. His Majesty, expecting an easy occupation of Palestine by the Arab regulars, whose leaders had looked with scorn on what they considered to be bands of unprofessional amateurs, ill-equipped and scantily armed, was deeply shaken. Some action had to be taken.

Farouk was not the kind of personality to indulge in recrimination and accusation. He did not blame the Americans or the British for the defeat of his armies. He did not waste breath accusing his unreliable and tricky Arab allies. True to form, his pride, and possibly his concern for Egyptian grandeur, led him to accept in silence the post-defeat manoeuvres of many to lay the blame at his door. He was clearly aware that his protégé, Mohammed Heydar Pasha, was largely at fault, the army having had to call on another general, Sadek Pasha, to extricate its forces from encirclement by the Israelis. Farouk emerged from the conflict with a firm determination to engage in fundamental army reforms. The Heydar clique, he realized, would have to go, but before this could happen a secret programme and time-table for the necessary moves would have to be formulated. Above all, Heydar Pasha must be kept in the dark about His Majesty's intentions. This was going to be made particularly difficult in the light of the fact that Princess Fawzia's new husband, Ismail Shirine, was both a nephew of Heydar's and a dedicated lobbyist for him within the Palace. Quite naturally, Ismail Shirine could be expected to defend his uncle's interests.

It was these deliberations which hatched the scheme to bring General Artur Schmitt, formerly one of Rommel's commanding generals at the time of Auchinleck's 'Crusader' offensive in the desert, clandestinely from Germany to Egypt to act as a guiding spirit in the creation of a new Egyptian army. The concern for total secrecy had meanwhile brought Azzam Pasha into the picture. The Arab League was an organization quite distinct from the Egyptian government, and particularly from the Ministry of Foreign Affairs, while Azzam had himself become a target for the same accusations being levelled against the King. I was present at the highly interesting presentation of the political and military report that Azzam made verbally to His Majesty a few days after General Schmitt's arrival. Azzam began by rapidly reviewing the reasons for our defeat (this account being based on the notes I made for the King at the time):

We must all share the blame for misjudging the strength of the Jews and trusting too much in the power of our regular armies. After all, the latter were made up of professional soldiers and full-time officers. They should easily have been able to dispose of Israel's settler army. We were wrong. The Israelis were resourceful, fought well, were absolutely dedicated to their struggle. Of the Arab armies, only the Egyptian could be said to have really fought; the Jordanians abandoned the battlefield without warning and left a vacuum on our right flank which was exploited by the Jews, who succeeded in surrounding us at Faloudja. We tried to fight the war in a conventional manner and in the process frustrated the work of our irregular forces who had entered Palestine well before the regular army. We suffered the loss of one of our most competent officers, Colonel Ahmad Abd el Aziz, commander of our irregulars, who was in a position to invest Gaza before the arrival of the regular army. Cairo refused to allow him to do so, considering Gaza a prize for the regular army – another example of internal army intrigue. Abd el Aziz was killed by mistake, by an Egyptian sentry.

Other reasons for our failure can be situated in the command structure of the Arab armies as well as in catastrophic deficiences in the logistics sector. There was no unified command and no machinery existed whereby the full co-ordinated weight of the several Arab armies could have been thrown into battle. In effect, the political aims of component nations overruled the common loyalties. As far as the logistical preparation for war was concerned, it was virtually nil. Whereas the Israelis will have thrown some 70 per cent of their resources into their war effort, the Arabs did not even use 1 per cent. Had we mobilized a modest 10 per cent of our potential reserves, we could have had a modern army of a million men at our disposal and a commensurately powerful air force.

There is no reason to cry over spilt milk. We should now look ahead and formulate a new policy for Palestine, based on our experiences. Two basic requirements must be fulfilled. The first of these is to tighten the links between the various Arab states in such a manner that all armed forces come under a unified command which will be in charge of training, stores, logistics and, most important, battle. To achieve this we should seriously consider converting the League of Arab States into a large and unified Federal Arab State with a central parliament and a federal war cabinet.

As far as the armed forces are concerned, a major rebuilding job will be necessary. A completely modern, up-to-date army of *one million men* should be aimed for. It should be organized and trained in accordance with the latest experiences of war. Likewise, an air force of some 2,000 to 3,000 combat planes should be created. All of this is well within the range of our unified Arab resources. If we can succeed here, there will be no further need for war, and if a certain level of diplomacy was used and the Israelis were ready to accept the liberal and open proposals that we made at the United Nations in 1947, then we should be ready to invite them to join our federation.

In 1949, this was revolutionary talk. The fact of having access to first-class German officers who could be asked to design and train a model division was a positive factor, and Farouk here decided to set the ball rolling. Clearly he thought that if Egypt could start on the much-needed military reforms, then the army which would emerge would itself become an important binding factor between the Arabs.

The King was fully in accord with Azzam Pasha's views, and the latter was at pains to stress the danger which might emerge if such views were to surface prematurely. We could expect dangerous reactions from the Western powers, since we were working on a programme that would completely change the balance of power in the Mediterranean. It was therefore decided that a total security blanket be maintained over the whole issue and the presence of Schmitt in Cairo be kept hidden from the army, from the government, and, above all, from British and American intelligence. It had meanwhile fallen to me to be responsible for Schmitt.

21. Getting to Know the General

When General Leutnant Artur Wilhelm Schmitt arrived in Cairo on 11 July 1949, I was detailed to greet him at Cairo Airport. The King had advised Azzam that the general was to be received in the strictest secrecy and a total security blanket was to be applied. Not even Heydar Pasha was to be aware of his arrival or, indeed, of his existence. The only people in the know were Azzam Pasha, myself and the Egyptian Ambassador in Berne, who had issued him with false Egyptian papers. These latter had been drafted in the name of Goldestein, and it was as Herr Goldestein that General Schmitt arrived in Egypt. The general, needless to say, was unhappy with his pseudonym and felt we were carrying security beyond reasonable limits. The name was therefore soon changed to Müller.

I was not sure what to expect as I drove to the airport to receive him. Would he be a tall blond Nordic specimen of the type of whom Hitler used to approve? His descent from the aircraft went almost unnoticed. He did not, at first sight, look like anything we were expecting. He was, as I have already described him in the Prologue, short, stocky and strongly built, bullet-headed with close-cropped hair, practically no neck and fierce pale-blue eyes. I rushed him through the arrival formalities and we were soon speeding on our way to Cairo, where Azzam Pasha received us. The general booked into the Hotel Claridge, a modest establishment in the centre of town. We lost no time over starting the briefing session prior to his reception by the King.

The general's initial views were taken down. He saw himself as a modern version of the late General Colmar von der Goltz, who had been adviser to the Turkish Army in the First World War. He was offering his full services to Egypt and was ready

176

to adopt Egyptian nationality and wear a fez if necessary. In the German Army, no distinction existed between *Panzer* generals or infantry generals, the rank simply meaning that its holder was capable of conducting every type of warfare and fulfilling every type of function that might be required. A general is a specialist in command. Schmitt therefore saw his mission in Egypt not as adviser, but as a trainer of men to fight a modern war. The experiences of the *Wehrmacht* during the recent hostilities would be made available to the Egyptians and, when necessary, élite German specialist officers would be brought out to help in the task of forming an ultra-modern Egyptian army, organized on the basis of actual modern fighting experience. Secret German reports on weapons training, troop utilization and deployment would be made available. The potential anchor-man in Germany was Field Marshall Guderian, and Schmitt proposed that another general, General Speidel, be approached to take on the task of chief-of-staff of a training command. Speidel was subsequently to become Commander of NATO forces.

I reported the whole briefing to Farouk and His Majesty was clearly delighted with the general.

'At last,' he said to me, 'we will be doing something positive for the army. Tell the general,' he continued, 'that I fully support his viewpoints and am already studying the methods whereby we may put proposals on to a practical footing. I am inclined to believe that what we should do is create an experimental training unit, formed and structured in accordance with German experience, this unit to be under the direct command of General Schmitt. Once it is formed and trained, we should then pass regular army units through its training process and gradually reform the whole army. It will be a *Nizam Gedid*, and we will call it so . . .'

The King was, of course, alluding to the great reform of the forces in the days of his forebear Mohammed Ali. Then, too, the new army had been called the *Nizam Gedid* or 'New Order'.

This, in brief, was the general line of thinking and discussion that occurred between Schmitt and Farouk when they came to meet shortly afterwards. The general was impressed by the King's knowledge and grasp of the problems of the armed forces and by his genuine concern for the army. The principal point advanced by Schmitt was that there was really no need to replace by German methods the ordinary drill, marching order and so forth of the troops, which generally followed those of the British Army. The reforms should be of a rather broader character.

Modern practice tended towards an integrated formation in which armour, artillery and infantry assault forces were present on a battalion level. Thus a mixed formation should be aimed for, and could be initially organized on a brigade level. The existing structure should be discarded in favour of the mixed formation. The notions advanced by Heydar Pasha, who was thinking in terms of separate tank, infantry and artillery divisions, were in Schmitt's opinion, absurd and suggested an ignorance of fighting conditions. How, he asked, could an effective *Schwerpunktbildung* (concentration of forces) be achieved under such circumstances? Nothing should get in the way of the ability of a commander to throw maximum firepower on to a given breakthrough point. Divisional systems, like that suggested, could only hamper and weaken an attack.

The King, in conclusion, asked Schmitt to start work on his programme and offered every support and facility.

'What requests do you have, general?' he asked.

Schmitt replied, 'I have two requests. (a) I wish to study the Egyptian Army and would like to have access to the staff reports and the critique of the recent war, (b) I wish to have the right to select German officers and approve them. I do not want to have former members of SS formations collaborating with me. What the army needs most is a thorough training in the field under conditions close to those of war.'

An army fighting spirit like that which Clausewitz called *l'ésprit militaire* was essential, and what Schmitt had seen of Egyptian forces made him feel optimistic that this could be achieved. The men should have confidence in the leadership and abilities of their officers, and the officers should have confidence in the capacity of the High Command to lead.

There was no doubting the credentials of General-Lieutenant Artur Schmitt in this respect. He was the sort of officer who could only have been produced by the German military system, with its traditions and outlook completely intertwined with the spirit of Frederick the Great and Otto von Bismarck. A native of the Rhineland Palatinate, Schmitt had first seen service in the Royal Bavarian Lieb Regiment, the crack bodyguard of the Wittelsbach kings. Something of a young romantic, he transferred from this blue-blooded regiment to the Imperial German *Schütztruppe*, commanded at the time by the legendary General von Lettow Vorbeck. The *Schütztruppe* had been formed as the élite colonial force of the German Empire. It was an imperial body directly dependent on Berlin and taking its recruits from all over the great conglomerate of German kingdoms and petty principalities. Notwithstanding this, it flew the red, white and black Imperial Prussian standard.

Schmitt campaigned in Africa in a war lasting longer than the war in Europe and ending twelve days after the Armistice on 23 November 1918 with the surrender of an undefeated *Schütztruppe*. Back in Germany, he joined those elements of the German Army who fought the Communists in East Germany, this being followed by service in the 100,000-man Seeckt Army created post-Versailles. In 1936, Schmitt commanded the first German regiment to cross the Rhine bridges at demilitarized Cologne. 'Our troops came over without a round of ammunition among them,' he commented. 'Any Allied counter-move would have been followed by our humiliating withdrawal.'

With the outbreak of the Second World War, Schmitt found himself in command of the battle force detailed to occupy Strasburg and force the Maginot Line in that area. Sensing the French demoralization as a result of Dunkirk and the defeat of the Allied forces in Belgium and north-western France, Schmitt, with his ADC, two sergeants and two motor-bikes with side-cars, used bluff to take Strasburg by *coup de main*. This was achieved by the simple procedure of crossing the Rhine clandestinely in rubber boats and waylaying the first French dispatch rider encountered on the Strasburg highway. At gun-point, the latter was then made to precede the two German vehicles, with the general prominently visible in the first one, through the French lines and directly to the doors of the Hôtel de Ville at the city centre.

Here the surprised French colonel in charge suddenly found

himself confronting the new self-styled German Military Commander of Strasburg. Assuming the worst, he quickly obeyed orders and mobilized the Strasburg police cyclists to deliver an ultimatum to the various French fortresses and units so successfully bypassed. All this was done six hours before the German fighting forces were due to cross the river, and the whole operation took place without a single casualty, some 120,000 men being taken prisoner. For this feat of tactics, Schmitt received one of the highest German military decorations, the Iron Cross with oak leaves. The fall of Strasburg had an important bearing on subsequent events. The extreme eastern wing of the Maginot Line had been turned and German contingency plans to force a passage through Switzerland to attack those formidable defences from the flank and rear rendered unnecessary, thanks to Schmitt's *coup de main.*

'Operation Barbarossa', Hitler's Russian campaign, found Schmitt on the staff of Field Marshal von Kluge. He was in command of the logistics and support echelons of the Armies of the Central Front advancing on Moscow. Meanwhile a friend and fellow graduate of his cadet days, Marshal Erwin Rommel, had landed in Libya with the Afrika Korps, and a request was soon on the way for the transfer of Schmitt to the post of General Commanding Libya Military Zone, thus giving him an important supporting role in Rommel's drive on Egypt.

The defence of the Bardia-Solloum-Capuzzo position by Schmitt, operating from his HQ at Bardia, was undoubtedly the key operation that ultimately frustrated Auchinleck's 'Crusader' offensive and gave Rommel time to fall back on Benghazi without suffering the defeat of the Afrika Korps, as might well have occurred had the British been able to throw the full weight of their superior forces against the retreating Germans. No less than two army corps were engaged by the British in the battle, each one being the equivalent in numbers and fire-power to the whole of the Afrika Korps. Meanwhile reinforcements in tanks were flowing from the United States and the fighting saw the arrival on the field of the new American Stuart tanks.

This considerable force, representing roughly twice the firepower of the combined Italo-German forces, was delayed by the continuing resistance, astride the Egyptian frontiers, of General Schmitt's mixed force of Italians and Germans entrenched in the Bardia-Solloum-Capuzzo triangle. Commanding at Solloum was the valiant Major Bach, who emerged with far more publicity than Schmitt. Nevertheless Schmitt earned the *Ritterkreuz* (Knight's Cross to the Iron Cross) the highest German field decoration, for his rearguard stance designed to give Rommel a chance to fall back and re-form at Benghazi. Bardia fell after this was accomplished, and Schmitt, captured by the South Africans, was sent to Canada. There he made himself memorable to the Canadians as the successful German commander of the mutiny and take-over of the POW camp, Camp Bowmanville. Here, for a while at least, he successfully held down substantial units of Canadians.

Schmitt had ended the war a frustrated man. While still relatively young, he was captured by the enemy and, as a prisoner of war, obliged to spend the last two and a half years of war in Canada. When he did return to Germany, his political innocence was confirmed and he was soon discharged by the Allied authorities. But although he was no admirer of the Nazis, he was nevertheless unemployed and unemployable.

The conflict between Egypt and Israel, in which his sympathies lay with the Egyptians, was in the nature of a challenge to his adventurous spirit. In addition, the German Army had a long tradition of service with the Muslims. The great Field Marshal von Moltke had been an adviser to the armies of the Caliph in Istanbul in 1839. Later, Generals Colmar von der Goltz, Liman von Sanders and Kress von Kressenstein served and commanded Muslim armies during the First World War. Schmitt was therefore following in an honourable tradition when he offered his services personally to King Farouk. The King, likewise, was conforming to an old and effective practice. Mohammed Ali himself, as we saw, bore witness to the services rendered to Egypt by Farouk's ancestor, Suleyman Pasha the Frenchman.

Such was the background to the Schmitt mission to Egypt from 1949 to 1951, and such was the man who had offered his services to King Farouk.

22. Keeping the General Happy

Schmitt's initial view on the requirements of the Egyptian Army was that it should be highly mobile, enjoying the maximum autonomy in freedom of movement and manoeuvre. This called for a standardized and integrated mixed division. Artillery, tanks and mobile infantry in armoured personnel carriers should be trained into a single formation possessing a high degree of potential for interaction. An efficient logistics echelon, likewise highly mobile and capable of anti-aircraft and field defence, should be part of this division, which might be described as an updated evolution based on the German *Panzergrenadier* formation.

There would be available to us *Wehrmacht* reports on all aspects of organization, armament and training, and the lessons of the desert campaigns of the Afrika Korps as well as of the in-depth fighting on the Russian Front would be given to the organizers of this experimental force. Specially selected former *Wehrmacht* officers would be recruited as instructors to work jointly with specially selected Egyptian officers. It was understood that the role of the German instructors would be *strictly non-political,* since Germany in 1949 had no political ambitions or plans in the Middle East. It was, however, necessary to grant German instructors the authority to give orders and see they were obeyed. If any questions of Egyptian sovereignty were to arise, then the German instructors would be required to assume Egyptian nationality on a temporary basis. *In no way was the Bundesrepublik to be involved in this venture.* So far as German personnel were concerned, it was a private arrangement for which individual German officers were alone responsible.

The object of the exercise was to form an experimental

fighting division which, besides its professional potential, could be regarded as a *training unit*, capable of engaging in the military build-up of a new Arab army. It was therefore something in the nature of a highly technical modern and practical military college.

These were the broad lines of the agreement reached between General Schmitt and King Farouk, discussed and put into effect by the King's personal order to Schmitt. Schmitt's acceptance of his commission had meanwhile required the King's agreement to two points:

1. All German officers to be subject to screening by a selection committee jointly formed by Egyptian and senior German officers (the name of Field Marshal Guderian here being proposed by Schmitt), the final confirmation of an appointment to be done by General Schmitt himself.
2. Since, after every war, armies produce analytical and detailed reports on the reasons for victory or the causes of failure, Schmitt requested that he be given the report of the Egyptian Army on the causes of the 1948 defeat, together with copies of the main army orders issued by the High Command.

Farouk agreed, and said that this would be seen to, and a rough outline for the implementation of the military programme was also discussed. Azzam Pasha was of the opinion that a suitably remote site in the Western Desert should be prepared to accommodate the division. This would need to be totally isolated from the Nile Valley and the Delta, and the Farafra, Dakhla and Kharga oases should be evaluated as the most likely areas for the project. Here selected men from the regular army, representing the different arms divisions, would be formed on a regimental or battalion basis as a preliminary sub-unit to serve as the foundation for the divisional structure. These were, of course, the days before satellite surveillance, and it was felt that, given reasonable precautions, the first division could be created in the minimum time-scale with the maximum security. Politically it was felt that, despite the objections to the scheme that could be anticipated in Washington, once the plans had reached an advanced state of development, the *fait accompli* would be accepted.

The most major problem to emerge was Heydar Pasha himself, Azzam arguing that since, after all, he carried the responsibility for the defeat of 1948, he could hardly be expected to collaborate with a foreign officer whose initial job was to investigate his conduct of operations. The King said that he understood this situation and promised that Heydar Pasha would be removed.

There now followed several months of hesitation, during which Farouk seems to have lacked the necessary decisiveness. In the end, he was to ask Schmitt to work along with Heydar – a decision that might with justice be described as one of the most disastrous ever taken by His Majesty since it ultimately cost him his throne.

It now came about that the need to implement the agreement meant that the security cordon around Schmitt must be lifted to allow Heydar Pasha to be informed so that he could in turn co-operate with the German. Needless to say, the revelation shook Heydar to the core. The request to study the causes of the 1948 defeat alarmed him even more, for, in effect, no report had been made and Heydar was engaged in his campaign to put the responsibility for failure on to the shoulders of Farouk and Azzam. Heydar therefore tried to politicize the whole affair and claimed that bringing in Schmitt was a plot by Azzam to intrigue against him. It had of course nothing to do with a genuine desire to reform the army. A campaign of this kind of denigration was launched and supported by Farouk's enemies. The media, to whom Heydar had access, was also quite willing to play along. The King was accused of betraying the army by being involved in the purchase of condemned military stores, of being totally uninterested in the welfare of his troops, of going to night-clubs and amusing himself when men were dying. Indeed, a whole mythology against Farouk was created at this time, and it still survives in the memory of the public despite the fact that legal inquiries into these supposed crimes, both in Farouk's reign and under Nasser, exonerated His Majesty completely.

It was becoming quite clear that, so long as Heydar remained Commander-in-Chief of the Armed Forces, no serious reform of the army could be expected. I urgently requested a meeting with the King, who asked me to come to Montazah Palace.

He said: 'I know the situation. Tell Schmitt to be patient. Heydar will be dismissed soon. Meanwhile, Adel, you keep Schmitt happy.'

This keeping the general happy was going to be quite a job. In consultation with Azzam Pasha, two programmes were decided on. We would first ask Schmitt to conduct a military survey of Egypt's western frontiers with Libya, to be used as a basic study paper on behalf of Egypt's western defences. This paper would be for the reference of the Egyptian delegation at the United Nations in the debate over Libyan independence. Since Schmitt had commanded Afrika Korps and Italian forces on the western Egyptian frontier in 1942, he was possibly the best qualified expert on the subject. Secondly, we would ask him to conduct a survey of the Syrian/Israeli front on the Golan Heights and prepare a military evaluation of the situation.

For the 'western approaches' study, our itinerary was Alexandria, Alamein, Mersa Matruh, Halfaya Pass and Solloum, finishing at Siwa Oasis. The army gave us a Chevrolet pick-up, and I took along my Dodge weapons carrier FWD super-Jeep, which carried radio equipment and generators. We had two drivers, an army man and Ismail, a tough Circassian jack-of-all-trades with a particular penchant for motor cars and mechanical and electronic machinery. Azzam had also landed us with six Libyans who had been part of the Arab League irregular forces fighting in Palestine and needed to get home. These had no papers, had left Libya clandestinely, and of necessity must be sent back clandestinely.

With the brisk setting out of our convoy that day in April 1950, General Schmitt was at last in his element. Binoculars at the ready, clipboard in hand, he diligently noted the terrain we followed in relation to its tactical character. Our crew of mixed Libyans, Circassians and Egyptians complained bitterly at the general's regime: no drinking, no stopping till sundown, and a tablet of salt for lunch. The drivers would dearly have liked a sweet cup of Turkish coffee at one of the few wayside inns, and were very unhappy. Luckily, we had no salt with us, and thereby avoided what would certainly have been a rather grim culinary experience. It was an uneventful journey until we were past Mersa Matruh.

To unload our Libyans, we used the famous Halfaya Pass to lead us to the Libyan border, represented by a ruined barbed-wire fence. Our friends crossed safely and were quickly on their way, and so we turned back down the pass, which was a narrow track through unswept minefields. In the distance, we could see the ruined hulks of burned-out tanks, still inaccessible and very likely still containing the remnants of their crews. We entered Solloum by the main road, and were enchanted by the picturesque little fishing village nestling at the foot of the high Libyan escarpment overlooking the Bay of Solloum. Solloum was then something of a centre for sponge-diving, and was regularly visited by Greek sponge boats.

At Solloum we were received by the colonel commanding the small frontier force there, who had received no notification of our imminent arrival and was furthermore highly perturbed by General Schmitt's intimate knowledge of the strategic features of the area. We were placed under veiled arrest, mainly in the officers' mess, where we were given lunch while frantic telephone contact was made with the Mersa Matruh command. We were then released after a motor tour of the frontier, and were soon on our way to Siwa.

Travelling in the desert with General Schmitt was never less than an interesting experience. As we passed through thick scrub on the track to Siwa Oasis, the general waxed enthusiastic.

'Fine ground for a holding defence [*hinhaltungs der wieder-stand*],' he commented. 'This scrub makes an efficient cover for heavy-machine-gun positions. Elite troops could hold up an army here. Of course, they should be intensively trained and enjoy "climate compatibility". Here, indeed, the Egyptian soldier should excel.'

We had further back passed an army camp where troops were being drilled under the blazing sun.

'Mr Sabit,' said the general, 'this is British-style drilling, not so rigid as ours, but good. Since your army uses British forms, these should not be changed.'

Siwa, where we spent two uneventful days, is something of a paradise on earth: a lovely, luxuriant oasis of palm, olive and fig trees. A large clear pool, whose waters bubble up from below ground, is supposed to be cool at noon and warm at midnight. Fruits fall from trees, figs and dates dropping at your feet, and the population is of an incomparable gentleness, probably because of the high incidence of homosexuality that prevails. The general, unaware of this phenomenon, bestowed salutations as he went along, and was surprised when told that the nubile young Siwan who followed us wherever we went, and to whom the general had directed his Bavarian nobleman's greetings in the form of sideways hand gestures popular with the Wittlesbach nobility, was offering an intimate relationship.

'Mr Sabit,' declared the general. 'We call these people breech-loaders.'

When, in the following month, it came to our second venture, to attempt a military assessment of the Golan Heights from the Syrian side, we travelled first to Beirut on the American liner *Excambion*, an air-conditioned ship that possessed possibly the most complete menu of any vessel afloat. Precooked refrigerated culinary masterpieces awaited us in the enormous deep freezes of its hull. Meals by Maxim's of Paris, the products of the world's most prestigious restaurants, were there for the asking, suspended in time by arctic temperatures. Lobster thermidor and *turbot braise à la Maurice Chevalier* from France, braised lamb *hazar pasand* from India, *tagliatelli verdi alla Genovese* from Italy and the delicious boned-duck *Ba bao ya* of Nanking, China; all these and many more exotic dishes were available on this remarkable ship.

Yet when we landed in Beirut we heard disturbing news. A young Egyptian assassin, Hussein Tewfik, had tried to murder the Syrian dictator, General Shishekly, two days before, thereby provoking a major crisis in Damascus. Rumours were abroad that Azzam Pasha had been behind the assassination attempt. The moment we arrived in the Syrian capital, I realized that a state of acute crisis prevailed and decided to park my general in a relatively inexpensive hotel, the Regent, where he might pass for an inoffensive German journalist. I myself went to the Orient Palace Hotel, the scene of various crimes, including the murder of a Colonel Stirling some months previously. This hotel was the top establishment in

Damascus at the time, though it catered for a colourful and rather dangerous clientele. As I arrived I was instantly identified by a Syrian police informer, who had worked in the Arab League in Cairo, as Azzam Pasha's right-hand man. Two police agents were detailed on the spot to follow me around.

Then as I was going up to my room, I ran into the British legal counsellor in Cairo, Mr Besly, who knew me well and greeted me warmly. Besly was, of course, regarded as something big in M15 by the suspicious Syrians. A fresh blow fell when I was informed that General Shishekly had taken refuge in the Presidential Palace and was seeing nobody. He had surrounded himself with the entire armoured might of the Syrian Army. The Prime Minister, Nazim Kudsy, likewise, had disappeared from view, though nobody knew where. All of this left me as a man marked by the Syrian Intelligence Service, apparently consorting with suspicious Germans, hobnobbing with British agents and sent by Azzam Pasha on some possibly desperate but unidentifiable mission. Unless I managed to deliver Azzam's two letters, one to Shishekly and the other to Mr Kudsy, I could find myself in deep trouble.

They ransacked my room while I was having lunch next day, but naturally found nothing since I was carrying my papers on my person. It must, however, have deepened the appearance of suspicions against me when I accidentally discovered that the Prime Minister was on the third floor of the hotel, surrounded by bodyguards. So, immediately after lunch, I went to the third floor, where, by some miracle, the guards had all gone off duty to eat, leaving just one elderly seedy-looking policeman to doze outside the Premier's door. I rang the bell to his suite and an attractive nurse came out. I told her I had a letter from Azzam for Mr Kudsy and gave it to her. She sat me down in the salon to the apartment and went in to the Prime Minister. A few minutes later she re-emerged and led me to the Prime Minister's bedroom, which I entered to discover Mr Kudsy trembling with terror.

'Who are you? I don't know you!' he bawled out in a high-pitched voice.

He obviously thought I was about to liquidate him. Since I was untypical for an Arab, and could easily have passed for a European killer, this was perhaps natural, but such niceties were far from my mind. I just felt angry that Azzam Pasha's courier should be treated in this manner, and showed it. Kudsy regained his aplomb when he saw that I was not about to murder him and said, 'Sit down. What's all this! Is Azzam mad to send a German general at this time to inspect the front? You want Shishekly. You'll need to break into him. But take my advice and get out of Damascus as quickly as possible – it's dangerous here.'

I returned to the general at the Regent Hotel and briefed him. 'Mr Sabit,' he said, 'we are not here to indulge in adventures. We should leave.'

There was, unfortunately, no way of leaving the country before the next morning. I braced myself to spend a second night at the Orient Palace, knowing the secret police were bound to have another and more determined go at getting my papers. I therefore went to my room early. At nine o'clock there came a knock on the door. The young lady was very beautiful: lovely black hair cascaded down her back and she wore an unmistakable Parisian dress of green velvet corduroy. Her necklace could only have come from Cartier.

'Can I help you?' she asked.

'How?' I said.

'I am the night maid.'

Hard as it may seem, I had very reluctantly to refuse her services. The tension was building up, I felt. Should I fall asleep, they would break in and try to steal my papers. And since they had a reputation for killing people 'by mistake' and apologizing later, I decided sleep would be unwise. I would therefore carry the challenge to the enemy. The night indeed passed sleeplessly as I left my door partly open with the screen hiding me from outside and all the lights full on. That way they would probably think I was armed and waiting. All night long I heard an impatient coming and going outside my door as they wondered if I could be a dangerous, expert killer.

By daybreak I had survived the night, the Syrian intelligence people having decided that discretion was the better part of valour some time around dawn. I collected General Schmitt and we headed for Beirut, where we spent the rest of the day in the King David Hotel swimming pool, luxuriating beneath the blue Mediterranean sky.

These two adventures kept Schmitt happy for a while, though the general's happiness was destined to be short-lived. We continued to send messages to Farouk, who continued to counsel patience. In the meantime, we had been increasingly witnessing Farouk's inability to fulfil the wishes of his new German general. Repeated requests to see the staff report on the recent war had continued to go unanswered, Heydar Pasha being understandably more interested in a cover-up operation to prevent any critical analysis of his own capacities or those of his officers. In fact, and possibly most damningly, no such report existed for the same reasons. The pressures applied by the King had earlier in the year prompted a visit from one of Heydar's officers, Colonel Hamdy Heyba, who was detailed to explain the war to Schmitt. Since Heyba had been away as a military attaché in Washington at the time of the conflict, his account in no way satisfied the needs of the German officer, who was, moreover, surprised and a little mystified by Heyba's attempts to lecture him on warfare in general.

'Mr Sabit,' he had said at the time, 'I cannot understand the colonel. Does he take me for a raw recruit from the country-side? I do not need persons to deliver elementary military platitudes to me. I wish to study and evaluate Egyptian general staff strategy with regard to the 1948 war, the methods of the transmission of orders, the orders themselves, the manner in which officers at all levels interpret such orders, and the degree of personal initiative and decision that is encouraged. In my opinion, these matters and the training of troops are the decisive factors of warfare, far more important than the obtention of weapons.'

It seemed obvious that the gap between Heydar and Schmitt was fated to remain unbridgeable and that the King, despite every effort, was increasingly facing the operation of a palace clique headed by Heydar Pasha. The day eventually came, in June 1950, when instructions arrived from the Palace that we should now go to see Heydar Pasha, who had finally agreed, on the King's insistence, to meet Schmitt and assist him with his task. I escorted the general to Heydar's office in the former British barracks of Kasr el Nil, the site today of the Nile Hilton Hotel. Heydar discourteously received Schmitt sitting down behind his desk. Though he was well able to speak English, and would have had no difficulty in engaging in direct conversation, he preferred to speak Arabic and leave me to interpret.

'Ask him what he wants . . . An office? All right, this will be provided! We will give him the wheel-house of the Nile steamer anchored outside Kasr el Nil. An officer? Lieutenant-Colonel Mustapha will be placed at his disposal. Here he is, talk to him.'

Thus were we summarily dismissed from Heydar's presence. Clearly His Majesty's wishes were being applied with the maximum bad grace and the minimum courtesy.

Next morning, at nine o'clock promptly, Schmitt arrived at his makeshift office in the wheel-house of one of those old Nile steamers which had, in their youth, carried General Wolseley's expedition to relieve Gordon at Khartoum. The accommodation was, to say the least, picturesque if rather sketchy. But Schmitt took his new office in good grace.

'Mr Sabit,' he said, 'these offices are certainly more luxurious than the headquarters we occupied in the Gazala battles in the desert. A general must be ready to work effectively under any conditions. We must thank General Heydar for his hospitality. But where is my new *Einz A*?' he asked, referring to the 'chief assistant' officer, Colonel Mustapha, who had been assigned to him and who had not yet arrived. 'Mr Sabit, this is very grave. The least an officer can do is arrive on time. He should be there before the general.'

But no! The minutes passed and still no colonel. At 9.15 precisely the general stood up and said, 'I will not wait any longer.'

We disembarked from our steamer and marched out to our waiting car. Just then Colonel Mustapha arrived and stepped hastily from his car, full of apologies. 'I had two punctures on the way,' he explained.

The general turned to him with a smile. 'I am very sorry, colonel. In the German Army there is no excuse valid for an officer. I regret I shall have to report you to your commanding officer! And now, please excuse me. I must go.'

This exchange precipitated a classic example of palace intrigue at work. Later in the day I received an excited phone call from Ismail Shirine, who said, 'Your general has insulted the Egyptian Army. The King is angry and tells me to tell you to deliver the general to my office, since I shall take him over. But first I would like him to send me his *curriculum vitae* since we understand he is only a supply general, and I shall want to know more about him before I make any decisions.'

I decided to go to see Ismail, because clearly any requests along these lines would, if presented to Schmitt, cause him to abort his Egyptian plans and return to Germany. The general, for his part, had meanwhile decided that Heydar was an intractable opponent and that there was really no future in carrying on conversations with him, his staff or members of his family. Henceforth, he said, he would deal with His Majesty directly. He had given the King his word and had received His Majesty's personal guarantee.

My own interview with Ismail was inconclusive. He expressed 'shock' at Schmitt's insulting attitudes and went on to warn me that the army would not tolerate direct or indirect criticisms of their much-loved Commander-in-Chief, Heydar Pasha. 'After all, I understand he is merely a supply general. If we found him useful we would be willing to take him on as some sort of adviser, but there is no question of giving him the right to command Egyptian forces, even for training purposes. If the King insists on supporting him, then he must expect consequences within the armed forces.'

As a result of these events, in July 1950 Schmitt drafted a letter of resignation to the King. Since it makes interesting and somewhat prophetic reading, I give the draft in full, transcribed from Schmitt's own handwriting and preserving his rather idiosyncratic English, in Appendix One (page 220). The King's response was still to advise patience. His Majesty was intending to dismiss Heydar Pasha in the near future and we should wait.

Azzam Pasha himself endorsed the advice, and the wait lasted nearly a further year until an event occurred that finally made Schmitt decide he should leave. One morning I received a call from the Ministry of Defence. The Minister, Nosrat Pasha, wished to see the general, so could he present himself at the Ministry next day at nine o'clock. We duly arrived at the Ministry of Defence next morning at nine, to be ushered into the office of the Minister's bureau chief, a plump colonel of infantry. The colonel gazed at Schmitt with surprise, until suddenly it dawned on him that there had been a mistake. 'No,' said he, 'not this one. We expect the other one.'

I at once engaged in an investigation and discovered what could only be seen as the ultimate betrayal. Unbeknown to the King, and behind our backs, the American CIA had been approached with a request for a 'German general' – in fact, already on the scene in the person of General Farmbacher, who had been, as the last German Commander of the French port of Brest, taken prisoner by the Americans after D-Day. Farmbacher's role was to provide the Heydar clique with a counter to Schmitt so that they could confront the King with an alternative and more convenient officer.

Faced with this fresh contingency, we were obliged to review our own position. CIA involvement meant that the Israelis were now in the picture and that all our painstaking and effective security arrangements had been blown and the secret made known to the enemy by the actual leaders of Farouk's army.[*] The ultimate victim in all of this was to be Farouk himself, since his regime could scarcely be expected to survive when betrayal and treachery on this scale was being practised in the highest echelons.

Schmitt packed his bags, and within the week left Egypt, on 5 June 1951, a little over a year before the Nasser revolution broke out on 22 July 1952 and precipitated Farouk's abdication four days later. The general's departure could well be regarded as the end to any hopes the regime might have had of forestalling a military rebellion. It could also be seen as marking the beginning of the closing chapter of King Farouk's reign.

---

[*]Indeed, it later emerged that the 'deal' had been done with General Gehlen through a CIA agent, Pat Eichelberger, the collaboration of Mossad, the Israeli intelligence agency, being an informed assumption. The relations of Mossad with the Gehlen organization, which in due course became the official West German intelligence service, have been well-publicized. Not only did Israeli agents penetrate the Gehlen organization, but Gehlen himself was a willing accomplice. See further, Richard Deacon, *The Israeli Secret Service*, Hamish Hamilton, London, 1977.

23. The Free Officers and the American Connection

It was in April 1947, when I was in New York, that Azzam Pasha called me to say, 'I am sending you a young American, Kermit Roosevelt. He's going to Cairo and would like to meet people there. Could you give him some introductions?' I therefore provided Kermit with letters to several friends, among them the Princess Faiza and her husband, Bulent Mohammed Ali Rauf. Presumably this set off a process that would nearly five years later make Kermit Roosevelt a so-called sponsor of the Egyptian revolution.

In 1962, Andrew Tully published his book, *Central Intelligence Agency: The Inside Story*, evidently with official blessing since I was sent a copy with the compliments of the US Embassy. According to Tully, 'CIA assisted in the ousting of King Farouk and then found itself forced to deal with a vain, power-hungry and unpredictable ruler named Nasser.'[*] Tully's account, however, needs to be looked at alongside that given by the former CIA director Miles Copeland in his 1969 book, *The Game of Nations*. Copeland tells us that Kermit Roosevelt had, in fact, been in close contact with King Farouk during the war years to encourage him to feel he could rely on American backing for a post-war Egypt free from British domination. Kermit then returned to Cairo in January 1952, just six months before the Free Officers' rebellion, with a brief to promote a ' "peaceful revolution" project', under the monarchy.[†]

---

[*] Andrew Tully, *Central Intelligence Agency: The Inside Story*, Arthur Barker, London, 1962, p. 102.
[†] Miles Copeland, *The Game of Nations*, Weidenfeld & Nicolson, London, 1969, pp. 51–2.

Tully concludes that it was probably about the time of the riots in Cairo in January 1952 that 'the United States and Great Britain decided that Farouk would have to go'.* On the other hand, Copeland tells us that it was not till May that Roosevelt 'threw up his hands' in despair at Farouk's inability to stick to the point or resist being side-tracked into irrelevant schemes and counter-plots, 'and agreed with the assessment of the then American Ambassador in Cairo, Jefferson Caffery: that only the Army could cope with the deteriorating situation and establish a government with whom the Western powers could talk sense'.† Once the *coup* had taken place, says Copeland, 'Roosevelt and members of his special committee refrained from any direct contact with Nasser and were content to watch developments in Egypt from afar. This was partly to avoid any suggestion of connivance, and partly because things were moving smoothly along predicted and approved paths.'‡

If we are to give credence to these accounts, then we may justifiably conclude that a level of collusion did indeed exist between US intelligence officials and the Free Officers. As Tully clearly states:

> Nasser . . . made no move until he had consulted people he considered more expert on such things as military *coups*. This was CIA, which had sent a number of skilled operatives to Cairo to keep a close watch on the weakening Farouk regime. Among these operatives were former Army intelligence officers who had spent most of their careers in the Middle East and with whom Nasser felt at home . . . CIA gave the word late in July 1952, and Nasser's Free Officers' Corps swung into action.§

Relying purely on American reports and published information still leaves the motivations obscure. The reasonable inference, however, is that the American objective was to end the Palestine hostilities through a peace between Egypt and

* Tully, op. cit., p. 104.
† Copeland, op. cit., p. 52.
‡ Ibid., p. 63.
§ Tully, op. cit., p. 107.

Israel at the same time as frustrating any plans Egypt may have had to launch a second war. Farouk's dedication to the Palestinian cause, and, as we shall see, his refusal to be bribed, represented an insurmountable obstacle to any such approach. The elimination of Farouk thus became a logical conclusion against which the American position seems clear and understandable. The fact that the palace clique and the Heydar Pasha team were successful in preventing Farouk from developing any personal contact with the younger officers of the army, so promoting within the officer community resentment and hostility at the King's aloofness, offered the US State Department a situation ripe for exploitation.

In this respect, the role of an intelligent young journalist, Hassanein Heykel, trained at the American University in Cairo and an ex-employee of the US Embassy Press Section in Cairo, takes on a special significance. Miles Copeland states plainly that Bill Lakeland, the US Embassy's senior political officer, 'first became friendly with Nasser's Free Officers through Mohammed Hassanein Heykel'.[*]Heykel then supposedly played a prominent part as a link between the Americans and the Egyptian officers in the months leading up to the abdication. Had the various spy trials that became a feature of the Nasser era known their equivalent during Farouk's reign, then Heykel and his associates could well have received, over and above the consequences of accusations of high treason against the monarchy, life sentences for exchanging intelligence with the enemy and plotting revolution in collusion with a foreign power closely associated with Israel.

An interesting aside here concerns the death, already mentioned, of one of the original founders of the Free Officers' movement, Colonel Ahmad Abd el Aziz, who was killed by an Egyptian sentry in Palestine in an obscure shooting accident. The colonel was a charismatic and exceptionally courageous commander who, shortly before his death, commanded irregular army units that penetrated into Palestine before the end of the British Mandate and were, by the outbreak of the 1948 war, poised to invest Gaza well before the bulk of the main army. Had he survived, the army movement could well

[*] Copeland, op. cit., p. 63.

have taken a different form and the *coup d'état* been averted. He would certainly have scorned any collaboration with the Americans, though, most important in this context, he was highly critical of Heydar Pasha's conduct of the war. To this day, there are those in Egypt who believe that it was murder rather than accident that caused Colonel Abd el Aziz's death. There is no denying that a remarkable amount of cover-up was applied to many incidents preceding the abdication. Future historians may well find themselves constructing an interesting new account of these remarkable events.

As we have seen, for their own good reason the Americans decided early in 1952 that they must do something about Farouk. Kermit Roosevelt was sent to Cairo in January 1952 by Allen Dulles on orders from General Bedell Smith. Roosevelt, according to Copeland's claim, began by working with Farouk for a 'peaceful revolution', but this, in any language, has the look of a curious objective. To come to Cairo in the first place presupposes some sort of motivation, and to do so in company with others who include such CIA operatives as Miles Copeland and Pat Eichelberger makes the whole enterprise begin to look suspiciously like the arrival of a CIA 'hit team'.

These facts on their own tend naturally towards confirming the writings of Copeland, Tully and, more recently, John Ranelagh, whose *The Agency: The Rise and Fall of the CIA* was described by the *Washington Times* as 'the most objective history and assessment of the CIA we shall have by a non-professional'; and by the *Boston Globe* as the 'fairest and most reliable history of the CIA that has been published'. Kermit Roosevelt is revealingly quoted by Mr Ranelagh as saying, apropos of his active involvement in Iran, where he helped to unseat Dr Mosaddeq in 1953, 'this operation succeeded because people, but most of all the army, wanted the same thing we did and therefore it was something that could be done by clandestine means . . . and I said, if you don't want something that the people and the army want, don't give it to clandestine operations, give it to the marines'.*

* John Ranelagh, *The Agency: The Rise and Fall of the CIA*, Hodder & Stoughton, London, 1988, p. 264.

In Egypt, the Free Officers wanted very positively to get rid of Farouk, and therefore 'clandestine operations' could be expected to be the order of the day; as Ranelagh confirms, Nasser had the backing of the CIA in attaining power:

Kermit Roosevelt had advised and funded the *coup* leaders in secret and against the British policy of trying to make the monarchy of King Farouk work. To the Dulles brothers, however, British attempts to hold on to colonial prototypes were more than an invitation to communist nationalists: they were a directive to them.*

If we want to read colourful accounts of 'Roosevelt's Egyptian exploits', Mr Ranelagh suggests we consult Miles Copeland's *The Game of Nations* and *The Real Spy World*, as well as Wilbur Crane Eveland's *Ropes of Sand* for a more detailed account of the role of the CIA in Egypt in the early 1950s.†

Eveland, says Ranelagh, while 'acknowledging CIA involvement, . . . wryly recalled Kermit Roosevelt's modesty on the subject'. Another matter of some importance that seems to invite further investigation and clarification is an allegation that the CIA made a gift of $12 million to the Free Officers. If such money was indeed offered by a clandestine operations organization, then this must in turn presuppose a political motivation going well beyond normal international exchanges. According to Ranelagh:

In a gesture of defiance, Nasser used CIA money – reputedly part of the $12 million given to his colleague General Naguib who had been co-leader of the *coup* against Farouk – to build the Cairo Tower, known privately to Nasser and his friends as the 'CIA monument' and 'Roosevelt's erection' after Kermit Roosevelt's efforts in Egypt. Bribery on a

* Ranelagh, op. cit., p. 297.
† Miles Copeland, op.cit. pp. 62–4; *The Real Spy World* Sphere, London, 1978, pp. 60–64; Wilbur Crane Eveland, *Ropes of Sand*, W.W. Norton, New York, 1980, pp. 95–105.

massive scale had been a hallmark of the CIA in the Middle East.*

On the face of it, the operation with regard to Farouk seems to have been carried out with ambiguous motivations. It looks as if Roosevelt was unconvinced at the outset of the usefulness of what he proposed to undertake. The decision to work with Nasser and against Farouk was likewise curious, revealing an unusual flexibility of thinking in that Roosevelt was at one moment presumably working to protect and maintain Farouk, but at the next working to get rid of him – surely a capricious way of conducting a political action that was likely, by its very nature, to cost lives.

Another aspect to reflect on is the seemingly rather loosely kept secret that the British were informed of how the Americans were working with the officers against Farouk. It was Julian Amery who told me in London that Pat Domville, a former RAF intelligence officer, had seen him in London before the *coup* to advise him of this fact, but that when the message was passed to Anthony Eden, the Foreign Secretary replied, 'Our information is that the army officers are all loyal to the King.' Pat Domville's source was most probably among the Free Officers, and we do not need to look too far for an Egyptian motive. In seeking to advise the British of American involvement on their side, the officers would have been guarding against any movements of British forces to Cairo from the Canal Zone. Hence the implication is clear that the British knew about the CIA move against Farouk well before the abdication.

Yet another question that comes to mind concerns Heydar Pasha's request for a German general. Again in London, I was informed by a former member of the Kermit Roosevelt 'hit team' that General Farmbacher had been brought to Egypt by James H. Critchfield, a CIA operative in Germany. Here, as well, the pieces of the puzzle fit together snugly, for the request for a German general must have been passed to General Gehlen, former chief of Wehrmacht Intelligence, who was,

†Ranelagh, op. cit., p. 301

according to Ranelagh,* installed as early as 1949 as head of the German Federal Government's intelligence service, the BND (Bundesnachrichtendienst), at his base at Pullich, outside Munich. From here he was working closely with the Americans, a CIA office also being based at Pullich and headed at the time by Critchfield. Gehlen, moreover, had well-established links with the Israeli intelligence services, as his much-publicized role in helping to plant in Cairo the Israeli spy, Wolfgang Lotz, bears witness.†

There are therefore various sets of questions still demanding answers in this whole affair, most especially from the US government, and these may be summarized as follows:

1. When and how did the Americans discover the presence of Farouk's General Schmitt in Egypt? Does the United States continue to disclaim involvement in recruiting General Farmbacher?
2. If involvement is now admitted, how and through whom was the request for an alternative German general made and subsequently processed? What was the US rationale behind complying with the request? Was General Farmbacher perceived simply as an adviser, or did he act more positively as a US/Israeli agent? (Gehlen, of course, is especially suspect here, in the light of his known contribution to the Lotz spy affair.)
3. What was the background to the decision by Bedell Smith and Allen Dulles to promote revolution against Farouk? Did such a directive originate at a very high level? What, in any case, were the reasoned motivations behind the decision to send Kermit Roosevelt to Cairo and what were his precise instructions? Following on from this, what role and what activities in the field of anti-Farouk operations were fulfilled by Ambassador Caffery at the US Embassy?
4. What was the timetable for Kermit Roosevelt's activities in Cairo? Did a rumoured meeting between him and Nasser in

*Ranelagh, op. cit., p. 770, n. 54.
†For further information on Mossad infiltration of the Gehlen organization, as well as Gehlen's complicity with the Israelis, see Deacon, *The Israeli Secret Service*, op. cit., pp. 141ff.

Cyprus (which sounds unlikely) ever take place? To what extent was there co-ordination between the CIA team and the Egyptians, and what finance, if any, was made available to Naguib before the *coup*? What were the circumstances and reasoning behind a gift of $12 million to the Free Officers, if it indeed existed?

Approaching forty years have passed since these events and it has become a duty, from the viewpoint of historic truth, to seek to present the unvarnished facts. The time has come when the door should finally be closed on exaggerations and unwarranted conclusions by releasing accurate, factual information. My purpose here is to raise the questions in the hope that future researchers will benefit.

In the present state of our knowledge, the question of who manipulated whom remains unanswered, but it would be wrong to jump to the conclusion that the CIA played any really effective role in the Egyptian revolution. The army takeover was essentially an Egyptian affair, and in no way did Roosevelt's activities influence the outcome against Farouk. The whole CIA venture may best be seen as representing an interesting game of political judo. Kermit Roosevelt and his associates were attractive young amateurs whose sense of adventure, supported by the enormous resources of the United States, provided them with a prestige and reputation that far overshadowed their actual effectiveness. Miles Copeland, in his curious book *The Game of Nations*, demonstrates clearly the degree of self-delusion that may be generated in these circumstances. One gains the impression from his account that it was the CIA that masterminded the revolution against Farouk; that a startling degree of intimacy had developed between Nasser and the CIA operatives; that the British, those old hands at Middle East affairs, found themselves outgunned, and so forth.

It seems far more convincing to suggest that the Free Officers applied, with resounding success, a policy directive first used by Farouk, namely, playing off the Americans against the British. In planning the *coup*, one major problem needed to be faced. This was the presence of a considerable British force in the Canal Zone, a bare hour away from Cairo.

201

It is rumoured that late in 1951 Farouk made an approach to the British through his new Chief of Cabinet, the Anglophile Hafiz Afifi Pasha, to seek assurances of British intervention in the event of trouble in Cairo. This move was thought to have been followed, in turn, by a meeting in Paris, on Farouk's instructions, between the Egyptian Ambassador Abd el Fattah Amr Pasha (formally withdrawn from London on Egyptian protest) and Anthony Eden. Such a sequence of events would have obliged the Free Officers to see a British intervention in the event of a *coup* as a real possibility. Thus the only way of blocking a British move was to use the Americans. Kermit Roosevelt's presence and Ambassador Caffery's vouched-for ambition to achieve peace between Egypt and Israel represented factors that could be positively mobilized against the King. This, apparently, was what happened, and it is only possible to admire the skill with which the young and inexperienced army officers were able to outflank the veteran diplomats of a superpower; as may be deduced from the fact that they fully achieved their objectives but in exchange gave nothing.

One of the most prominent Egyptian officers of the time was Wing Commander Ali Sabry, chief of Egyptian Air Force Intelligence. In answer to the questions I put to him, Sabry had this to say: 'It would not have been possible for the Free Officers to have any dealings with the CIA because we considered that the Americans were on the side of the King. Whatever contacts existed were mainly of a social nature, and naturally the Americans were interested in the events taking place in Egypt. For my part, I enjoyed good social relations with them, not only through being Chief of Air Force Intelligence but also from having taken advanced courses in the United States. In all our conversations with the Americans, we were careful to keep them un-informed about our intentions and to feed them with misleading information. This was especially the case when they questioned us about the crisis surrounding the elections to the Officers' Club [a key event in triggering the revolution]. We then told them that this was an internal matter, circumscribed completely by the club issue and carrying no other implications.

'To the question of whether the Americans were played off

against the British, it was not so much a matter of playing as of using the Americans as a channel of information to the British. This was done immediately after the *coup*, the message we gave the Americans to transmit being that we were neither Communist nor Fascist, that we were against the King for known reasons and that we strongly advised the British not to interfere. Should they do so, we had prepared contingency plans which would have plunged the country into a major guerrilla war. For my part, I had good personal relations with the US air attaché, who was a friend. I personally heard him inform Caffery of our viewpoint, and I do not doubt that the message was transmitted to London, where it had the desired effect.'

Needless to say, an inflated assessment of the importance of American links with the Nasser regime continued to be endemic in American circles. The present author himself had confirmation thrust on him at the time by the US counsellor of the Embassy, Bill Lakeland, and Ambassador Caffery, who tended to regard the successful *coup d'état* against Farouk as a personal triumph. Caffery would push his intimacy with the Free Officers to the point of referring to them as 'my boys'; while Lakeland, as senior political officer at the Embassy, kept referring in our conversations to the Free Officers as 'we' in a way that showed he identified himself with them completely.

A CIA operative whose conscience appeared to trouble him more than most, broke down one evening at Princess Faiza's home and confessed to having been trained at a CIA centre in the United States to organize revolution in Middle East countries. He had received so much kindness and hospitality from the princess that he felt guilty in the knowledge of having worked against her and her brother. But the outstanding question is still why the United States, a foreign power which initially enjoyed excellent relations with Farouk, should suddenly side with a group of dissident army officers. How could this possibly have been justified as serving American interests, especially when we consider the way in which the Egyptian revolution brought Egypt into bitter conflict with the United States – a conflict leading to an alarming penetration of Soviet influence into Egypt; a penetration which, in turn, led directly to a near takeover of the Egyptian economy by COMECON?

Yet another question that may justifiably be asked is how was it possible for the Egyptian Commander-in-Chief to collaborate so closely, against his own king and in time of war, with a foreign power whose intimate connections with Israel were well known? And leading on from this, there remains the final and equally important question: what exactly was the deep grievance which alone could have justified such a betrayal by Heydar?

To seek an answer to these questions I made it my business to seek out various people, and asked, among them, Hilmy Bey Moussalem for his view. Hilmy Bey was a veteran Ottoman diplomat, former secretary to the Grand Vizir, Said Halim, as well as political officer on the staff of General Kress von Kressenstein with the Turkish forces on the Suez Canal in 1916. An Egyptian of Kurdish origin who had joined the Young Turks on the eve of the First World War, he was a tall distinguished figure whose angular height and rather gaunt physique was emphasized by the high fez and long military greatcoat he habitually wore. He was an acute observer of the political scene in Egypt and the Middle East while also being the representative of a rather mysterious Kurdish organization based in Paris.

This was what Hilmy Bey had to say: 'There is, in my opinion, little doubt that Farouk's bid, with the active collaboration of Abd el Rahman Azzam, to create a new form of Arab union based on a Federal superpower, to enrol German military advisers and assistants to build a model training division as a pattern for a million-man Arab army and the construction of a 2,000-plane air force, and above all the obvious feasibility of such an operation, was enough to alarm Israel and its American supporters. The full, or indeed partial, success of such a plan would have seriously upset the balance of power in the area and posed a serious threat to Israel's survival.

'What I do not understand is the naïvety of Farouk's and Azzam's thinking. Did Azzam and the King really believe they could get away with it? Possibly, if total secrecy had been applied to it, the operation might have progressed sufficiently to survive international opposition. But in informing Heydar

Pasha of his plans and of the presence of Schmitt, could not the King have anticipated Heydar's reaction?'

It so happened that, in the summer of 1950, a Jewish friend of mine, Mr Roby Hemsy, president of Alexandria Bonded Warehouses, a company with quayside warehouses in Haifa, Marseilles and elsewhere, had approached me with a strange proposal. He was about to celebrate the lifting of the sequestration of his company, which, being Jewish, had been temporarily taken over because of the 1948 war with Israel. Now he was planning to throw a big 'end of sequestrations' party in his luxury apartment in Sidi Bishr.

'Everyone will be there,' he told me. 'Omar Fathy Pasha, the King's principal ADC, the Garrison Commander of Alexandria, senior officials of the government, and the top people of Alexandria. There's no one who wouldn't like to see an end to this ridiculous war with Israel. May we speak freely about it?'

'Of course,' I said.

'A great friend of mine, Mr Jefferson Caffery, is soon arriving here. As you may know, he is one of America's top ambassadors. Cairo will be his last post, and his great ambition is to promote a peace between Egypt and Israel. He has great faith in King Farouk's ability to lead the Arab world in making an acceptable peace treaty. The Americans are very worried at the threat of Communism in the Middle East, and they know Farouk shares these apprehensions. The continued conflict with Israel can only strengthen the Communist threat. It therefore follows that Farouk should collaborate with us in this. I am in a good position to play a part here, being a friend of Caffery's as well as a friend of the Israeli Minister of Justice, who is ready and willing to collaborate. Would you, Adel, be interested in establishing contact with Azzam and the King in this matter?'

I went to Azzam, who advised caution, but suggested we extract more information. Therefore I saw Roby a second time, late at night in one of Alexandria's night clubs. He drew an alarming picture: most of King Farouk's entourage as well as his army generals had been sounded out. They all agreed that peace should be made. Unfortunately, Farouk was idealistic, obstinate and, it went without saying, above bribery.

The one man who could influence him in this direction was Abd el Rahman Azzam.

'Could you, Adel, establish contact with him, and that would allow us to arrange a top-secret meeting in Paris with the Israeli Minister?'

I promised to do what I could. When, next day, I saw Azzam, he said to me, 'What you tell me is confirmed by our intelligence services. You can't trust anybody. We must regard the offer of secret transactions in Paris with Israeli ministers as constituting the promise of a financial "deal". I do not think the King will agree to anything of the kind.'

When I brought the matter up with Farouk a few days later, the King said, laughing, 'So they think they can bribe me. How strange!'

I went to Hemsy's party, and by chance two British MP friends, Billy Maclean and Julian Amery, were in Alexandria at the time, so I took them along as well. I had the impression they were surprised to see the 'mateyness' which existed between the sequestrated, presumed enemy, Roby Hemsy, and so many senior Egyptians who had only a few weeks before been his controllers.

Later, thanks to Roby, I met Jefferson Caffery in Cairo just after his arrival, when he assured me of his admiration for Farouk and his conviction that the King was destined to play an important part in the defence of the Middle East against Communism. Shortly after my meeting with Caffery, *Time* magazine featured Farouk on its cover, its contents more or less following Caffery's line. Needless to say, all these attempts to break the King's loyalty to the Palestine cause failed. The only alternative they had was therefore to incite revolution against him!

Azzam Pasha, to whom I made my reports, did not altogether blame the Americans. In terms of their own thinking, they were fully justified and logical in their determination to get rid of Farouk. Before the war, the King had been the leader of the Arab war party; despite strong pressures, he had decided to remain faithful to the Palestinian cause. At Inchass, he had forced the hand of such redoubtable Arab leaders as the veteran Nuri el Said of Iraq and the crafty Abdullah of Jordan into rallying to the cause of war. Egypt, albeit inefficiently, had committed her professional army to the 1948 war, and now, after her defeat, Farouk was actively plotting revenge on a scale which could represent a crushing defeat for the Israelis and a serious international upheaval for the West. Caffery tried at first to enrol Farouk in a peace process at the expense of the Palestinians. The King, however, refused to countenance what he regarded as a betrayal of the Palestinian Arabs, and he did so in the face of 'advice' from his closest associates. He was clearly an incorruptible idealist; those ready to betray the Palestinians needed to be sought in other quarters.

Where the Free Officers themselves were concerned, their quarrel with Farouk seems to have emerged with growing strength only at what they assumed to be his responsibility for the mismanagement of the 1948 war. The secrecy surrounding higher policy, and their own political indirection, had kept them guessing where the true nature of Farouk's activity and aims was concerned.

I brought this matter up some years later with a friend who had been prominent in the Free Officers' *coup*. He commented: 'The secrecy surrounding Farouk's "higher policy" and our lack of contact with him obviously kept us in the dark with regard to any patriotic activity on which he may have been working. The picture we had of him was a bad one, induced by Heydar's bid to put on him the blame for defeat. If it was the King's intention to prepare effectively for a second round, he certainly did not deign to confide in his officers. Instead, he allowed the palace clique to isolate him from us. Our only interlocutors were people like Karim Sabit and the King's brother-in-law, Ismail Shirine, and even they were not informed of the King's plans and tended to criticize him behind his back. Thus our image of Farouk was that of a pleasure-loving, corrupt and irresponsible monarch who had better be eliminated before he could lead Egypt to a final disaster even worse than our defeat in 1948.'

Farouk's palace mafia, which effectively isolated him from the rest of the country, had played an even more mischievous role. Heydar Pasha should have been axed immediately after the fiasco, but was kept on through the energetic lobbying of Ismail Shirine. The King once said to me, rather facetiously, 'You know, Adel, Ismail claims that Heydar is so loved by the army that if I were to get rid of him there would be an army revolt!'

That the contrary was the truth we all knew, but still Farouk hesitated. Heydar Pasha's role here was ambiguous, as he played a double game with the King. On the one hand, he appeared to be loyal to His Majesty, while on the other he campaigned against him and, what was worse, did his best to minimize the danger of revolt. Heydar was well aware of the intentions of the Free Officers, but nevertheless actively lulled the King's suspicions.

There seemed to be little doubt that, while the army officers regarded Heydar Pasha as Farouk's henchman, who had led them into an impossible military situation, they even so saw him as a useful ally with the King. After the Schmitt mission was wound up and the general had returned to Germany, all hope for an effective army reform was lost. Farouk showed himself to be impotent against the palace intrigues, while the maintaining in power of Heydar Pasha meant that we could expect further defeats at the hands of the Israelis. If the officers blamed Farouk for this, they were fully justified.

24. The Last Year

It was learning that another German general was being imported into Egypt that made Schmitt decide to leave. The arrival of the new general Farmbacher, brought about by courtesy of the CIA, could only be seen as a cheap betrayal by Heydar Pasha and his associates of the King's undertakings with regard to Schmitt. The fact that His Majesty had done nothing, and presumably acquiesced, was sufficient cause for us all, Azzam, Schmitt and myself, to lose confidence in Farouk and abandon efforts to promote change. Events were, in any case, moving towards a climax.

In June 1951, I accompanied Azzam Pasha on his official visit to Turkey. The decision to go was part of Farouk's new-face policies. *Rapprochement* with Turkey, long deferred, was now to be made, and our visit took place in an atmosphere of remarkable cordiality. Arriving in Istanbul, Azzam purposely decided to wear the fez, though his staff stayed bareheaded on his instructions. Before we disembarked, an extremely well-attended press conference was held on board, at which Azzam, a veteran of the Young Turk revolution, spoke Turkish. He told the Turks that he felt he was coming home, that Turkey was a country admired by all Muslims, the Turks having been the redoubtable shield of the Muslims facing Europe. We would never forget this.

His reception by the Turkish press was enthusiastic. No dissonant voice was raised. Even Ahmed Amin Yalman of the semi-Jewish Dunme sect wrote an exceedingly friendly article in his paper *Vatan*. A number of papers headlined the reflection that Turkey might do better to leave NATO and the Europeans and join the Arab League. Thus were the years of keeping the Egyptians and the Turks apart – long a mainstay of

British policy – broken at last. Good relations with Turkey were essential if a federal Arab state was to be created. As sovereign of Egypt, Farouk stood at the forefront of Turkish commendations.

But other more ominous events were brewing. October of that year saw the final breakdown of Anglo-Egyptian talks over the final evacuation of British troops. The Wafdist government of Nahas Pasha, back in office after the 1951 elections, now decided to play the nationalist line. In a last-minute effort to find a compromise over retaining the Suez Canal base for the West, in particular for NATO, Egypt was offered a *primum inter pares* status in a new organization to be called the Middle East Defence Pact. Here Egypt would be on a par with Britain, the United States and France, together with other Commonwealth nations, jointly administering the Suez Canal base with these countries. The proposal was rejected by the Egyptian government, who logically objected to the omission of other Arab League member states, whose concern for Middle East defence was, to say the least, more justifiable and more important than that of New Zealand, Australia, and other countries less directly involved. Egypt could not betray other members of the Arab League by joining such a pact. The Wafdist government, well aware of having reached the end of the road so far as Anglo-Egyptian negotiations were concerned, now decided to abrogate the 1936 Treaty with Britain. They also solemnly proclaimed Farouk as King of Egypt and the Sudan, denouncing in the process the condominium arrangement that had prevailed ever since the reconquest by Kitchener of the Sudan in the late nineteenth century. These measures were tantamount to a declaration of war against the British presence in the Suez Canal Zone.

As soon as the parliamentary session promoting the measures had ended, Azzam called me to say: 'Tell the King that things have now reached a climax. He must take the lead in this new struggle against the British. He should not allow the Wafdists to master-mind the conflict. If he does not lead the fight against Britain, he will forfeit his position and probably lose his throne.'

I dutifully transmitted the message. But, by now, the 'Little Egypt' palace clique was firmly established in its position and

Farouk was panicking. As a consequence of the denunciation of the treaty and worsening security in the Canal Zone, Egypt had withdrawn from London Ambassador Abd el Fattah Amr Pasha. In the meantime, the UN General Assembly was meeting in Paris with the Anglo-Egyptian crisis at the forefront of its agenda. A bitter and acrimonious debate was unleashed against the British.

At this point Farouk's actions took on a particularly distasteful form. The Anglophile Hafiz Afifi Pasha was nominated Chief of the Royal Cabinet in Cairo and allegedly lost no time in proceeding to the British Embassy to sound them out on whether they would defend the King militarily if things got out of hand in Cairo. Farouk also instructed the Ambassador withdrawn from London to meet and talk with Anthony Eden in Paris, in the precincts of the British Embassy on the Faubourg St-Honoré. (The Free Officers themselves suspected that Eden had sent reassuring messages to Cairo.) For those of us who were attending the debate at the United Nations, this looked like the ultimate betrayal. Henceforward Farouk lost the support of every right-thinking Egyptian.

The year 1951 was drawing to a close in a state of semi-chaos. Violent guerrilla war erupted against the British Canal Zone and, unforeseen by Britain, almost the entire Egyptian labour force working on the base – some 100,000 men – withdrew. The British Suez Canal garrison was now virtually cut off from the rest of the country. Irregular warfare being the order of the day, the Egyptian government opened its arsenals to supply the citizens with weapons. The future looked black indeed.

Yet Paris that November was a heady and stimulating city as it hosted the meeting of the UN General Assembly. The Arab League was poised to raise the question of the independence of the North African trio of states, Morocco, Algeria and Tunisia. Azzam had received a mandate from the leading political parties of these countries to negotiate their independence from France. I was myself a member of the committee that included all the political leaders of the Magreb. An Arab League, ultimately to become an Arab state, was the secret stimulus. Modern Libya, Morocco, Tunisia and Algeria were to be so many new national entities likely to join the federation in due course. France, at whose expense the independence of North Africa was to be obtained, stood by.

Azzam had earlier been invited to discuss North Africa at the Quai d'Orsay by M. Chauvel, the French Ambassador in London. Now that he came with a mandate to negotiate, the French cold-shouldered him and informed him tersely that these were non-negotiable matters of internal French concern. Recourse to the United Nations had therefore been decided on, and it seemed a fortuitous coincidence that the General Assembly should be meeting at the Palais de Chaillot in the French capital.

The debate – soon, in 1956, to wrest Moroccan independence from France – was under way, and we were treated to one of the most inspiring demonstrations of oratory when Ambassador Adly Andraos, a brilliant Francophile Egyptian delegate, took on M. Schumann, the French Foreign Minister. Andraos's oratory in French was outstanding. Using a subtle blend of history and a flattery of France, its culture and civilization, while adopting French principles and attitudes, Andraos demolished the French case, so winning the enthusiastic applause of a mainly French audience. A motion condemning French colonialism was on the verge of being voted, and only an impassioned intervention by the French delegate, ending with the words: '*Je vous en supplie ne condamné-pas la France,*' saved the day.

The effectiveness of the Arab League as an international diplomatic instrument of liberation was clearly demonstrated in the assembly. All the Arab delegations worked smoothly together under the leadership of Azzam, the Egyptian, and, ironically, the only flawed case was that of Egypt herself. The Egyptian delegation was having to pursue its case against Britain in the knowledge that the King was already negotiating with the British behind its back.

I was dispatched to London by Azzam and Mohammed Salah el Din, the Egyptian Foreign Minister, to sound out British reactions and report back to Paris. The message I was asked to deliver was: 'The Egyptians you call extremists today, you will regard as moderates tomorrow.' My friends in the Foreign Office were not forthcoming. One Foreign Office spokesman said to me: 'We are tired of hearing you people talk

212

about Egyptian nationalism. It simply does not exist. It is a myth created by your politicians to cover up their mistakes and their corruption.'

Through the good offices of a friend, the French Military Attaché, I was able to secure a more reasonable British reaction when they told him: 'We do know the Egyptians. The Wafdist government, like so many before, has promoted a public hysteria. They are arming the most undesirable elements and, in consequence, the internal security situation is deteriorating. As this process goes on, internal opposition in Egypt will rise against the government. Then a determined blow from us will bring the whole thing toppling down . . .'

In effect, that blow fell in January 1952, when the British forces in the Canal Zone destroyed a police outpost in Ismailia, using artillery and tanks and killing a score of virtually unarmed heroic defenders. The next day, in Cairo, the police went on strike and the citizenry went on a burning spree. Responsibility for the rioting was attributed to a variety of sources, ranging from the Communists to the Muslim Brothers, even to the King. His Majesty was that day entertaining army officers at a banquet in Abdin. Through the splendid baroque windows of Abdin Palace the flames of Cairo burning were clearly to be seen, yet Farouk withheld the order for military intervention until the burnings were well advanced. The Wafdist government could only look on impotently as His Majesty's banquet proceeded. Then, at four o'clock in the afternoon, the army invested a smouldering city. Inevitably, the Wafdist government resigned, and the prophecy heard in London was fulfilled. Farouk was now well embarked on the slope that would lead to his abdication.

As the UN General Assembly ended its Paris sessions in the spring of 1952, another important development occurred. The Soviet Union, which had until then chosen to ignore the Arab League as an instrument of covert British colonialism, suddenly discovered that, with the debate on Moroccan independence and the Egyptian case against Britain, the whole system had turned against the Western powers. Clearly the Arab League deserved Russian recognition, and no less a person than Mr Vishinsky came forward to propose a meeting between the Russians and the Egyptians. This was attended by

Mr Vishinsky and Bogomolov of the Soviet Embassy in Paris, the Egyptians being represented by Azzam Pasha and Mohammed Salah el Din. At the meeting Mr Vishinsky informed our delegation of Russian readiness to help in the struggle against the British and other imperialists, and it needs to be stressed that this Soviet move, eventually to bring about a major *rapprochement* with Egypt, took place well before the advent of Abd el Nasser and was handled by representatives of the old regime.

We returned to a Cairo still subjected to curfew, and a scene of devastation presented itself. Disaffection was everywhere; the King had become the main object of resentment. In the Palace a war of intrigue was going on, the King himself at the centre of an army controversy. On the one hand, the Heydar Pasha clique was desperately trying to retain the King's trust, and on the other a group headed by General Hussein Sirry Amer was supplying His Majesty with accurate reports on the Free Officers.

An incident recounted to me by one of the latter seems worth recalling: 'Hussein Sirry Amer had managed to produce a full report, with names, on the doings and ambitions of the Nasser group. We knew the report was a damning one, and that it was on its way to Farouk in Alexandria, where he had gone to inspect the Royal Yacht *Mahroussa*, which had just finished a complete modernization and refurbishing in Italy. Something had to be done, since there was always the fear that Farouk might take action. We knew that Heydar Pasha was worried about the rise of Hussein Sirry Amer's position in royal estimation, so we sent Abd el Hakim Amer, one of us and a member of Heydar Pasha's family, to warn him that Amer was inventing stories about the Free Officers to curry favour with Farouk. Heydar's response was, "I know what you are plotting. You are naughty boys and are playing a very dangerous game." [By this stage, Heydar was aligning himself with the army rebels against Farouk, since he well knew that his career was ending.] Heydar immediately took off for Alexandria to inform the King that Amer's report was tendentious and untrue and so dissuaded Farouk from taking action at that time, when he could have frustrated the whole operation. As a result, Farouk preferred to put things off until the real crisis with the army officers began to manifest itself in the summer.'

The precipitating event was the nomination of a new commandant for the Cairo Officers' Club, Farouk's candidate being General Hussein Sirry Amer. Nasser and his group, already influential in the corridors of the military, opposed the nomination and instead proposed General Mohammed Naguib. It was the first open revolt by the officers in the face of a royal request, and it convinced Farouk that Heydar Pasha's reassurances were false and General Amer correct. He at once moved to get Sirry Amer appointed as Minister of Defence, a position from which he expected him to take immediate action against the Free Officers. But these were by now in a position to put pressure on the government, and Hilali Pasha, when offered the Cabinet, refused to take on Sirry Amer. Another candidate Prime Minister, Hussein Sirry Pasha, Queen Farida's uncle, likewise refused when he was approached to form a Cabinet with General Hussein Sirry Amer as Minister of Defence. He had been tipped off to decline the nomination by his son-in-law, who was the brother of a Free Officer.

The King, finding all doors closed, decided on a compromise with the Free Officers. He would be ready to make Naguib the Minister of Defence if Sirry Amer could be commandant of the Officers' Club. This, of course, was a face-saving formula intended to reassure the Free Officers, but whether it could have worked at such a late hour is questionable. The offer, in any case, was never made, since there was no one to transmit it to the Free Officers, Heydar having refused to carry such a message in case it uncovered his own ambiguous position as a Minister of Defence whose resignation, though pending, was yet to be confirmed. Thanks to the long years of palace intrigue, the palace clique had painted itself into a corner. Farouk, isolated at this crucial point from his army by the barriers created by his courtiers, faced a total breakdown of communication with his officers.

In desperation, the King again called on Hilali Pasha to form a government, but the identity of the new Minister of Defence was only to be revealed at nine o'clock on that evening of 22 July 1952, when the Cabinet arrived at the Palace to take the oath. There they were duly told that Ismail Shirine, Heydar's nephew and the King's brother-in-law, would be the minister concerned. The bluff showed evidence of serious miscalculation by the King. It was obvious that Shirine was to provide the façade from behind which Hussein Sirry Amer and Mortada el Maraghi, the energetic new Minister for the Interior, were to take action against Nasser. Effectively an hour after the oath-taking at Alexandria, orders reached the Army High Command in Cairo to arrest the Free Officers.

Well informed by his army associates of the turn of events, Nasser had no choice but to take action. Even up till the last minute it remained touch and go. The senior officers were forestalled by minutes, the Nasser team having managed to take over Army HQ just in time to arrest the surprised senior officers as they arrived. The revolution had begun, triggered by Farouk's mishandling of the crisis.

25. A King Departs

The night of 22/23 July 1952 in Alexandria was balmy. Princess Faiza had decided to hold a picnic in Alexandria harbour, at White Sands, where we would fish for shrimps and other sea creatures. White Sands was a favourite swimming area in the harbour, where the rather shallower bottom was sandy. The harbour, that night, was a fairyland of luminescence. Ships' searchlights vied with the floodlit Ras el Tin Palace, built by Mohammed Ali in the early nineteenth century, a delightful domed construction in the kind of neo-rococo style then fashionable.

We sailed to our fishing grounds in one of the tall-masted open dhows that were able to carry at least thirty people in reasonable comfort. But possibly the most exciting element was the water itself. We could see luminous sea creatures including blue jelly fish and shoals of tiny fish that trailed minute phosphorescent traces and energetically criss-crossed in the dark waters. To dive into this sea of light and be transformed into a glamorous, luminous, god-like shape, swiftly plunging into the deeper, cooler water in a haze of incandescent bubbles, was something of a wondrous experience. We were a large party including, besides the princess and her husband, Bulent Mohammed Ali Rauf, the Marquis de Perinat, Jojo Naum, the son of the Grand Rabbi, Mira Wahba and the usual Zohria crowd. Here was a Cytherian ambience so aptly described by Verlaine the French poet: '*La tout est ordre et beauté, luxe, calme et volupté . . .*'

The fishing was fine that night. We could virtually pick the shrimps out of the water – and what shrimps! Five inches long, and bursting with clean white flesh. Champagne with shrimp and caviar – the food was of a sophistication appropriate to the occasion and the party was an unqualified success.

At four o'clock in the morning we slowly sailed back to the Royal Yacht Club moorings. As we passed two of the naval destroyers we heard the sound of bugles rousing their crews. Facetiously one of our number remarked, 'What keenness! The Egyptian Navy outdoes the British in its early-morning reveilles.'

And another, more cynical, said, 'There must be yet another government crisis and things have been put on alert.'

When we reached the cars parked outside the club we were surprised to notice a small crowd of naval cadets in the street. They looked at us curiously. Clearly there was tension in the air. However, it was four in the morning and we could think of nothing else but bed. I went home, but at seven o'clock precisely was woken by a colleague from the Arab League, who informed me that something had happened overnight in Cairo.

If Farouk had, that first morning of the *coup d'état*, taken his car and driven straight to the Alexandria Garrison HQ at Mustapha Pasha Barracks, he would have been able to assume command of a substantial military force which considerably outnumbered the Cairo rebels. In addition, the Egyptian Navy remained loyal and could be counted on to intervene on His Majesty's behalf. But he preferred to remain inactive and let events overtake him. Some years later I expressed my astonishment at this passive inaction to Ismail Shirine, who was presumably one of the royal advisers at the time when the crisis erupted, and received this curious answer: 'There would have been bloodshed and people would have died . . .' – as if a King had no right to defend his throne. Clearly, the same inertia and lack of decision that caused the army to lose the 1948 war was as prevalent as ever.

It took the Nasser team a bare forty-eight hours to secure their position and transfer from Cairo sufficient loyal forces to confirm their hold on Alexandria. Once this was achieved, the next step was to demand the King's abdication. Events moved with startling rapidity. Within three days of the *coup* Farouk was poised to leave, his formal abdication taking place on 26 July. The Royal Yacht had been ordered to stand by and a formal ceremony of departure was organized at Ras el Tin, to be attended by General Naguib, the nominal head of the *coup d'état*, and other officers of the revolutionary junta.

Nasser would be conspicuous by his absence. Two other persons, however, would not. These were the Princesses Fawzia and Faiza, who, against the better judgement of their frightened husbands, decided they must see their brother before he left the country. They appealed to me, and I thoroughly approved of their determination and, it has to be said, their courage in the face of a dangerous, unknown revolutionary group. I went to see Azzam Pasha, who at once got on the phone to Ali Maher, whom the Free Officers had invited to form the first revolutionary cabinet.

Ali Maher spoke to Anwar el Sadat, who in turn referred the matter to Nasser. Within minutes the princesses' request had been granted. They should be at Montazah Palace at four o'clock in the afternoon to bid their brother farewell.

That afternoon, the American Ambassador, Mr Caffery, was accompanied by Anwar el Sadat and our friend Bob Simpson as they, too, went on their way for the Farouk departure.

Mr Caffery asked: 'Well, colonel, are you going to make peace with Israel now?'

Anwar el Sadat answered: 'As soon as we clean up the corruption, we will do it.'

And he did, thirty years later.

Appendix One:

Transcription of General Schmitt's Draft Letter of Resignation (the original written in his hand)

Alexandria, 28th July 1950

Dear Adel,

When you communicated about two months ago that the position as adviser in ordnance to the Minister of War had been offered to me, but this, according to Karim Tabel Pasha, without having any authority, I asked you to arrange under these circumstances my release – your way.

The reasons for my request were the following:

By this offer I am recognizing that one has in the Egyptian Army no idea of what can be offered to a German lieutenant-general. Otherwise I ought to regard the offer as offending.

I was induced to stay so long in Egypt only because my Egyptian friends ever and again referred, when I became impatient, upon the fact that I could rely on the word of His Majesty the King, who had promised me an independent unit under his direct command.

It seems to me now that I am considered as a suppliant who is still glad to receive such an offer, being unworthy of his rank. I have got the impression that the motives for the offering of my services cannot be recognized in this country.

Therefore, I must underline that the task to be expected by or attracted to an old officer with African experiences in two world wars, when I was asked in March by the go-between if I were willing to serve the Royal Egyptian government, I had hoped to be able to do efficient work in the army. As it is known in my country of a pro-German state. Especially as was since my first stay in Egypt and from the recent failure of the

Palestinian campaign that the services of German officers in the Egyptian armed forces could be a profitable field to the activity of new striving to attain high arms.

During my stay in Egypt I could always see, if recognized as German, how great the sympathies are which nearly all orders of the Egyptian population show towards us Germans, no difference if these were simple men of the street or educated ones. I had also the same experience with some officers including colonel rank, of whom I made the acquaintance incidentally, these latter declared they would much welcome German officers in leading army positions. I had the very contrary experience meeting the Commander-in-Chief of the Egyptian armed forces. I would not like to be unfair, but I cannot help but take the conclusion after careful consideration that this officer felt threatened by me since the moment I asked him for permission to study the Palestinian war and that he feared I should point to the made war blunders and to the still existing defects in training and organization of the army which might prejudice his authority with the King.

It was characteristic that he first agreed to send me an officer for this purpose and that he was for many months delaying and preventing me when I tried to study this campaign for being able to draw the lessons from this last fighting. Today I am of the absolute opinion that the war against the Jews has been lost by uncapable generalship. In that, I was confirmed also by the reading of the book His Majesty graciously sent to me about the war in Palestine, although this book, as written by a Jew and glorifying the Jewish army, naturally is very one sided. But that in the later weeks and months Jewish superiority in arms or defective ammunition of the Egyptian forces or disloyal behaviour of the Arab Legion could contribute to the failure, this was only the consequence of the uncapable Egyptian leadership not being able to make use of the advantages of the first week, to force the law of action upon the Jews and to extinguish the Israeli state by a blitz campaign of at most two weeks.

If the C-in-Chief were truly anxious about the good training and the high state of the army, why did he sabotage my intentions of studying the Palestine campaign although he had learned from me that I received His Majesty's permission for it? Ought he not to be glad to get the judgement of a war-experienced officer, if his unselfish aim is the best possible condition of the armed forces entrusted to him? This the more, as till this day the army has not taken the lessons out of the campaign must be considered a grave neglect.

I have been living long enough in Egypt and I have heard and seen enough to know that I should have the possibility of useful work only in case of being given authority, especially considering the residence to be expected from the side of C.-in-Ch. and his staff. I am convinced that my work would be welcomed by most Egyptian officers, surely by most younger officers, and that at least by all who want to serve their country and to create a real army. I am also persuaded that the most senior officers would not have resisted me as it was not my intention to act as a schoolmaster, but to gain confidence and attachment.

It is evident, however, that I cannot work usefully against the hostility of the C.-in-Ch. shown to me in a tactless and ungentlemanlike manner. After the conversations with Karim Tabel Pasha (who had told me all has been settled!), unless I am independent from the C.-in-Ch. and endowed with authority.

In the proposed position I should be only a *Geschaftsempfänger* [salary-receiver], as we in the German Army contemptuously used to name an officer whose performance did not correspond with his salary.

Such a job is out of the question for me.

Dear Adel, shortly after the above-mentioned conversation with you, you asked for permission of delivering my letter to His Majesty some days later as Colonel Ismail Shirine wished to speak with you about my affair. I agreed to it, but the conversation did not bring any news. Astonishing, however, was to me the again proved ignorance about the German Army. The colonel thought I was a 'supply general' not knowing that I could not have been appointed *General Leutnant* unless I should have proved able as a *Truppenführer* [a leader of forces] at the front. I could show the colonel here two letters of General Rommel acknowledging my merits as a tried *Truppenführer*. Furthermore it was self-evident in the German Army that an officer was not employed continually as staff or as administration positions, as the fighting forces always must be the most important part of a real army. Thus I was taken by General Rommel from my position as chief administrative officer of the Afrika Korps in Tripoli after I was staying there for only three days, and immediately I (my opposite number in Cairo was then General Robertson, now C.-in-Ch. in Fayed) appointed leader of the independent Salloum front (Halfaya-Salloum-Bardia) with the German-Italian division Bardia and the Italian division Savona, whilst the other parts of Rommel's forces were sent in to conquer Tobruk.

If the C.-in-Ch. or any officers of his staff should have shown interest, I would have informed them that I got in the First World War the Iron Crosses II and I class and I gained in the Second World War as *Abschnitts-Kommandeur* (commander of front line of some 20 km) on the Upper Rhine front the Iron Cross II (*Spangezüm EkII*), as leader of the battle group Strassburg the Iron Cross I (*Spangezüm Ek I*), and finally as leader of the Salloum front on proposal of General Rommel the Knight's Cross of the Iron Cross, the 1939-founded highest German war decoration, for my defence-victory at Bardia Dec. 1941. As is well known in military circles, the Iron Crosses and especially the *Ritterkreuz* (Knight's Cross) could be gained only by outstanding bravery and excellent leadership. A 'supply general' could not get even the Iron Cross II, let alone the Knight Cross.

Dear Adel, I told you earlier that my long stay in Egypt had a very disadvantageous effect for me in personal respect. Therefore I ask you after all to make the necessary preparations for me and my wife's return journey to Germany. Since Azzam Pasha expressed the opinion I should still wait a while as His Majesty probably had not had time to come to a decision from reasons not recognizable to us outside the new political events, I beg to tell him that I cannot afford to neglect my personal interests any longer and that my dignity as a German general requires me to bring an end to my stay here and to avoid further opportunities in which I have to expose myself to an unworthy treatment.

I think I was showing all the time a considerable patience and I regret to be forced to write this resolution. Above all, because I am of the opinion that I could have had a deep effect with the assistance of other German officers upon the Egyptian armed forces and, furthermore, because I perceived that this army never under the present system will play the role which it rightfully could play, be it against the Jews or be it as a power factor in the imminent Third World War. I need only think of the defective centralization of the training of the staff of the C.-in-Ch. which destroyed every responsibility and independence of the other generals and by which the training of the generals themselves, that is of the officers who in a future war have to lead the forces, will become illusory.

On the other hand, I have learned about the Jewish army that it makes use of the fighting lessons, that it is pursuing steadily its aims and does not waste money what a military expert can affirm about the Egyptian Army if he is following the newspaper information about army matters.

What the experts in European countries or in the USA think of the Egyptian armed forces as factors in the strategy of the big powers, has been shown some days ago in an article of the English *Economist* on 'Defenders of the Middle East'. It says 'on paper the Egyptian Army is a force to be taken into serious consideration as a bulwark of Middle East defence' but for various reasons, 'unfortunately, its efficiency is enormously impaired'. The 'principal reason for this estimate is concealed not to hurt personal feelings: it is the fact that the Egyptian Army has at the top an amateurish directorship neither trained nor qualified for this position, full of responsibility and besides after the failure of the Palestine War failing the general confidence of the officers and soldiers'.

Dear Adel, I always declared you that I should want to hold myself out of the policy especially the internal matters of your country. The soldier has the only duty to be faithful to the supreme commander, His Majesty the King. If I now, determined to leave Egypt, was more frank and plain [spoken] in this letter, I did so, because I gave my parole of honour, when I offered my service to serve Egypt like to my own fatherland. Desiring the well-being of Egypt, I respect it my duty to tell the truth, as I have recognized it and point at things which will turn out in not so far a time unfavourably. I am not the least interested in the persons, I only care about the matter, a principle always impressed upon us officers of the old German Army, but not very often understood in the Orient.

Asking you to express Azzam Pasha my warm thanks for his friendship towards my fatherland for his kind benevolence for my person, I am, dear Adel, Yours truly . . .

Appendix Two:
A Note on the Historical and Political Background to the Egyptian Monarchy

The Kingdom of Egypt was set up in 1923 at a time when the country still came under British occupation. The granting of independent sovereign status was, in theory, to follow later with the signing of the 1936 Treaty with Britain. Yet in practice this instrument allowed Britain, among various other rights, the right to occupy the country militarily and to establish, for what were described as reasons of imperial security, a war base in the area of the Suez Canal.

The Treaty nevertheless did convert the British representation in Egypt from a High Commissariat to an Embassy status. It had the effect of reducing the powerful proconsular figure of Sir Miles Lampson (later Lord Killearn) from High Commissioner to Ambassador, though in practice this turned out to be largely a 'cosmetic' arrangement.

One dominant feature of Egyptian politics stems from the 1923 Constitution put together under British suzerainty. This instrument has been criticized in Egypt for having been drafted with the idea of a balance of power in mind. It contained an area of ambiguity concerning the relative authority of the King and the Cabinet, thus ensuring a continuous bickering between these two elements and leaving the British in an advantageous position from which they could play off one party against the other.

There was, moreover, a certain bitterness to be discerned within the ranks of the Egyptian nationalists, who argued that the principle of constitutional reform had already been achieved during the 1880s, when the Cherif Constitution was carried by vote in the National Assembly and effectively withdrew executive authority from the sovereign. In the light of this, the 1923 Constitution was seen as retrogressive and drafted mainly along the lines of British convenience. Without doubt the situation promoted a virtually permanent discord between the King and the Wafd, the majority national party. This, in turn, promoted a latent republicanism in the country and ultimately led to the disappearance of the monarchy.

Both King Fuad and King Farouk tended towards an autocratic outlook which ill-accorded with the Egyptian party system, dominated largely by the Wafd. Likewise it encouraged dissident or ambitious Wafdist political figures to detach themselves from their mother party to join with palace-sponsored entities that clashed with the Wafd. Among this category were the Sa'dist party, the Ittihad party and the Liberal Constitutional party.

The name 'Wafd' simply means 'delegation', the party having been formed out of the National Delegation led by Zaghloul Pasha to negotiate the terms of independence after the First World War. At that stage the Wafd enjoyed the enthusiastic support of the whole of the Egyptian people, a fact allowing it to master-mind the 1919 revolution against the British, which had, in turn, been a prime factor leading to independence.

From being what might have been termed a 'national front' entity, the Wafd was seriously eroded by the defection of many of its leaders into the palace alignment. Nevertheless the mother party was, from the time of King Fuad onwards, able to continue to represent the national aspirations of the people, largely through the continuing momentum of the 1919 revolution, the retention of the name 'Wafd' and its inheritance of the original national electoral organization. The retention of the name 'Wafd' quite possibly became its single most valuable asset.

It was the Second World War that provoked a showdown in the basic confrontation. With the Abdin Incident of 1942, in which the British Ambassador foisted on Farouk a Wafdist government under threat of an enforced abdication, the true nature of the Anglo-Egyptian alliance was exposed and a serious internal imbalance set in motion. The Wafd found itself seriously discredited through its role as a British 'agency' and through accusations of corruption made by one of its most important members, William Makram Ebeid. When the Wafd's British support was withdrawn with the ending of the war in 1945, Farouk found it a simple matter to dismiss it from power.

With the British out of the picture as a result of their post-war preoccupations, Farouk took over the ruling of the country. He became the main executive authority in Egypt and governed through the palace-inclined parties against a somewhat weakened Wafd opposition. But on 12 January 1950, the Wafd returned to power, reportedly under British pressure. The rationale behind this was Britain's need to negotiate with Egypt a new treaty on a strong popular foundation. It was during this period that Egypt led the Arab world in its opposition to the founding of the state of Israel, clashed with Britain at the United Nations and suffered defeat in the ill-fated 1948 war in Palestine.

The year 1951 was a watershed year, marking the beginning of the end for Farouk. Following on the failure of negotiations in London, the recently elected Wafdist government proceeded to provoke the most serious crisis with Britain since the days of Arabi. That October, they denounced the 1936 Treaty and the Sudan condominium arrangements and declared a guerrilla war against British forces in the Canal Zone. The brutal British response was the massacre of an Egyptian police outpost in Ismailia, which in turn led to the burning of Cairo, the fall of the Wafdist government and, a few short months later, the abdication of Farouk and the establishment of a military hegemony.

So the historic Palace/Wafd confrontation ended with the dissolution of both parties. It also marked the end of the game of the balance of power, all three contestants eliminating themselves from the scene. In the long run, the only survivor of the game turned out to be the Wafd party, which has in recent years been able to make an unexpected come-back on the Egyptian political scene.

One of the more curious after-effects of the 1923 Consti-tution turned out to be the manner in which it facilitated the imposition of totalitarian rule in Egypt. With the successful conclusion of the military takeover of 1952, President Nasser found himself constitutionally in the enviable position of being able to accumulate unto himself the political power and prestige of the British Ambassador, the King of Egypt, the parliamentary and party systems and, in the final analysis, the executive authority, for no constitutional machinery existed to contest his power to nominate Prime Ministers and dismiss Cabinets.

Thus did the rule of the Mohammed Ali family in Egypt come to a close. It had begun with Mohammed Ali, who was first Ottoman *Governor* then *Viceroy* of Egypt. After his death, his successors were given the title *Khedive*, a practice that continued up to the outbreak of the First World War when Lord Kitchener deposed Khedive Abbas Helmi and *Sultan* Hussein was proclaimed sovereign. The dynasty of kings started with King Fuad in 1923 and ended with the abdication of his son Farouk in 1952. Had the process of constitutional reform started by King Farouk's ancestor, Mohammed Cherif Pasha, and Sheikh el Tahtawy in 1879 been allowed to continue, then it seems likely that the monarchy could have survived in Egypt, albeit on the British pattern.

Index